# FILM
# SCHOOL
## CONFIDENTIAL

# FILM
# SCHOOL
# CONFIDENTIAL

## An Insider's Guide
## to Film Schools

Tom Edgar and Karin Kelly

A Perigee Book

A PERIGEE BOOK
Published by the Penguin Group
Penguin Group (USA) Inc.
375 Hudson Street, New York, New York 10014, USA
Penguin Group (Canada), 90 Eglinton Avenue East, Suite 700, Toronto, Ontario M4P 2Y3,
  Canada (a division of Pearson Penguin Canada Inc.)
Penguin Books Ltd., 80 Strand, London WC2R 0RL, England
Penguin Group Ireland, 25 St. Stephen's Green, Dublin 2, Ireland (a division of Penguin
  Books Ltd.)
Penguin Group (Australia), 250 Camberwell Road, Camberwell, Victoria 3124, Australia
(a division of Pearson Australia Group Pty. Ltd.)
Penguin Books India Pvt. Ltd., 11 Community Centre, Panchsheel Park, New Delhi—
  110 017, India
Penguin Group (NZ), 67 Apollo Drive, Mairangi Bay, Auckland 1311, New Zealand (a divi-
  sion of Pearson New Zealand Ltd.)
Penguin Books (South Africa) (Pty.) Ltd., 24 Sturdee Avenue, Rosebank, Johannesburg
  2196, South Africa

Penguin Books Ltd., Registered Offices: 80 Strand, London WC2R 0RL, England

While the author has made every effort to provide accurate telephone numbers and Internet
addresses at the time of publication, neither the publisher nor the author assumes any
responsibility for errors, or for changes that occur after publication. Further, the publisher
does not have any control over and does not assume any responsibility for author or third-
party websites or their content.

Copyright © 1997, 2007 by Tom Edgar and Karin Kelly
Cover art and design by Ben Gibson
Text design by Pauline Neuwirth

PRINTING HISTORY
Perigee trade paperback first edition / September 1997
Perigee trade paperback revised edition / April 2007

Perigee revised edition ISBN: 978-0-399-53319-8

The Library of Congress has cataloged the first Perigee edition as follows:

Kelly, Karin, 1961–
    Film school confidential : the insider's guide to film school / Tom Edgar and Karin Kelly —
1st ed.
    p. cm.
"A Perigee Book."
ISBN 0-399-52339-1
1. Motion pictures—Study and teaching (Graduate)—United States—Directories
    I. Edgar, Tom, 1963–    II. Title
PN1993.8.U5K46 1997                                             96-30032
791 43'071'173—dc21                                             CIP

PRINTED IN THE UNITED STATES OF AMERICA

10   9   8   7   6   5   4   3   2   1

Most Perigee Books are available at special quantity discounts for bulk purchases for sales
promotions, premiums, fund-raising, or educational use. Special books, or book excerpts,
can also be created to fit specific needs. For details, write: Special Markets, Penguin Group
(USA) Inc., 375 Hudson Street, New York, New York 10014.

# Contents

# Introduction
## to the Second Edition

It has been ten years since we researched and wrote the first edition of Film School Confidential, and the world of film has changed tremendously.

To a person pondering how to start a career making films in the twenty-first century, the way things were way back at the end of the twentieth century will matter little, so we'll try not to spend too much time on this. But forgive us if we take a moment to mention some of the more important changes since the first edition, as it may help illuminate the road ahead for you.

In the past ten years digital video has emerged as an accepted medium for shooting feature-length narrative films. New and improved DV formats such as 24p and HDV, which utilize small, inexpensive cameras but are better suited to theater projection than standard-definition video, make DV features better-looking all the time. With the release of Apple's Final Cut Pro application, nonlinear editing went from an expensive technology that only professionals could use to the standard way independent filmmakers cut their films. Production and postproduction audio have gone entirely digital as well. It is now possible for a filmmaker to do all of the postproduction on a film—including editing the picture, building the audio tracks, and even performing the final mix—on an inexpensive desktop or laptop computer.

Ten years ago cell phones were expensive luxuries that few possessed. And the Internet was only a rumbling in the distance, something that was discussed in computer journals as a possible replacement for dial-up online services such as AOL or CompuServe. Few foresaw that it would change the way films are made, marketed, and distributed.

Who knows what's coming in the next ten years? Certainly high-definition video will come into its own as a dominant medium for both production and distribution, and more and more of our entertainment will be distributed over the Internet. But enormous changes in the technology and technique of filmmaking are coming that we can't foresee.

One thing of which we can be sure: ten years from now we will look back and shake our heads at how limited our tools were back in the first decade of the twenty-first century, how backward and inefficient we all were, and how much has changed since then.

One striking change that we noticed while researching this second edition is how happy students are with their film school experiences. Ten years ago students we interviewed complained about everything: they hated their teachers, they never got enough time with the equipment, the equipment was old and constantly broke down.

We suspect this is primarily due to the emergence of digital equipment for production and postproduction. Ten years ago students edited their films on flatbed editing machines. Flatbed editing machines were expensive pieces of equipment—schools could rarely afford to buy enough to go around—and they broke down frequently. Film was a delicate medium that would break or scratch or be ruined in the processing. Today most film students shoot on inexpensive and reliable digital video cameras and edit on computers using Avid or Final Cut Pro. This equipment is inexpensive enough that even the most underfunded public school can afford to buy enough to go around, and it is reliable enough that students rarely lose work or time to equipment failure. Some students still shoot film, but they benefit as well; with most students shooting video, the film cameras see much less use and abuse, so they, too, are more reliable.

But beyond the equipment, the programs and professors are constantly evolving. As more film programs are created, all are looking for ways to distinguish themselves, to provide better educations, and to turn out better filmmakers. Based on our conversations with professors and students alike, it is clear to us that there has never been a better time to study film.

Another change from when we attended film school, and one so novel that it's a little hard for us to accept, is that an ability to make films has become a marketable skill, and an MFA from a well-known film school is in some situations an advantage.

At a time when outlets for visual material are multiplying—from satellite and cable networks offering hundreds of channels of programming, to flat-screen displays on buses and in supermarkets, to video-enabled cell phones and mp3 players, and so on—there is an ever-greater demand for video content and for people who can create eye-catching and entertaining content. Businesses and governments are increasingly dependent on video to disseminate information among their clients, employees, and constituents. And any website can contain video and animated material, all visible to millions of people. Grass-roots organizations with little or no money can, if they have someone with the right skills, broadcast their message to the world in a powerful way. The ability to make a film is akin to operating a printing press in an earlier era. It is a powerful and valuable skill, whether you use it to express your own or other people's ideas.

In the twentieth century, for someone seeking a job in corporate America, an MFA in film marked one as frivolous, unwilling or unable to study something useful such as business or law. But today a film degree can actually be an advantage. The *New York Times* in 2005 ran an article suggesting that an MFA in film may be what the MBA was not long ago.[1] We wouldn't go quite that far. But literacy in visual media—the ability to author it as well as understand it—is unarguably becoming more useful and valuable with every passing year.

As of this writing, there is much hand-wringing in the United States about the many jobs and industries moving to other countries. According to the economist Adam Smith, this is only sensible; that when China can make a better TV for less money than the United States, then China will of course make all of the TVs. Therefore, Smith would ask, what products does America make better than other countries? One answer to that question is motion pictures. There are large filmmaking industries in China, Korea, India, Germany, and Nigeria, to name only a few countries, and each makes films that are popular in regions of the world. Yet none of those countries' films are as popular with audiences the world over, or as profitable, as American films. As other industries are shrinking, entertainment is becoming an ever-larger part of the American economy, with more people finding gainful employment in movies. So to some degree, learning to make films today is a far more sensible thing to do than it was in the past.

---

1. Elizabeth Van Ness, "Is a Cinema Studies Degree the New M.B.A.?" (*New York Times*, March 6, 2005). The article argues that film production requires students to be fast on their feet, to be able to deal with chaotic situations, shifting information, and clashing egos, yet come out at the end with a polished product. This kind of adaptability, useful in any business, is not generally taught at business schools.

Another revolution, which is only in its earliest stages at this time, is in documentary. Though documentaries have been with us as long as the medium of film, they were traditionally so difficult and expensive to produce, and the audience for them so limited, that few filmmakers pursued the genre. But the advent of small, inexpensive, high-quality digital video cameras has made filming documentaries much easier and much less expensive. And the flowering of new film festivals and new methods of distribution has made it easier for documentaries to find audiences.

But the change we see from ten years ago that is likely to hit you the hardest will be what you face immediately after finishing film school, in how you then go about creating a career for yourself in film. Don't worry about this just yet; we'll discuss it at length in the "After Film School" section. For now, just sit back and relax and allow us to discuss the ins and outs of getting in and out of film school in one piece.[2]

This book contains objective and subjective information about schools in the United States that offer MFA degrees in film. This includes film directing programs plus some affiliated programs such as screenwriting and producing when we feel they merit inclusion. We obtained the objective information by talking with professors and administrators at the schools and by perusing the schools' various published materials. The subjective information comes from interviews with students and graduates from these schools. The views expressed are those of the interviewees and do not necessarily reflect the views of the authors. In the reviews of the individual schools, we're just here to pass on the opinions we hear; if students are happy with their film school experiences, we'll say so; if they're unhappy, we'll pass that

---

2. Are you reading this while standing in the aisle of a bookstore? That doesn't sound very pleasant! Think how much more comfortable you would be if you were to buy it and read it in the comfort of your own home!

on as well. Subjects we have strong opinions about are largely covered in the surrounding materials; we try not to let them slip into the coverage of individual schools.

Forgive us if we impart a dismal truth right up front. While everyone who goes to film school hopes to direct feature films, the odds of any one student coming straight out of film school and getting financial backing to direct a feature are very small. We don't mean to discourage you; if you are determined to make it in film, you probably will. But the purpose of this book is to fill you in on information that the schools themselves will not. By definition, much of this news will be bad; if it were good, you would read it on the schools' websites. By getting all the bad news at the start, you will be well-prepared to make the most out of the experience. And by hearing how other people have succeeded or failed in the situations you will be facing, you will be prepared to navigate safely through the many obstacles before you.

Film schools often do not have the best interests of their students in mind. Unlike almost every other kind of school, they provide little career guidance, few easy ways to find jobs or make contacts, and little or no help once diplomas are handed out. Film schools charge the same tuition as law or medical schools, yet offer little hope of the gainful employment after graduation that degrees from those other schools afford. They will offer you some classes, which may or may not teach you to make films, and they will give you access to some equipment with which to make some films. More importantly, they will give you the opportunity to form lasting collaborations with other aspiring filmmakers. This is the most you can expect from a film school.

Since no one else will be looking out for you in film school, our main objective in this book is to help you keep track of your own interests. We will tell you what you should bring with you into film school and what you should expect to get out of it. We will let you know what the various film schools seem to look for in applicants—and what Hollywood seems to look for in graduates.

If you are going to film school, you probably want to be a director. We will tell you the things to do in school that will most likely help you to direct once you are out of school. We will let graduates from the top schools tell you about the activities you should try to participate in and the pitfalls you should try to avoid.

Most of all, we will try to give you the career advice that the schools will not. We will tell you how to make film school work for you in your quest for success in the film industry.

So, everybody ready? Quiet on set! *Film School Confidential*. Scene 1, shot 1, take 2. Roll camera. Mark!

And—action!

# Film Schools and Hollywood:
## A Brief History

For most of the twentieth century, film schools were campus jokes. Though some universities offered courses in film as early as the 1920s, the programs that existed were not taken seriously by administrators. A few young directors working in Hollywood in the early 1970s had attended film school in the sixties—notably Martin Scorsese, who studied film as an undergraduate at NYU, and Francis Ford Coppola, who studied at UCLA—but they were making small, commercially unsuccessful films and had no more fame and no more power than anyone else in the industry. At the time many more young filmmakers were getting their start working for producers of low-budget exploitation films like Roger Corman or William Castle, not through film school.

The 1960s had seen the most revolutionary changes in the film industry since the advent of sound. With the dropping of the Hays Code in 1965, and the introduction of the MPAA film rating system three years later, filmmakers were free of the wholesomeness that had been forced on them, and many followed the lead of international filmmakers like Bergman, Polanski, and Kurosawa, packing as much pain and despair as they could into their films. The uncertainty of the times also fed into the mood of Hollywood, and for nearly ten years many of Hollywood's best and most influential films were rooted in existential despair. American filmmakers explored painful, emotionally charged subjects that their predecessors could not—and, perhaps more importantly, they explored subjects that television could not even hint at. Many great films were made in the late 1960s and early 1970s, but few were what you would call good-time entertainment. Even the movies of the era that were marketed as rollicking adventures—*Butch Cassidy and the Sundance Kid* (1969), for instance, or *Bonnie and Clyde* (1967) or *Easy Rider* (1969)—ended when the heroes died in a hail of bullets.

But then a pack of graduates from Southern California film schools got the chance to make movies. Most of these guys did not have a whole lot to say about the world, but all of them knew how to show an audience a good time. The early films of Steven Spielberg (Cal State, Long Beach) and George Lucas (USC) were not especially deep, but they were enormously entertaining, and audiences ate them up. Audiences had been subjected to cinematic explorations of oblivion and nothingness for so long that these movies made them feel they were discovering real entertainment for the first time. It is hard to appreciate today how astonishing the joyful energy of Lucas's *American Graffiti* (1973) was, or how invigorating the sheer joy of spinning a story evident in Spielberg's *Jaws* (1975) was. Perhaps most astonishing of all was the trend toward a more simplistic view of good and evil. By 1977, the nation that had been through the Vietnam War and Watergate had nearly forgotten how to differentiate between the heroes and the villains. *Star Wars* (1977) was not popular just because it was a science fiction spectacular the likes of which no one had seen before. It was popular because it was a throwback to the simple good versus evil stories typical of Hollywood Westerns. To audiences accustomed to the depressing entertainment of Hollywood in the sixties and too young to remember the Westerns of the forties and fifties, *Star Wars* was something entirely new. All these elements came together at once, and these film students' movies made more money than anyone in Hollywood had ever imagined was possible. No one had seen audiences wait in line for five hours to see a movie before, and yet that's exactly what happened at *American Graffiti, Jaws, Star Wars, Close Encounters of the Third Kind* (1977), *Raiders of the Lost Ark* (1981), and *E.T.* (1982). Hollywood recognized that young audiences were the key to enormous profits and that young filmmakers were the key to young audiences. And Hollywood studios started signing recent graduates to make films.

Universities, too, began to recognize the benefits of turning out students who could create such hugely popular entertainment. In the short run, these luminaries gave their schools free publicity. In the long run, successful graduates would give generous donations back to their schools. As the existing film programs grew, new programs popped up at colleges and universities everywhere.

University administrators and Hollywood studio executives were not the only ones awestruck by these young filmmakers. Newspapers and magazines were quick to publish stories about the new auteurs, complete with glossy photos of the twenty-five-year-old millionaires in jeans and tennis shoes striking poses of directorial authority on glamorous movie sets. Suddenly millions of high school students had a new goal in life: they wanted to be filmmakers.

If public interest in film as an art form grew a little in the seventies with the unprecedented celebrity of directors like Spielberg and Lucas, it exploded in the early eighties when anyone could become an authority on film for about three hundred bucks. With the introduction of the VCR it was suddenly possible to see *The Third Man* (1949) without having to go to a seedy art house in a bad part of town. It was possible to see *Lawrence of Arabia* (1962) on your own TV without commercials, or *Citizen Kane* (1941) in a crisp new print without scratches or breaks in the film. And it was possible to study those films over and over again.

But by the time the next generation of students finished film school, the industry had changed. Whereas the huge success of *Star Wars* had been a fabulous surprise to studio executives in 1977, by the early eighties success along those lines—success beyond anyone's dreams—was expected. *Star Wars* had completely changed the way Hollywood made films. Prior to *Star Wars*, a hit movie was one with broad appeal, one that people of all ages would see once: *The Sound of Music* (1965), for instance, or *West Side Story* (1961). After *Star Wars*, a hit movie was one that teenage boys would see fifteen or twenty times. *Star Wars* also changed Hollywood's business priorities; while the film grossed around $350 million in domestic ticket sales in its original release, toys and other *Star Wars* merchandise have grossed more than $4 billion. Films ceased to be works that stood by themselves and instead became pieces of global marketing campaigns aimed at selling toys.

After *Star Wars*, studios were no longer interested in intelligent, low-budget films that made respectable profits. They only wanted the next megahit; the next *Star Wars*, the next *Raiders of the Lost Ark* (1981), the next *E.T.* (1982). Film students were still hired to make films, but if their first films weren't huge hits, they rarely got a chance to make a second. Film students, whose youthful energy had given Hollywood unprecedented success, eventually became passé.

Frustrated film school graduates looked for other alternatives, but the Southern California film schools didn't prepare their students for any kind of filmmaking except Hollywood filmmaking. These schools prepared students to pitch scripts and take meetings; not how to write grants or raise funds from friends and family. So the next generation of film students to make features was not graduates of USC or AFI, they were students who had learned down-and-dirty filmmaking techniques from schools that specialized in down-and-dirty filmmaking, like NYU. Following the lead of independent filmmakers like John Cassavetes and John Sayles, film students like Spike Lee and Jim Jarmusch raised their own funds and made challenging, personal films on extremely small budgets. These film school graduates made daring films that became critical successes and made money on a smaller scale. They were not the blockbusters that the studios had come to count on from young filmmakers, but they were profitable. And with Lucas and Coppola releasing big-budget flops like *Howard the Duck* (1986) and *One from the Heart* (1982), even modest profits started to look good again to the studios.

This low-budget era lasted for a few years in the late eighties, when the economy was strong and investors were willing to risk their money on small films. During this time a number of young filmmakers were hired to write and direct films shortly after graduation; some were even recruited while still in school. But many of these films were disasters, and it was not long before film school graduates were again ignored by Hollywood. (In 1985, Todd Solondz was signed to a three-picture deal while still a student at NYU, based on his second-year film. The feature he made, *Fear Anxiety and Depression* [1989], was such a disaster that it ended not just his deal but a lot of other students' deals as well. It would be six years before he would be able to make *Welcome to the Dollhouse* [1996] and get his career going again.) With the recession that spread across America in 1990, film school graduates found that no one was interested in them anymore. Independent filmmaking came to a near standstill as even proven filmmakers found they could not get financing to make their films. By 1995 things began to improve, but only after thousands of film school students had graduated only to find themselves deeply in debt and essentially unemployable.

When the economy showed signs of recovery, film production began to pick up again. Digital video cameras became available, and independent filmmakers began making feature-length films with them—most notably Lars von Trier, Thomas Vinterburg, and the members of their Dogme 95 movement. Other new technologies that were similar to film emerged, which demanded new kinds of directors and writers, people experienced with both acetate and silicon. Video games, computer-generated animation and effects, and even the World Wide Web needed technically aware people with a knack for visual storytelling. Film schools quickly added new media to their film and television programs, and soon film school graduates were more employable than they ever had been before, working for start-ups in the dot-com bubble. And that lasted until, oh, about March of 2000.

Since 2000, digital video and high definition have changed how independent movies are made, and DVD has changed how they are marketed. It has never been easier to make a movie or to get it into people's homes. But because so many films are being made, it is difficult for any one film to stand out from the crowd. In the 1980s a slight but likable film like Spike Lee's debut, *She's Gotta Have It* (1986), could find an audience. Today it might not even be accepted into a film festival.

The demographics of a hit have reverted to what they were pre–*Star Wars*. Now that the DVD of a movie is released two or three months after its release in theaters, movies no longer have to appeal to the small segment of the audience who will pay to see a movie again and again in the theater. Now movies are made to appeal to anyone who might buy it on DVD. So while large-budget films are still aimed primarily at teenage boys, the stories are deliberately expanded to appeal to other demographics. If you look at any major film franchise these days—Lord of the Rings, Spiderman, Batman, Superman, X-Men, Harry Potter, etc.—every movie includes the same basic cast of characters: a heroic young man, of course, but also at least one strong young woman who has her own story. No longer just a love interest, the heroine now has needs of her own, in order to make the film more appealing to young women in the audience. And there will always be some older characters played by well-known actors of previous generations. So *Batman Begins* (2005) sells not only to the boys who like the Batmobile, but also to the girls who identify with the Katie Holmes character. Gary Oldman and Liam Neeson sell the film to audiences in their thirties and forties, and Michael Caine's presence sells it to audiences in their fifties and sixties. The least-known actor in the cast of these films is often the lead; the teenage male audience doesn't see movies for the stars, so this allows the studios to save some money by hiring someone inexpensive, say Christian Bale or Brandon Routh.

We only go into this to indicate the way big-budget movies are made these days. A newly graduated film student has little hope of directing a big-budget feature. Most of the current directors of A-list movies worked their way up after starting out making low-budget independent films. A few first-time directors will be hired by Hollywood to make inexpensive children's movies or lowest-common-denominator comedies (and many find their careers badly damaged after their first major film is something like *Herbie Fully Loaded* [2005]). But in general you don't get to make a big movie until you've made small ones. You don't get to direct *The Matrix* (1999) until you've already made *Bound* (1996); you don't get to direct *Superman Returns* (2006) until after you've made *The Usual Suspects* (1995); you don't get to make *The Lord of the Rings* until after you've made *Heavenly Creatures* (1994).

For the most part, film school graduates have to put together their own first features and work their way up into larger-budget movies from there. And that's a subject we'll delve into later.

# Before You Go

▶ **WHY GO TO FILM SCHOOL?**

This is a question that has been asked since the first film school was founded. But while the question persists, the answer changes over time.

For instance, until only a few years ago the decision to go to film school was a matter of simple math. If you wanted to make a film, you needed access to very expensive equipment, including crystal sync motion picture cameras, Nagra audiotape recorders, flatbed film editing machines, and audio mixing facilities that could run multiple tracks of magnetic film simultaneously. At a time when annual tuition at a typical film school was around $10,000 a year, film school was simply the least expensive way to make a film. That film schools also taught you how to use the equipment, how to write screenplays, and how to direct actors was just icing on the cake; a nice bonus, but peripheral to the primary consideration, which was financial.

In the past decade that equation has reversed itself. Digital video, especially newer iterations such as 24p and high definition, now provides image quality that approaches or equals that of 16 mm film, yet at a tiny fraction of the cost of shooting on film. You can currently buy a high-quality digital video camera—24p or HDV—for around $5,000, and a computer fully pimped out as a film and sound editing workstation for under $5,000. So for less than $10,000 you can now *own* all the equipment you need to make your own films. At the same time, tuition has skyrocketed; tuition is now over $30,000 per year at many schools, and the price rises every year. So film school is no longer the obvious choice it once was in terms of cost versus access to equipment.

But film school does offer other benefits. Such as:

## Time

Making films is very difficult in the best of circumstances. If you and your crew are trying to make a film while working full-time jobs, you will find it nearly impossible. Film school allows you to step outside of ordinary life, to carve out a period of time wherein you can focus entirely on learning how to speak through the visual medium. It's very difficult to learn to make films any other way.

## Structure

Each film you complete makes you a better filmmaker. By giving you firm deadlines to meet in the making of your films, film school will allow you to complete a number of films in less time than it would take you to make one film on your own.

## Freedom

Specifically, the freedom to screw up and make a terrible film. In film school you will make many films. If you are lucky, one or two will be very good. But you can be certain that at least one of them will be very bad indeed. There is often no way to tell, while you are making a film, how good or bad the finished product will be. If you are out in the world and you spend all that time and money making a film, and it turns out to be terrible, you might never make another film. In film school nobody but you will care, and it won't be a problem even for you, because by the time you realize how bad it is, you will already be working on your next film.

## Guidance

Teachers have their role to play. Every professor won't be good, but you will probably find one professor in your time at film school who genuinely inspires you and who makes you want to exceed your own expectations. But beyond your professors, you will learn about film by making films; not just your own films, but, even more so, your classmates' films. Watching other people try things out on set and then seeing whether or not they work in the finished films is the best education you'll get in the art of filmmaking.

## Contacts

If you attend a major film school—especially one in Los Angeles or New York—you will meet people working in the industry. If you present yourself professionally, they may want to give you work. Many students at schools in New York or Los Angeles find themselves working in film before they have even finished school. If you were to move to Los Angeles right now, knowing nobody and with no professional experience in film, finding work would be a challenge. So film school can be beneficial, even if all you want is a job in film.

## Insurance

Film sets are dangerous places; heavy lights drawing thousands of watts of electricity can explode or blow out circuits; expensive equipment can be lost or stolen; fires can start. Any film production needs a liability policy to protect the filmmakers from disaster. Most film schools provide blanket liability insurance to all students. This seems to be changing; as insurance becomes more and more expensive, many schools are limiting or eliminating their policies. But, for now at least, this is a benefit you get from most film schools.

### Teaching Credentials

OK, this one may seem a bit out there, but it is worth remembering that an MFA makes you eligible to teach at the college level. At a time when new film programs are sprouting up like weeds, being able to teach film can be a remunerative skill and is a nice fallback job for the periods when you can't get your movies funded. If you drop by one of the many for-profit, unaccredited film schools (the ones you see advertised in the backs of magazines) and talk to the teachers, you will find most of them are recent graduates from the nearest accredited film school. The New York Film Academy might as well have a shuttle bus to bring NYU students straight over to start teaching after they graduate; UCLA and USC graduates teach at half a dozen such schools in the Los Angeles area.

### Community

While this is probably the last thing you think about as a benefit of film school, in our experience it actually is the one that will have the greatest impact on your life. The people you befriend and collaborate with in film school will be your closest allies in the filmmaking world after you graduate. You will continue to work with them throughout the rest of your life, helping one another out through good times and bad, keeping one another focused on your careers in film. From what we've seen, people who continue to work with their classmates in the years after finishing film school are far more likely to have lasting careers in film than people who try to go it alone.

Do these benefits merit three or four years of your life and a crushing load of student debt? That's your decision to make. Many people make the perfectly reasonable decision to skip film school and just find an entry-level job in film. Some decide to take the $30,000 they would have spent on tuition and spend it to hire a crew and make a movie. Others have realized that a two-year program in screenwriting or producing provides most of the benefits listed above, but in less time and at less cost. (It is for this reason that we are including in this edition information on screenwriting and producing programs that, ten years ago, we deemed outside of our scope.) All of these are perfectly reasonable options for certain people in certain circumstances. Are any the right one for you? We can't tell you. But we hope the information in the pages that follow will help you to make an informed decision.

### ▶ WHAT ABOUT UNDERGRADUATE FILM SCHOOL?

In the last edition of this book we dismissed the idea of undergraduate film school entirely. But with the skyrocketing cost of film school and the new inexpensive filmmaking technologies, we can no longer be so dismissive. People are looking for less-expensive alternatives to graduate film school, and undergraduate film school is certainly not the worst of the alternatives. But we still have many reservations. We can't give you a firm recommendation on whether or not to go to undergrad film school; all we can do is go through the pros and cons for you.

A number of arguments can be made in favor of undergraduate film school. Probably the strongest is financial; if you're going to college anyway, getting a bachelor's degree in film takes no additional time or money. An undergraduate film student, with only undergraduate student debt and half of his twenties ahead of him, can afford to take an internship or entry-level job that will help him move into a career in film. People who finish graduate film school today often find themselves in deep debt and older than a lot of the competition. MFA graduates worry much more than undergrads. They worry about things that people in their early thirties always worry about: security, finding a mate, starting a family, escaping debt, saving for the future, and living like adults. These people can't afford to take jobs that don't pay well, so if they can't get feature films going quickly after graduation, they generally wind up taking nine-to-five jobs to pay their bills. Many spend the rest of their lives in cubicles, paying off their loans or saving for their children's education, daydreaming about films they never got to make.

The downside of studying film as an undergraduate is that you may not be ready to make a film at the time you get the opportunity. You may come out of school able to speak through the powerful language of cinema, but, with very little life experience, you might have nothing to say that would interest other people. If you have ever wondered why so many dumb, pointless films are made, this is one reason. Hollywood hires twenty-something writers and directors for their cheapest films because they will do the work for very little pay. However, having no experience in the real world, they often bring nothing recognizably real to their movies and simply regurgitate things they've seen in other movies. And once a filmmaker has made a terrible movie this way, it can be difficult for her to get funding to make another when she is older and has things to say.

Now, we were in our twenties not that long ago, and if at that time someone had said this to us, we would have replied unequivocally that we were ready to make a film. Looking back, we can say unequivocally that we were not. We're happy we didn't get the chance to make a movie when we were in our twenties; we certainly would have made terrible films. (Of course, ten years later, when we were ready, the opportunity didn't come either, but that's a separate issue.)

But we have seen people who were not like us; undergraduates who did have the maturity and worldliness to make great films. We've also seen people who still did not have that maturity and worldliness even after graduate school. We can't make a blanket judgment here that would apply to everyone. Just try to be realistic about your knowledge, experience, and talents, and take the advice of people you trust.

Here are a few things we can say with certainty: Don't get both an undergraduate and a graduate degree in film. If you decide in advance that you will study film as a graduate student, study something else as an undergrad and get a well-rounded college education. If on the other hand you decide to study film as an undergrad, then don't think about going to graduate film school; you'll be spending a huge amount of additional money just to take most of the same classes over again. Better that you get what you can out of college and then go use it in the world. And if you do major in film as an undergraduate, be sure to do so at a large university where you can get a broad liberal arts education at the same time. If you go to, say, CalArts or Art Center Pasadena as an undergrad, you will not be able to study anything but art. If you go to UCLA or Columbia, on the other hand, you will be exposed to a wide range of arts and sciences. A well-rounded education like that is crucial for anyone who wants to tell stories.

## ▶ WHAT ABOUT THE FILM SCHOOLS THAT ADVERTISE IN THE BACK OF MAGAZINES?

So, as we were saying, a graduate education takes a lot of time and costs a lot of money. As such, many people look longingly at quick and inexpensive schools such as the New York Film Academy or the Los Angeles Film School.

It's understandable; the classes last weeks or months, not years, and cost a tiny fraction of university tuition. And the names sound the same; a lot of people don't know the difference between the New York Film Academy and New York University, or between the L.A. Film School and UCLA Film School.

In these schools, a recent graduate from UCLA or NYU will teach you how to use a camera. And that can be a good thing. But learning how to use a camera is not the point of film school; learning how to tell compelling stories in the visual medium is the point of film school, and that takes time. Learning how to use a film camera makes you a filmmaker to the same degree that learning how to type makes you a writer.

It's great to know how to use the tools. But knowing the tools is not equivalent to knowing how to use them to tell moving and meaningful stories. A school like the Los Angeles Film School is not a substitute for a school like UCLA; it is at best a prerequisite.

### ▶ WHAT ABOUT PROGRAMS IN SCREENWRITING?

Many film schools, in addition to programs in directing, offer separate programs in screenwriting. Other schools have screenwriting tracks within the filmmaking major. As you'll see when we discuss the individual programs, we think highly of many of these programs. They often give 90 percent of the benefit of attending film school, but at about half the cost and in half the time.

To a great degree, whether a director establishes a lasting career in film comes down to whether or not she has a bank of good screenplays ready to go into production. Some of the best filmmakers started out as writers. In Hollywood, the first successful screenwriter to become a successful director was Preston Sturges; soon after, Billy Wilder got into directing. Neither had the distinctive visual style of contemporaries like Hitchcock or Orson Welles. But their stories were so strong, their dialogue so sharp, and their ideas so forcefully expressed that their films were every bit as brilliant. In recent years, successful screenwriters such as Paul Schrader, Robert Towne, Stephen Gaghan, and Paul Haggis have moved from writing into directing.

So writing is a perfectly valid entry point into directing. In Hollywood there's even a rule of thumb: *write three, direct one*. That's not a law, mind you, but frequently a screenwriter who has written three successful films will be able to get funding to direct a film.

If you are looking to save time and money, a screenwriting program might be a great alternative. At USC, UCLA, and AFI, screenwriting students work closely with students in the producing programs; many establish relationships that carry on after school and into real-world films.

## ▶ WHAT ABOUT PRODUCING PROGRAMS?

There are good programs dedicated purely to producing at USC, UCLA, AFI, and NYU. These programs tend to be more like business schools than film schools; they focus on the legal and business aspects of filmmaking: on contracts and financial agreements, and on schedules and budgets.

The USC producing program is angled toward Hollywood, as many of its graduates work to become studio executives as producers after graduation. The UCLA program teaches the concept of the *creative producer*: someone who conceives and develops ideas for projects, finds collaborators and funds to get those projects made, and sees them through completion, marketing, and distribution. UCLA graduates are more likely to work alone, producing small independent productions after graduation, than to go work at an existing production company or studio.

Several of the producing programs make an effort to move their students into the industry; the programs at USC and UCLA hold most of their classes in the evening and encourage students to work in internships or entry-level jobs during the day.

Producing is very different from the other aspects of filmmaking. It is much more business-oriented and requires energy, social skills, and business acumen. But for those who are suited to it, it's fun and rewarding. And as necessary as producers are, good producers are always in short supply. If you have the interest, the skills, and the personality to be a producer, a producing program may be exactly what you need.

## ▶ WHAT ABOUT SKIPPING FILM SCHOOL ENTIRELY?

Again, at a time when you can buy all your own equipment, it is always tempting to bypass film school. The main thing to ask yourself is, what do you want to do in film?

If you want to be a technician—a cinematographer, say, or an editor—you could move to Hollywood, find a job as a production assistant, and work your way up through the ranks into your desired field. Rather than pay tuition for four years as you learn your craft, you could be making money and making contacts. But attending film school can also be a good option. It will give you the opportunity to work with your classmates on countless films. By the time you graduate you will have an impressive reel of work and will have established close relationships with a number of young filmmakers who will hire you as they make films for years to come.

If you want a career directing films, there's only one thing that matters: your first feature film. Film school is one way of getting into a position where you can make your first feature, but it is not the only way. It is possible to simply make your first feature yourself as an ultralow-budget DV feature. Doing so could allow you to bypass film school completely.

But it's a very risky gamble. There are thousands of other people just like you making independent features in the U.S. every year, and Sundance only screens twenty-four of them (twelve in competition and twelve in the less prestigious American Spectrum). Of those, only three or four are likely to find distribution. And of those, at most one or two will ever see a profit. The odds of getting anywhere with a self-produced feature are very small, even if your film is good.

But if you've never made a film before, have not written screenplays and worked with actors and editors and cinematographers, your film is probably not going to be that good. It may not be bad; it may even be OK. But when you are competing with thousands of other films, your film has to be much better than OK. It has to be outstanding. (We'll go into more detail about the perils and pitfalls of the first feature in the "After Film School" section.)

In general, if you are determined to skip film school and go straight to your first feature, we recommend finding a happy medium: take some classes where you get the experience of writing and directing some short films and then seeing how they play in front of an audience. Take some acting classes on your own to learn about the craft of acting, and then try your hand at working with actors as a director. Direct a one-act play for the stage and get a feel for the craft. Watch as many great movies as you can—with an audience whenever possible. And when you go into production, make sure the people you hire as crew have a lot of experience, and be willing to accept their advice.

A common misconception about directing is that the director should be a dictator who creates every detail of the movie. In fact, directing is mostly delegation; a good director hires talented artists and collaborators and trusts them to make most of the decisions.

## ▶ WHY ARE THERE SO MANY
## FILM SCHOOLS ANYWAY?

The personal computer has made it much easier to be creative. Digital technology has given writers, composers, photographers, and filmmakers astounding creative tools. As a result, more people are creating work in these media than ever before. And the Internet has made it easier to promote and distribute personal creative works. Because of this, over the past two decades the market for creative works has changed; there is far more supply than ever before, and almost no demand.

Look at short fiction, as an example. Until a few decades ago, magazines that published short stories were enormously popular. Writers of short fiction such as John Cheever, W. Somerset Maugham, and Roald Dahl achieved international celebrity. And the magazines that published their stories were some of the best-selling of the time.

The few magazines devoted to short fiction that exist today barely scrape by. There are many reasons for this. Certainly new forms of entertainment and changing tastes have a role; the people who fifty years ago read short stories for entertainment are watching *American Idol* or playing "Halo 2" today. But there aren't many people today willing to pay to read other people's short stories. At the same time more and more people are *writing* short stories. A short fiction magazine that prints ten stories in an issue and sells five thousand copies of that issue is likely to receive nearly ten thousand submissions. So now you'll see short fiction magazines trying to make money off writers instead of readers, by offering writing workshops, writing retreats at fancy resorts, and writing contests.

The same is true of independent film. Far more people are making low-budget independent films today than the market for such films can sustain. It is said that during the California gold rush of 1849 few of the gold miners struck it rich, but the businessmen who transported the miners, who clothed them, fed them, and sold them supplies, did very well. There's virtually no money to be made in making independent films, but countless businesses turn a healthy profit by providing goods and services to filmmakers who, like the forty-niners, are pouring every penny they have ever earned—or will ever earn—into making their dreams come true.

One such business is the screenwriting symposium. You may have heard the names Syd Field or Robert McKee. People who dream of being screenwriters pay hundreds of dollars to hear these guys give lectures about how to be a screenwriter. They write books, charge large sums of money to give one-on-one story advice, and travel the world giving lectures. Neither has actually written a produced screenplay, mind you, a fact you would think might make people question the validity of their teachings.

Another such business is the for-profit film school. The Los Angeles Film School, to take one, is not there to help young people realize their potential as filmmakers. It is there to make money off the tens of thousands of aspiring filmmakers who move to Los Angeles every year with dreams of being the next Spielberg.

To be fair, the same dynamic is at work at university film schools, if not quite to the same mercenary extent. A lot of students want to learn to make films today, so schools that do not offer classes in filmmaking are at a disadvantage in attracting new students. As a result, film programs are popping up everywhere, at institutions both reputable and disreputable.

Many film festivals are also in on the scam. We hasten to add that reputable film festivals play an important role in helping aspiring filmmakers find their audience. But most film festivals are at base somewhat exploitative; independently produced films are screened to a paying public, but the filmmakers receive none of the box office. So the filmmakers have taken on all of the risk in the deal, paying to make films and to deliver them to the festival in a format suitable for screening—often paying for their own travel and lodging to attend the festival—but then the festival makes all the money.

The best-known festivals—the Sundances and Canneses and Torontos—offer a filmmaker a great deal in return for this expense. They offer the chance to network with important and powerful people in the filmmaking community, the chance to win awards and get reviews that will help the films move on toward the ultimate goal of distribution, and the filmmakers toward the ultimate goal of establishing a lasting career in film. But the majority of festivals are not there to help filmmakers; they are created by communities to benefit themselves: to drive tourism and boost their economies.

Some have even taken the exploitation a step further. There are businesses out there that call themselves film festivals, charge an application fee to filmmakers, and later announce winners, but do not actually screen any films for the public. The correct term for this would be *lottery*, not *film festival*. There also are festivals that will screen any film you send them as long as you pay them to. Watch out for these. A representative of the New York International Independent Film and Video Festival, to name one festival that works this way, will call you and tell you your film has been accepted into their festival. When you express delight she will then tell you that if you just send your film and a check for a few hundred dollars, then they will screen it. Sadly, the New York Independent Film and Video Festival screens quite a few films every year.

Again, it goes back to the gold rush. As long as there are people who dream of becoming famous filmmakers and are willing to make a big wager on achieving that dream, there will be others out there waiting to take their money away from them. Always keep this in mind as you move forward in your film career. Sooner or later someone will try to con you.

## ▶ SPEAKING OF FINANCIAL EXPLOITATION . . .

As we interviewed students and recent graduates for this second edition, one common theme came up again and again for students at all levels and across all schools: debt. Deep, deep debt. Over time it became increasingly clear to us that this is an enormous problem, and it is only getting worse.

It is our feeling that the U.S. has passed a tipping point, a shift that will make life after college much harder for college graduates in general and for film students in particular. The ramifications of this shift will certainly become clear in the next few years, but at the moment few seem to have noticed.

Three elements come into play here: the first is the skyrocketing cost of university tuition; the second, the aggressive marketing of student loans by the Student Loan Marketing Association, SLM Corporation (a quasigovernmental lending business that hides its cutthroat practices behind the folksy nickname SallieMae); the third is the rewriting of U.S. bankruptcy laws by Congress in 2005. The first two make it much easier for students to fall into irrecoverable debt; the latter punishes students who do.

Student loans can be a good thing. For someone studying a profession such as law or medicine, particularly at a prestigious university, going into debt to pay for tuition is not much of a risk. After graduation, the graduate will almost certainly find a six-figure job and will be able to pay off the debt in a few years. It is partly because of the clear financial benefits of professional degrees like these that tuition has risen so steeply in recent years.

But for many professions—particularly the arts and humanities—a degree carries no such benefit. When tuition was around $10,000 a year, it made sense to take on $30,000 or $40,000 of debt to cover college; when you graduated and got a $40,000-a-year job, if you planned carefully you could realistically pay your debt off in a decade. But with tuition now around $35,000 a year at many schools, many students come out of school with debt loads well into six figures. And while tuition has soared, wages have stagnated. So when, after graduation, students with $150,000 of debt find they can still only get a $40,000-a-year job, they realize that they will be slaves to SallieMae for decades to come.

As a film student, the danger is even greater. In addition to tuition, students often take out additional loans to help pay for their films. And, far from having an assured income after graduation, a young person trying to get into film can be nearly certain of having little or no income for at least several years after graduation. While in school, students often view their debt as something that kind of sits there until they finish school, after which it shrinks as they pay it off. But after graduation the debt does not sit there waiting to be paid off. It grows. Like a cancer. If you have $100,000 worth of debt at a 7 percent interest rate when you graduate, and you can't pay it off, after five years it will be $140,000. In just over ten years it will be $200,000. In just over twenty years it will be $400,000.

The founders of this country saw fit to write bankruptcy into the first article of the Constitution. They had seen people fall into debt they could not escape and wind up in actual poorhouses, debtors' prisons where they worked as indentured servants to their creditors for the remainder of their lives. The founders saw that such servitude did not benefit a country or a people, and that, on the contrary, countries often benefited when people felt free to take financial risks. So the founders made it possible for people in irrecoverable debt to declare bankruptcy, freeing themselves from that debt and enabling themselves to start over. There was a time when this was a celebrated fact of American life; R. H. Macy famously went bankrupt several times before eventually succeeding with the dry goods store that became Macy's department store.

But in 2005 the U.S. Congress passed a bill called the Bankruptcy Abuse Prevention and Consumer Protection Act of 2005. Despite the name, the effect of the law is to make it nearly impossible for individuals to declare personal bankruptcy for any reason. The claim was that the bill cracks down on people who abuse the system, who deliberately rack up debt and then try to escape it through bankruptcy. But the bill specifically and deliberately did not provide ways out for people who went into debt because of misfortune.

Students are being encouraged to go much deeper into debt than ever before, while largely unaware that the safety net that protected their parents and even their older siblings is no longer there. We have not yet seen the result, but when it comes it will probably be drastic. Many of today's students will find themselves laboring the remainder of their lives toward no end but paying off their creditors.

It's likely that nobody has even mentioned this to you. People who went to college a few years ago will probably tell you that student loans are no problem, unaware that things have changed substantially since they were in school. The schools need students to be able to pay their ever-rising tuition, so it is not in their interest to warn you against the debt. And SallieMae wants you to take out more loans than you can easily pay. The longer you go without paying off your debt, the more money SallieMae makes.

So it's entirely up to you. Please, be careful. You need to know what your limit is, and you need to make sure you don't take debt beyond that limit. Nobody else is going to help you with this.

▶ **A NOTE TO OUR INTERNATIONAL READERS**

Many people come from other countries to attend film school in the United States. We spoke with quite a few international students while researching this book, and it occurred to us, based on experiences many of them related, that it would be worthwhile to mention some of their general insights here. (Easily offended U.S. residents might want to skip on to the next section.)

In the post-9/11 era, many U.S. schools automatically give international students a one-year deferral upon acceptance. This is because many students now have to go through a lengthy approval process by the U.S. Department of Homeland Security before being allowed to enter the country. If you are planning to come to film school in the United States, be sure to allow at least a year just for the approvals to go through after you are accepted.

Also be aware up front that, even with a weak dollar, universities in America are tremendously expensive. Many international students come to the United States without a clear understanding of just how expensive it will be and wind up having to drop out after one or two terms. Many schools now require incoming international students to provide financial documentation proving they can afford to pay the school's tuition.

One thing that surprises a lot of international students is the poor state of public transportation in the United States. In much of the country public transportation is so poor that it is simply not possible to get along without a car. Before you go to any school, be sure to look into the transportation situation around the school; if a car is indeed necessary (and we try to make this clear in our reviews in this book), then factor in the necessary time and money to purchase a car upon arrival as part of your relocation plan. The website Craigslist (www.craigslist.org) is a useful resource to see how much cars and apartments cost in specific cities where you might attend school.

Students who come to the United States from Asia are often shocked by American universities. In most Asian countries, relationships between students and teachers

are extremely formal. By comparison, American universities are anarchic; students and professors will fraternize
freely, will go to bars and get drunk together, will sometimes sleep together and not bother to try to keep it secret.

A number of students we spoke with looked at the *U.S.*
*News & World Report* rankings of film schools and simply applied to whatever film program was rated highest. (A
lot of U.S. citizens do this as well.) This is a real mistake,
given how many different kinds of film there are, and how
different the various programs are. Don't choose a school
because of its name or ranking. Read up on the various programs in the pages that follow, and choose a school that is
appropriate to the kind of films you want to make.

Finally, it pains us to write this, but several international
students told us that as an international student you may
be shunned by American students. Many international
students come to U.S. film schools hoping to meet and
work closely with American students. But the United
States is a country so large that many of its citizens, especially young people still in school, have never traveled
beyond its borders and are unaccustomed to people from
other countries who may not be fluent in English. Many
are uncomfortable around people from other cultures,
and in film school will find excuses not to work with
them. At some schools international students find themselves ignored by the American students and left to make
their films with crews made up entirely of other "for-
eigners." This isn't something you'll experience with
everyone you meet, but you're likely to notice it with a few
of your classmates.

## ▶ WHAT YOU SHOULD PLAN TO GET OUT OF FILM SCHOOL

It's easy to forget that film school is not the goal. The goal
is a lasting career making films, and the most important

first step toward that goal is making your first feature. Film school is one way to get closer to making that first feature, but it is not the only way. And whether it serves that purpose at all really depends on you.

In the first edition of this book we postulated that the way to make film school work for you is to come out at the end with a good feature-length screenplay you want to direct, and a strong short film—ideally similar in tone and content to the screenplay—to prove that you are capable of directing it.

This is still the best you can hope to take out of film school when you finish. If you have a strong screenplay, you may be able to convince a producer to back it. If you have a strong short to show that you know how to direct, it may convince the producer to allow you to direct it. And this does still happen occasionally (especially for animators and filmmakers who can use technology with a unique visual sense; *Sky Captain and the World of Tomorrow* [2005] was the first feature from CalArts graduate Kerry Conran, and *Monster House* [2006] was the first feature by UCLA graduate Gil Kennan); however, it does not happen as often as it used to. For most young filmmakers there is a new step that comes after film school and before getting backing for a feature; the festival circuit and the DV feature. Here's how it generally works.

After you have finished your thesis film you submit it to film festivals. Showing your short in festivals is an important first step for your career, not because you will meet someone to pay for your movies but because you need to meet and befriend the festival programmers. Festivals are vital to your success as a filmmaker, and the programmers of these festivals are your gateway to that world. If you get your short into important festivals, you can go and meet the programmers in person and make an impression on them. There is little other reason to attend a film festival with a short film, as the makers of short films are generally treated as second-class citizens. Go, attend a few parties, drink the free booze, meet some other filmmakers, see some movies, but don't expect anything big to happen for you as a result. Just be sure to make a good impression on the programmers; that's all that matters at this point.

Then rush back home and get back to work on your feature. The contacts with programmers will pay off when your feature is finished.

"Wait, what?" we hear you ask. "Feature? What feature?" This would be your self-financed feature shot on DV. We're sorry to have to break this to you, but it's the way the film world has reshaped itself in the digital-video era. You're going to have to make a feature on your own before anyone else will give you money to make one.

"I have to make a feature before I can make a feature?" we hear you asking. "Isn't that a catch-22?"

Well, yes. This has always been true to some degree; producers would rather back a filmmaker who has proven she can handle the pressures of directing a feature than one who has not. But the rise of the no-budget first feature is largely due to the emergence of digital video. It's barely more expensive to make a DV feature film than it is to make a DV short film; once you've got a camera and an editing system, and a small cast and crew willing to work for no pay, you might as well shoot for another week and make a feature. As a result, thousands of feature-length films are shot every year.

And every one of them is submitted to the Sundance Film Festival. In the early nineties, after the success of *sex, lies and videotape* (1989), Sundance ruled the world of American independent features. When Sundance received five or six hundred feature-length submissions a year and picked fifty or so to screen, they were screening most of the good independent films that were out there that year. With digital video, the number of submissions skyrocketed (Sundance received 3,148 feature-length submissions in 2006), and soon dozens, perhaps hundreds, of good films were being rejected by Sundance each year and were not getting their shot at reaching the public as a result. So other film festivals stepped up to become additional venues for new independent films, and to introduce new filmmakers to the public.

While Sundance retains the reputation as the best U.S festival to debut an American independent film, it is at this point only slightly less prestigious to debut in the New York, Telluride, South by Southwest, or Los Angeles film festivals. (Also, many American filmmakers forget that there is a world outside of the United States. On the global stage, Sundance is not a very important festival. Cannes, Berlin, Toronto, and Pusan are all much more important to the global film market than any U.S. festival, including Sundance.) It used to be that only a top prize at a major festival would be worth mentioning on a movie poster: "Winner! Palme D'Or, Cannes Film Festival!" surrounded by those little laurel parentheses; "Winner! Best Narrative Feature, Sundance Film Festival!" Today just being selected for a major festival merits placement within the laurels. We've even seen movie posters that trumpet such unremarkable accomplishments as "Official Selection, New York International Independent Film and Video Festival."

"OK," we hear you say with resignation, "I accept that I'll have to make a no-budget feature." Good for you, hypothetical you! "But," we hear you continuing, "how do I go about making it?" Have no fear; we're full of ideas on that subject, and we'll get into it later, in the "After Film School" section.

## ▶ THINGS TO THINK ABOUT WHEN APPLYING

Allow us to generalize for a moment: There are four kinds of film school: industry, independent, experimental, and documentary.

The industry schools, most typified by USC and AFI, train students to work in Hollywood. This means some will be given money by the school to direct films, but many will not, and will spend much of their time working as technicians on films that other people write and direct. The independent schools—UCLA, NYU, and Columbia for example—expect everyone to write and direct. But the school provides little financial assistance with the films, so students learn to strip down their filmmaking to the barest essentials and make do with what they have. The experimental schools like CalArts and the San Francisco Art Institute don't teach students to raise large amounts of money or to make feature films. They teach film as a medium for personal expression and encourage students to make art without any thought of the business of film. Documentary programs teach students not only the art of documentary filmmaking, but also the art of writing grants and raising funds.

To some degree the lines are blurring. USC is an industry school but has a good documentary division; at traditionally experimental schools like San Francisco State and CalArts, more and more students are working in independent-style narrative filmmaking.

None of these is better than the others; it's a matter of personal preference. But it's important that you know what kind of films you want to make and then choose an appropriate school. Many people see that *U.S. News & World Report* ranks USC as the number one film school, and just apply there, without ever stopping to wonder if USC's particular brand of industry-trade-school film-making is what they want to do with their lives.

The industry is hard to get into, and it restricts creativity to whatever is marketable, but once you are in you can be financially secure for life. Independent feature filmmaking is hard work and is financially risky, but it promises complete artistic control. Experimental filmmaking is a calling, not a living. Its chief practitioners do it because they are driven to express themselves, not because they expect to make money doing it. Documentary filmmaking was once a calling that was not a living, but today many filmmakers make a living in documentary, and a few have even become famous.

The independent schools encourage independence both in school and out of school. They provide their students with equipment, but the students have to come up with their own money to pay for film stock, transportation, food, and so on. The students have a great deal of freedom to make the films they choose, but the financial burden can be staggering.

It used to be that AFI and USC picked only half a dozen thesis films to be made each year; the school funded those films, and afterward the school held the copyright on those films. Nowadays these schools are more like the independent schools; most students who attend USC or AFI can make a thesis film if they want to, but the school does not pay for the films. But at the same time both schools continue to claim ownership of these films. Some students are surprised to learn that, after spending tens of thousands of dollars to make a film, they have no right to put that film into festivals or sell it on DVD. This does not represent nefarious intentions on the school's part, only a difference of opinion on the purpose of these films. At these schools, a student film is not intended as a work of mass entertainment; it is intended as a résumé piece. The intended audience for any of these films is a producer looking for someone to hire, not a cinema fan looking to be entertained.

Each variety of film school reflects that part of the real world in microcosm. The independent schools are microcosms of independent filmmaking, as filmmakers who never have quite enough money for what they want to do help one another out to make their films as best they can. The industry film schools are a microcosm of industry filmmaking, where films are the result of complicated processes of negotiation and compromise. The experimental schools are full of quiet, artistic people who mostly work alone on shadowy projects that few eyes ever see. And documentary film students trek the world in small packs following stories wherever they lead. As such, film school can teach you as much about the filmmaking way of life as about the technique of filmmaking.

### ▶ HOW MUCH IS THIS GOING TO COST?

Film school is expensive. Once you have paid your tuition, which can be as much as $34,000 a year for three years or more, and once you have paid for room and board for up to four years, you may still have to buy film stock, rent extra equipment or vehicles, feed large casts and crews, pay for locations, or reimburse people for damaged equipment or property. (Don't laugh—at the end of a shoot there is always damaged equipment or property.)

Most of the schools purposely play this aspect down. And for good reason. If you knew now what you will have spent by the end of film school, you may very likely chuck the whole idea.

This is not to say that it can't be done affordably. There are ways of saving money. There are inexpensive schools, and there are ways of getting through the expensive schools at a discount rate. There are even schools that have high tuition, but that pay that tuition for their students. For each school we will provide a rough estimate of how much the program costs and will give hints on how to save money along the way.

There are schools that are unbelievably expensive, and there are schools that are virtually free. But beware—the cheap ones are not always a bargain, and the expensive ones are not always a rip-off.

The inexpensive schools tend to be small. They will give you solitude in which to do your own thing. But you will be as much on your own after school as during school.

You will not have a large network of classmates to call on for advice or assistance, and your school will do nothing to promote you or your work. On the other hand, if you have a good film, and if you have the chutzpah to promote it, to enter it into festivals, and to show it to producers and agents, then you will be better off than the film students at the bigger schools, who often patiently wait in vain for their schools to promote them and provide them with contacts.

The most expensive schools are big schools—schools with too many students and not enough equipment for them all. These schools have to ration their equipment; they may have good equipment, but they will only give it to you for a week or two per year, which may or may not be enough time to shoot your film. These schools will surround you with a diverse and supportive community of filmmakers. You will work on your classmates' films, and they will work on yours, and through this interchange you will learn everything you need to know about filmmaking. These schools will provide better chances of making contacts in the outside world, and better exposure after graduation. Whether the contacts and exposure are worth the extra hundred thousand dollars is a difficult call.

There are other advantages and disadvantages that are hard to quantify. For instance, some schools have more cachet in Hollywood than others. If you tell a producer you went to USC he may smile grimly and change the subject. Because of the school's size and location, USC alumni— graduate and undergraduate—make up a large portion of the film community in Los Angeles. You can't throw a rock in Hollywood without hitting a USC graduate. So producers will often be impressed if you tell them you graduated from any school other than USC—from Columbia, or Florida State, of the Chicago Art Institute, or AFI. But, on the other hand, they are only impressed by schools they have heard of; you won't wow anyone in Hollywood by telling them you went to Ohio or Carbondale or Milwaukee.

Still, if you made a great film at Ohio or Carbondale or Milwaukee, and won awards, and had it shown in major festivals, then you won't need to wow them with your degree. A great short film is worth more than a certificate from the best film program (not to keep hammering this, but especially when it is accompanied by a great feature-length screenplay).

Student loans are available, but be careful. New York and Los Angeles are already stuffed with MFA graduates from respected institutions who write screenplays in the evenings while they temp or wait tables or fill out unemployment forms during the day.

### ▶ WILL FILM SCHOOL BRING YOU CLOSER TO YOUR GOALS?

Many people who want to go to film school don't have a specific career in mind, only a general desire to be in the movies. This can be unfortunate, as many ultimately decide to pursue a career they could have gotten into without a degree.

For instance, we know of several people who finished three years of graduate film school only to decide that they wanted to be film editors. It is likely that, had they known three years earlier that they wanted to be editors, they could have gotten jobs as assistant editors and worked their way up through the ranks for three years. Not only would they be much closer to their career goals at the end of the three years, but they also would have been making money, rather than spending money on film school.

Compared to directing, fields like editing, sound, cinematography, and producing are not hard to get into if you are certain you want to get into them. You can start as an intern or production assistant on any shoot, befriend the technicians in your chosen field, and get them to hire you as an assistant on their next film. It may be a few years before you work your way up to a position of any influence, but even that will certainly be sooner than it would take to finish film school and then pay off all of your loans.

If you want to be a cinematographer, film school has a lot to offer. Directing students always need good cinematographers, so if you are good, you can shoot your classmates' films, getting all the practice you can stand, putting together an impressive reel without spending a cent of your own money beyond tuition. And if any of the students whose films you shoot gets a chance to direct a feature, you might be hired to shoot it. On the other hand, you could be doing this without paying tuition; all you need to do is hang around a film school and offer to work for free on students' films. Also, it is not that difficult to become an assistant cameraperson in the real world. Once you are in that position, it might be a few years before you get to shoot your own footage, but it is almost certain to happen, and getting there is sure to be a lot less expensive than film school.

## ▶ ARE YOU KEEPING UP WITH THE NEW TECHNOLOGY?

The high-technology revolution that has reshaped so many industries has only relatively recently found its way into the film industry. It started slowly, when Japanese high-tech firms developed small, high-quality video cameras and recorders that replaced the 16 mm film cameras of television news programs. Then consumer electronics firms adapted the technology into consumer video camcorders to replace the Super 8 film cameras of amateur filmmakers. Then movie camera makers like Arriflex and Cinema Products started to put microprocessors inside their film cameras.

But for all the changes in camera technology, they still work about the same; you frame up and shoot. Where high technology has really changed how things work is in postproduction. In the entertainment industry most editing is now computerized. When you make a film the old-fashioned way, you shoot your negative, pay to have it processed, and then have a workprint made of the negative. Workprints are expensive; you essentially buy another roll of film, have it exposed from the negative, and then have that film processed. You then have to buy a lot of magnetic film and transfer your sound onto it. When you have your workprint and mag film ready, you rent expensive editing equipment to cut it, and when your cut is finished, you rent time in an incredibly expensive mixing studio to mix the soundtracks. The new technology has made workprints, flatbed editing machines, and mag film mixing studios unnecessary; you now telecine your negative directly to video and then digitize the video and audio tracks into a computer and edit them there. When you are happy with your cut, the program will spit out an edit decision list. A negative cutter can then cut your negative according to the EDL while you are still at your computer putting the final touches on the soundtrack.

This is a startling change from only a few years ago. Editing, sound design, and mixing of a twenty-minute film used to cost thousands of dollars, even tens of thousands of dollars, in materials and equipment rental. Now, you just pay for the processing of the negative and the telecine. If you go to a school that has this equipment, you can do everything else but the negative cut and the answer print for free.

The fields of sound editing and sound design have changed almost beyond recognition thanks to digital audio technology. Digital audio is higher quality than analog audiotape or mag film; it always runs at sync speed, and it is much easier to manipulate and mix. And audio can be manipulated on a computer in ways that were unthinkable only a few years ago: camera noise, once the bane of sound technicians' existence, is now easily removed from recordings using digital audio workstations. Audio effects that once took hours of tinkering to get right can now be manufactured in seconds and saved to disk for future use. Where mixing eight soundtracks used to mean stringing up eight different mag film tracks on enormous dubbers and praying they stayed in sync and that the mag film didn't break while you were mixing, a digital workstation can easily mix hundreds of audio tracks at once.

Many schools are taking this technological leap, but not all. Some schools are still wed to film—either because they have a lot of money invested in the equipment or because professors are not willing to give up skills they have spent decades perfecting—and students continue to shoot film and edit on Moviola or Steenbeck flatbed editing machines, cutting and taping picture and soundtracks by hand. But students at these schools find that the methods of filmmaking they learn in school are no longer marketable skills in the industry. An editor today must know how to use Avid and Final Cut Pro; cutting film on a flatbed is a dead art outside of film schools.

But if a school is still teaching film techniques, it's not the end of the world. You can buy yourself a Macintosh and a copy of Final Cut Pro and edit at home. The biggest problem with nonlinear editing systems is that they are incredibly complex, and it can take a long time to learn how to use them and keep them running optimally. Where the old film and tape method of editing was pretty easy to learn, the new method requires considerable knowledge of computer hardware and software, of video formats and film formats, of RAM modules and RAIDs, of SATA and SCSI and Firewire.

Beyond editing, new technologies have also opened up whole new fields for those who want to work in visual media. Digital effects work has become huge business in recent years, and digital animators are in such demand that they are recruited directly out of school like lawyers or MBAs. Lighting directors and production designers are needed for 3-D games. And even the Internet has proven to be an amazing visual medium. Today, young people who are both technologically proficient and skilled in visual storytelling can easily find challenging, well-paid work in almost any of these fields—and new fields are opening up all the time.

But in order to work in any of these fields you will need to choose a school that can teach you the new technologies. Remember that as you ponder which schools you want to apply to.

## ▶ PREPARATION FOR FILM SCHOOL

There are some things you can do before going to film school that will help you to get in and that will put you at an advantage once you get there.

### Take Some Writing Courses

Many film schools have come to the realization that if they are going to teach their students directing, lighting, editing, camera, and sound, then they will not have time to teach them to write. This realization has led to a policy at many schools of only accepting applicants who already show an ability to write. Consequently, we recommend that you work on your writing skills as much as possible now.

Writing is an indispensable skill in film school and in the industry. So few people know how to write well in America today that literacy has become a rare and valuable skill. When you apply, if you can show the ability to write an original story, it will put you miles ahead of most of the applicants you are competing with. Once you're in film school, if you can write good short screenplays, it will put you miles ahead of most of your classmates. After film school when you are out in the real world, if you can write good feature-length screenplays, it will put you miles ahead of everyone else in the industry.

Screenplays are power. Every person in the industry—actor, director, producer, cameraman, designer, and so on down the line—flatters himself that he is a creative genius. But in truth, if the film he works on is badly written, then his genius will never be noticed. It is the writer who creates the characters for which the actors take credit. It is the writer who creates the settings for which the designers take credit. It is the writer who creates the story and situations for which the director takes credit. In fact, the writer is the most truly creative person in the entire industry. All the other crafts merely build upon what the writer creates.

So while nobody in the industry will ever admit it, a good screenwriter is the most powerful person in Hollywood. We cannot encourage you strongly enough to take courses in writing and to keep cranking out stories and screenplays as energetically as you can.

**Take Some Acting Courses**

If you want to direct, you must take acting courses. Actors have a language of their own, and directors must be conversant in this language to be able to direct them. Audiences don't watch movies to see cool camera angles, they watch movies to see characters they can empathize with in situations they can relate to. The actors who portray these characters are the most important element in your film, and if you know how they work, how they talk, and how they feel, you will have a great advantage when it comes time to direct them.

It is a common mistake for first-time directors to concentrate on camera angles and effects and forget about the actors. This is unfortunate, as actors can be an emotional and contentious lot. Many need to be coddled and flattered if they are going to give good performances. When a director does not give an actor a script in advance of production, when a director makes an actor sit around for hours with nothing to eat while the crew sets up lights, when a director's only instructions to an actor are, "OK, in this shot I want you to walk over to that railing and look out at the sailboats with a sad yet whimsical smile," the actor gets cranky and looks unhappy on screen. And if the actor looks uncomfortable, then the audience will not be interested in the story, and nobody will care if you have cool camera angles or neat effects.

47

If you take acting courses, you will have a valuable appreciation of the actor's craft, and you will avoid a number of the worst mistakes that first-time filmmakers make.

## Make Some Films

The best way to learn how to make a film is to get out there and do it. If you have access to a video camera, go out and start making movies.

When we say you should make movies, we don't mean you should shoot bar mitzvahs or Little League games. Rather, we mean you should sit down and write a five- or ten-minute story that involves characters and action, and find friends to act in the roles. Then make people watch it. When someone sits and watches your film, you will find yourself saying, "Hey, that scene would have been better if I'd shot it in close-up," or, "There's too much going on in this scene. I should have simplified it," or "Gee, my sister is a lousy actress—I'll have to cast someone better next time." That is how you learn to make films; by making mistakes and then figuring out how to do it better next time.

If you are at a school that offers film courses, you would do well to take one or two courses where you can shoot films or videos. This is a great opportunity to experiment with writing and directing, and it is a great opportunity to get feedback from a receptive audience of classmates. Some film schools like to see examples of work from their applicants, so this could also help you to get into film school.

This is also a good opportunity to befriend the people in the equipment room, but we'll come back to that later.

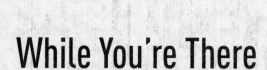

# While You're There

Let's say you've been accepted into film school. Congratulations!

So, you move to that school, you enroll, you pay your tuition, and you start taking classes. Now what?

The first thing you will notice is that your bank account is emptying out faster than you ever dreamed possible. Here are some suggestions for how to deal with that.

## ▶ SAVE MONEY

The single best way to save money (and at the same time make money) is to become a teaching assistant. Most universities pay part or all of their TAs' tuition and pay a stipend on top of that. Because TAs work closely with the faculty, they can often get more equipment than they deserve when it is time to shoot their films, so they do not have to spend money on renting additional equipment. And when a school decides to give out a cash award to some lucky student, it often goes to a TA.

You can also save a lot of money on housing by becoming a resident assistant (RA) in a school's dormitories. RAs get free housing and all the free dormitory food they can stand. Rent and food are so outrageously expensive in New York that you could probably pay for all of your films just with the money you save by being an RA. Rent is cheaper in other cities, so being an RA may not be as good a deal, depending on where you are living. But no matter where you are in the country, free room and board is nothing to scoff at.

When it comes time to make your thesis film, do not fall into the common misconception that expensive effects or complicated shots will make your film good. Many students have made films for next to nothing, shooting entirely in their own apartments or in their parents' houses, that have gone on to wide acclaim. These students knew that the secret to a good film is not in the technology but in the writing and the performances. If the characters are vivid, if the situations they get into are realistic and intriguing, then fancy camera shots are not necessary. It costs nothing to write a good story, but no amount of cool camera effects will make a bad story into a good film.

You can save money on film stock. There are companies in New York and Los Angeles that buy unused stock from professional film shoots and resell it at a significant discount. This is a great way to save as much as 25 percent off the going price of raw stock, but it has a downside; if you shoot short ends, you'll have to piece your film together from tiny bits of film. Better still, you can shoot on digital video. Today, 24p video has about 90 percent of the quality of 16 mm film but costs about 1 percent as much money to shoot.

## ▶ MAKE MONEY

There are a number of ways to make money while you are in school. The first thing to do is apply for financial aid—if you can get an all-expense-paid fellowship, then you will not have to worry about money at all. If you can't get a fellowship, then try to get a teaching assistantship. Assistantships pay fairly well, and what work they involve usually has something to do with your studies.

Most schools offer work-study programs where students are paid close to minimum wage for working as projectionists or in the equipment room. These are a better deal in the less expensive parts of the country than in New York or San Francisco or Los Angeles. In these large expensive cities, work-study hardly seems worth the effort—the pay is usually less than what jobs outside the school pay, and the work is usually pretty dull. The main benefit of a work-study position is it might get you closer to the faculty and thus into a better position to get a teaching assistantship.

Most anywhere you go, you can make more money working outside the school than within the school. But the jobs need to be flexible enough to allow you to go to school.

It is also possible to work in film in many of the cities where there are film schools. New York, Los Angeles, Miami, Chicago, and San Francisco all have film and TV production on a regular basis—both local work like commercials and industrial films, and the occasional feature. Production companies will sometimes post notices on school bulletin boards looking for people to work as production assistants. PA work will generally pay from $100 to $200 per day to start, and as you get better at it you can ask for more. In Los Angeles work in the film industry is more plentiful, but you have to compete with undergrads who are still living off their parents and who can afford to work for free as interns. PA work is a good way to learn how a real film shoot operates, and to learn about gaffing and grip equipment (which is something you won't learn much about at a lot of schools). The drawbacks of PA work are the gruelingly long hours (which always seem to conflict with classes) and stultifying work (expect to spend most of your time running errands or restocking the crew's snack table).

## ▶ SHOOT VIDEO

The quality of video has improved dramatically in the past few years. First digital video came along, which dramatically improved quality over analog video. Then new formats came along that provided clearer images: 24p, high definition, and HDV (which has the resolution of high definition, but is heavily compressed so it can fit onto mini-DV tapes). The use of video has grown astoundingly in recent years. In one decade video has displaced film as the medium of choice for most productions.

There are many reasons for this. One is that most productions are intended to be seen only on video. Whether television shows, commercials, music videos, corporate films, industrial films, or multimedia presentations, these productions will never be seen anywhere but on a television screen, so there is little benefit to shooting them on film. Thanks to the high cost of the silver halides used in motion picture film, and of the chemicals required to process them, film is much more expensive than video. And with video there is no lag time between shooting and screening. If a DP on a set is worried about how a take looks, she need not wait until dailies return the next morning to find out; she can just rewind the tape and look at it.

One issue with video is that there are so many different standards around the world. If you shoot NTSC video, converting it to the PAL or SECAM standards used in other countries will degrade the image noticeably. Many network television shows are shot on film only because the final film print can be used as a high-quality master from which any standard of video copy can be made with no loss of quality. But high-definition video can be used the same way, so more and more television shows are being shot in that.

### ▶ KEEP IT SHORT

Film students like to show off by making the biggest, longest, most impressive films they can. If a project is supposed to be ten minutes long, a lot of students will want to make it half an hour; if a project is supposed to be half an hour long, a lot of students will want to make it feature-length. It's an understandable impulse; the goal is to make feature films, so it seems logical that the closer a student film is in length to a feature, the more likely its maker will be hired to direct features.

It doesn't work this way, though. Today, the primary forum for short films is the film festival circuit. It is true that cable networks like IFC and the Sundance Channel screen shorts, but they largely screen shorts that have won awards in film festivals. So getting into festivals is vital. The more festivals your short screens in, the more exposure you will get, and the more likely it will be that you will go on to a career making films.

Film festival programmers want their programs to include a wide variety of films and filmmakers. When faced with a choice between screening one thirty-minute film or three ten-minute films, a programmer will almost always program the ten-minute films. So, all other things being equal, a strong ten-minute film is at least three times more likely to be accepted into a festival than an equally strong thirty-minute film. A strong five-minute film might play in every festival in the world. On the other hand, a forty-five-minute-long film won't screen anywhere; too short to be programmed as a feature but too long to be programmed as a short, a film of this length would never be seen by anyone but the filmmaker's friends and family.

So don't feel a need to make long and complicated films while you're in film school. The most important thing is to be seen, and the shorter your film is, the more people will see it. And, anyway, people who know about film know that it takes great skill to make a genuinely moving five-minute-long film. To the people who matter, a strong five-minute film is far more impressive than a half-hour-long student film that wishes it were a feature.

## ▶ BEFRIEND THE PEOPLE IN THE EQUIPMENT ROOM

If you want to make films while you are in school, these people are the best friends you can have. If they like you, they will loan you the best equipment available. If they really like you, they will bend the rules for you. They will help you out of many of the pinches you get into.

On the other hand, if they do not like you they can make your life hell. They will give you the worst equipment available. You and your films will suffer. Even if they don't actively dislike you, they can still compromise your film; they will give the best equipment to the people they really like, and you will wind up with the camera that scratches film sometimes or the DAT recorder with the battery that only lasts ten minutes.

Once you have befriended the people in the equipment room, you may not have to depend on the school much. You can bug your new friends and get equipment any time you want and make the films you want to make without interference from the school. The more films you make, the more you will know the craft of filmmaking. And the more you know the craft of filmmaking, the better off you will be when it comes time to make your thesis.

If you get into one of the big film schools, the equipment is almost constantly in use, so there isn't much opportunity to get equipment on the sly in this way. But the people in the equipment room can still be very helpful with the quality and quantity of the equipment you receive when you are allowed to borrow it.

This may be the most important thing we say in this book, so keep it in mind. Wherever you are, and whatever you do, always be nice to the people in the equipment room.

# The Schools

We have broken down our descriptions of each of the schools into three sections: "The Program," "The Price," and "The Lowdown."

**THE PROGRAM** describes the basic facts about the school and the film program: what the focus is, how long it takes, how classes are organized, what are the specific requirements for graduation, and so on.

**THE PRICE** includes a rough estimate of how much the school will cost and some specific suggestions on how to save money and make money. The calculation is only a very rough estimate based on many variables, including tuition, length of stay, approximate rents, approximate film budgets, whether or not you will need a car, etc. Apart from tuition, we have based all of these calculations on anecdotal information; average rents and film budgets according to the students we spoke with at the schools. *These figures are not intended to be the final word on how much each school will ultimately cost, only a very rough indication for the sake of comparison.*

**THE LOWDOWN** includes the nitty-gritty information about the school: comments and advice, complaints and recommendations from students who have gone there.

This section includes a discussion of the schools' best and worst features, information about the schools' equipment and facilities, and what the schools look for in applicants.

In addition, we group the schools into four categories; industry, independent, experimental, and documentary. These categories are described in detail in "Things to Think About when Applying" (page 36).

# AMERICAN FILM INSTITUTE

The American Film Institute Conservatory
2021 North Western Avenue
Los Angeles, CA 90027-1657
323-856-7600
www.afi.com/education/conservatory

| | |
|---|---|
| **Tuition:** | **$29,975** |
| **Enrollment:** | **28 directors** |
| | **28 producers** |
| | **28 screenwriters** |
| | **28 cinematographers** |
| | **14 editors** |
| | **8 production designers** |
| **Deadline:** | **December 16** |
| **Focus:** | **Industry** |

## ▶ THE PROGRAM

The American Film Institute is much more than a film school. It is a large organization with three main purposes: preservation (through the National Center for Film and Video Preservation), advocacy (through lobbying and through the sponsorship of restorations, special screenings, and film festivals), and training (through the AFI Conservatory). The conservatory is in Los Angeles, housed in Spanish-style buildings that once belonged to a parochial school on a hill overlooking Hollywood.

The program consists of six divisions—Screenwriting, Producing, Directing, Editing, Cinematography, and Production Design—but fellows in all departments work together so closely that it's essentially one program, not six separate programs. There is also a program in Digital Media, but apart from occasionally doing titles or effects for films, the Digital Media fellows largely work apart from the film production department.

Each division accepts twenty-eight fellows per year, except for Editing and Production Design, which accept fewer. These are ideal numbers; while hundreds of people apply to be directors and cinematographers every year, the school often has trouble finding twenty-eight acceptable producers or eight acceptable production designers and accepts fewer.

This is a rigidly structured, five-term/two-and-one-half-year program, which is intended for people who already have real-world experience in film. Most of the applicants accepted as directing fellows have already made movies elsewhere. This allows the school to launch straight into fairly advanced filmmaking as of the first day. There are no courses in film theory and criticism; AFI's program is about making movies, no more and no less.

At the beginning of first year, students introduce themselves by screening films they have made before. This is followed by the first of a series of boot camps designed to get the students accustomed to working together as production teams. In boot camp, students are assigned to groups—one student from each division—who work together to shoot scenes. Each group is given the same two- or three-page scene to shoot, and is given four hours to shoot it and four hours to edit it. In any given year there will be two or three boot camps—it changes from year to year—and then students will move on to the cycle projects.

Where the boot camps are made from scripts provided by the school, cycle projects are created and produced entirely by students. Producers, directors, and screenwriters are asked to have two ideas for short films in mind when they arrive at the school; the school divides these students up into twenty-eight groups, with one writer, one producer, and one screenwriter, and each group has to decide on an idea to turn into a film as a group. Once a group has decided on a project, they then recruit an editor, cinematographer, and production designer to work with them. Each group is given four days to shoot the cycle project and about ten days to edit it. Each student screens the project for classmates within his specialty, and then the film is screened before the entire class in the Narrative Workshop. In this class, a film is screened, and then its crew sits onstage and listens quietly while a professor leads a discussion about it with the other students. Later, the professor discusses the film privately with the crew. Students go through three separate cycle projects before the end of the year, which frequently overlap; students frequently find themselves trying to find a team for the second cycle project while still editing the first. One major restriction on the cycle projects is that when finished they cannot be screened outside of the school.

All of these first-year projects—the cycle projects and the boot camps—are shot on digital video and generally run between twenty and thirty minutes. The school provides production equipment and $3,250 in cash for each cycle project. Students frequently augment this budget to make their projects more impressive. The school asks that students not spend more than $2,000 of their own money on each of these projects, but in reality, most spend more. Where this extra money comes from varies for each film. AFI is very much an industry school, and these films are produced as if they were Hollywood features; the producer is expected to raise the necessary money, while the other crew members focus on shooting and completing postproduction on the project. Most crew members wind up contributing some of their own money toward these projects. The school has strong ties to unions, and students may only cast their films using actors from the SAG Conservatory, located on the AFI campus. Cinematographers accustomed to low-budget productions are often surprised to learn that they are not allowed to operate the cameras on these projects and are required to work with camera operators. Therefore, on any given cycle project there will be two cinematography students; one the cinematographer, the other the camera operator.

At the end of first year, all students have a Year One Portfolio Review, a formal interview/interrogation with faculty in their respective disciplines. Students can only continue on into second year if they are invited back by the faculty. There was a time not long ago when more than half of the first-year students were not invited back, regardless of the quality of their work, but these days almost everyone is invited back. Only people who really screw up during their first year are not invited back today.

The end of first year is also when thesis projects are arranged. This is a strange and complex process, somewhere between a mating ritual and a feeding frenzy. We fear our words may not come close to describing the reality, but here goes: Only twenty or so thesis films are made each year. In April, every student submits to the faculty the script of a project he would like to make as a thesis film in second year. All students can submit projects, including cinematographers and production designers, though the majority of projects chosen will be director-, producer-, or screenwriter-initiated. On a Friday afternoon in mid-May the faculty posts a list of the projects that they have "green-lighted." Scripts for the green-lighted projects are posted online and in the school's library, so everyone can read them. Green-lighted projects may then proceed toward production in second year. Students with green-lit projects have to scramble to get the cinematographers, editors, and production designers they want before those people commit to other projects. Many students do not get green lights on their films and have to work on other people's films; a director who does not get a green light must find a producer-initiated project that does not yet have a director and try to talk his way into directing it.

After the green lights are announced, the faculty disappears for twenty-four hours. They are unreachable by phone or e-mail, so the students are left to fight it out on their own. Those who have green-lit projects fight to get the best crew to commit to their projects. Those who do not have green-lit projects fight to get onto the best projects they can. People call one another at two, three, and four in the morning, pleading, threatening, crying, doing whatever it takes to get onto good projects. Some students learn how popular they are with their fellow students, and have to choose between many different projects; others discover how unpopular they are with their fellow students when nobody calls. And every year some people are left without a thesis project to work on, and with nothing to do in second year, they leave the program. By Saturday afternoon crews have congealed around the green-lit thesis projects, and, one way or another, everyone knows what they'll be doing in second year. Saturday evening faculty members start answering their phones again.

Students then begin work on their productions and present complete production packages to the faculty. The faculty assigns dates to these projects: not just start dates for production, but dates for completion of the initial edit, for reshoot days, for picture lock, and for final delivery. Each thesis crew is required to go through a three-week preproduction track under faculty advisement. Students who are set to shoot before Thanksgiving of second year are required to do this during the summer. For the others, nothing much happens during the summer. There are no classes, so some students work during this time; cinematographers and production designers in particular are in demand by students at other Los Angeles film schools, where the technical training is not as good as at AFI. Directors and producers are likely to spend the summer rewriting and preparing to shoot their thesis projects.

Second year revolves around the thesis films. Each production receives $12,000 in cash; students are allowed to raise additional funds, but the total budget on these films cannot exceed $65,000. Students are allowed to shoot a total of six days within a fourteen-day window. They must schedule one break day within the six shooting days. The school is well-stocked with DV and high-definition cameras, thanks to a generous donation from Sony, so many students work in digital. The school has one 35 mm camera package, which was donated by Panavision. However, students who shoot film almost always rent complete production packages from local rental houses. A number of houses have relationships with AFI and will let students use their gear for almost nothing.

When a thesis film is complete, the students who made it are expected to arrange a gala screening and to invite agents and producers to come see it.

While students get to keep copies of the films they make, the school claims ownership of every film made there. Students are given a window of eighteen months after completion of a project during which they can freely submit it to film festivals and awards programs. After that time, all films are handled by Shorts International, which has an exclusive contract to distribute AFI student films.

While thesis films are assigned a completion date at the same time they are assigned a start date, many students do not deliver their films on time. Students may continue working on their films through the summer and fall, but all films must be completed and delivered to the school by December 15. While all students walk through graduation ceremonies in June of their second year, few are actually finished at that time. For those students, there is a hard graduation date of December 31.

## ▶ THE PRICE

| | |
|---|---|
| $29,975 tuition for two years | $59,950 |
| $15,000 per year rent and living expenses for three years | $45,000 |
| $2,000 per year maintenance and insurance on a car in Los Angeles for three years | $6,000 |
| First-year films | $5,000 |
| Average thesis film costs | $20,000 |
| **Total** | **$135,950** |

You will need a car in Los Angeles. Students with cars can work on any shoot they like, while students without cars are regarded as something of a burden and are, to a certain extent, shunned by their classmates.

The campus is on the eastern edge of Hollywood in an area called Los Feliz. Housing in this area is expensive compared with other cities, but only a little above average for Los Angeles. There are many apartment buildings in the area. One-bedroom apartments within walking distance of the school go for as little as $1,000 a month; two-bedrooms go for around $1,400; studios for $800 or so. We're told there's one apartment building near the campus that only accepts AFI fellows as tenants.

A handful of scholarships are available. Kodak gives out grants of free film stock to several students a year, and Photochem, a local film processing laboratory, gives two thesis films free processing services. Beyond the grants, both are happy to give deep discounts to AFI thesis students.

## ▶ THE LOWDOWN

We were told this story: One recent year, the faculty decided to demonstrate to the incoming first-year students how a team should work together on the boot camp exercises. Six professors, the heads of each department, got up onto a stage in front of the whole incoming class and proceeded to plan and then shoot a scene as a team. But after only a few minutes one professor made a cutting remark about another's choices, and before long it devolved into something of a shouting match. It may not have worked out as planned, but the students all agreed it was highly educational.

Unlike the majority of schools we cover, AFI largely accepts only people who already have experience in film. It is not an introductory film program at all, rather a place where experienced filmmakers and technicians go to polish their existing skills or learn additional skills in the hope of making the transition to directing. An unusually large number of AFI students come from other countries; between a quarter and a third of any class will be from outside the United States.

For the directing division, AFI accepts submissions of films with applications. In fact, the school really only considers applicants who have already made films on their own. Generally, if you cannot send in a good film that you directed, you have little chance of getting into the directing program. In any given year a number of directing fellows will have already made features or worked in television. Most have a great deal of experience; indeed, students say that they learn far more from one another than they do from professors.

Competition is fierce to get into the directing, screenwriting, and cinematography programs. There is less competition to get into editing and production design; if you know you want to be an editor and have a reel to show, you have a good shot of getting in. Producing and production design are the only departments that actually have trouble finding enough qualified applicants every year.

AFI's producing program is very different from the producing programs at UCLA and USC. Where those programs are largely about creative producing—about finding an idea and nurturing it over the long term, collecting collaborators and financiers and seeing a project through production, completion, and distribution—AFI is mostly about line-producing. AFI producers learn a great deal about managing the day-to-day details of a shoot but less about having an overall vision for a creative project and carrying it over the course of years from conception to completion.

Many of the students we spoke with did not get in the first time they applied but did get in on the second after revising and improving their application materials. If you want to direct, do not apply to one of the other divisions thinking you can switch into directing later. But if you want to study editing or cinematography or production design, AFI is a very good place to study. The cost is low compared to many schools, the opportunities to work are many, and much of the equipment is first-rate.

Sony has endowed AFI with a digital media center and gives a large chunk of money to the school every year, with which the school can buy new equipment. Avid keeps the school stocked with sufficient Avid editing workstations for the editors. The school has one soundstage, a basement space with a low ceiling and creaky wooden floors.

The school is deeply entrenched in Hollywood and operates by many of its rules. For instance, all actors in AFI films must be members of the Screen Actors Guild. As a result, SAG's union regulations dictate a great deal about how student shoots must be scheduled and executed. But an advantage of this is that any member of SAG can appear in an AFI film. If you want to make a student film that stars Harrison Ford and Meryl Streep, and have the connections to reach them and ask, you'll have no objection from the school or the union.

The school has in recent years been making more of an effort to introduce graduates to Hollywood. The school screens all student thesis films for the industry at a theater in Hollywood every year, and screenwriters are given an opportunity to pitch their screenplays to producers, agents, and development executives. The producing fellows are required to work as interns at the annual American Film Market event in Santa Monica. And even within the school all second-year students are assigned first-year students to mentor and advise.

For the most part students speak highly of first year as a solid year of intense creative experience. But as the thesis green-lighting approaches in May, students start eyeing one another nervously, trying to determine who will be a friend and who will be an enemy when the day comes. Many students try to negotiate deals to work on one another's theses in advance of the date; however, those deals tend to fall apart when faced with the reality of the green lights. Several students described a polarization that occurs as the stress of the program increases, where some students become more and more benevolent, helping others out however they can, while others become more and more solitary and defensive. Needless to say it is the former who have a good experience at AFI, and the latter who tend to leave the program before second year starts.

*Some of the worst things about the program:* Many students are frustrated that they do not own the films they make. The faculty members are working professionals—sometimes not-working professionals—and occasionally seem more interested in their own careers than in those of their students.

*Some of the best things about the program:* It begins very well, with a screening of all of the films the students sent in with their applications, and then with the boot camps. For people who have already been working in film and just want a program that will allow them to move upward in the industry, AFI is a great school.

# AMERICAN UNIVERSITY

School of Communication
4400 Massachusetts Avenue NW
Washington, DC 20016-8002
202-885-2060
www.soc.american.edu

| | |
|---|---|
| Tuition: | $17,802 |
| Enrollment: | 34 |
| Deadline: | Fall: February 1 |
| | Spring: November 15 |
| Focus: | Independent Documentary |

## ▶ THE PROGRAM

American University established its MFA in Film and Electronic Media in 1997. The three-year program is documentary-focused and provides a general knowledge across the landscape of media.

There are twenty-seven credits of core courses. These include film program standards like production fundamentals, producing, history, theory, and writing, as well as some not-so-standard classes in teaching media arts, animation, and a required internship. Some classes might be taken with undergraduates. Those with no prior experience in photography must also take a basic black-and-white photography course before taking any advanced courses in media production. These three credits do not count toward the degree requirements.

Students meet early on with a faculty advisor who assists in creating a plan of study that allows them to fulfill requirements and to possibly choose an overall focus in media studies or production and writing. Students who do not wish to focus can continue to take their required elective credits within the School of Communication or even liberal or performing arts. With advisor approval there is opportunity to tailor the program electives according to the interests of the individual student. Classes need not be taken in any particular order other than taking pre-requisite courses when necessary. Students generally begin with twelve credits the first semester, then scale back to between six and nine credits for the remaining semesters.

The program encourages students to make as many films as possible both within and outside of classes. More than half of the students devote themselves to documentary filmmaking, and long-form journalism documentaries are not uncommon. Depending on the course of study a student develops, he can have four to five short films for which he is responsible by the end of the program. If ambitious, he will also work in key positions on many more of his classmates' films. Once in awhile students join forces and shoot a longer project. Thesis films should be no more than thirty minutes but this rule is not strictly enforced. The program views students' creative portfolios as the most valuable asset with which they depart.

In the late nineties American University established an international program at FAMU, the Academy of Dramatic Arts in Prague Film Academy. A large number of American students accept the option to attend a semester of twelve credits of either intermediate or advanced training in Prague. All of the credits are transferable, so students can return to the States and still be on track for their degree. There is, however, an additional $5,000 fee for housing and staff assistance (like English translators in all classes). Partial funding is provided for all production classes taken while abroad.

A mentor program is in place to match interested students with specific alumni. There is a very active internship program. And although only one is required, most students take the maximum of three internships either locally or in Los Angeles. The West Coast positions are secured through a summer program in Los Angeles that introduces students to West Coast alumni who work as media producers and executives. Through these contacts, students network their internships. Many have positions locked down before they even arrive in Los Angeles.

The Center for Environmental Filmmaking invites students to take advantage of "Classroom in the Wild," a spring break program that focuses on "extreme filmmaking." They have the opportunity to travel to locations like the Florida Everglades or the Chesapeake Bay to work on film projects. The center has a relationship with REI to conduct training sessions in kayaking and climbing or rappelling or other skills necessary for filming in the outdoors. The Center for Social Media is another supportive environment that sponsors film series, workshops, and research for social documentaries.

Alumni judge the Visions student film festival, which screens the best graduate and undergraduate films each spring. There is a large networking party beforehand. The program sometimes holds screenings at the AFI Theatre in Silver Spring, MD, and also does periodic screenings in L.A., New York, and Washington, DC.

▶ THE PRICE

| | |
|---|---|
| $989 per credit for fifty-one credits over three years | $50,439 |
| $12,000 per year rent and living expenses for three years | $36,000 |
| Average film costs | $10,000 |
| **Total** | **$96,439** |

In addition to tuition there are lab fees that provide minimal film stock and cash for some production courses. There are some finishing funds available. Students pay for all other film costs, including additional stock, tape, and even batteries for light meters. Luckily, there are few 16 mm courses, so costs can be kept to a minimum.

Eleven merit awards of varying amounts are given to incoming students. The max is eighteen hours of tuition with an $8,000 stipend. There is a cash award for a U.S. minority student that includes twelve hours of tuition credit and $4,200 in cash. Twenty-four credits of tuition are broken into various combinations for international students. Tuition-only awards of nine credit hours are available to continuing MFA students. Students who are not given merit awards are offered teaching, lab, or research assistant positions at an hourly wage of $13.

The scenic campus of American University is classified as a national arboretum. It is located near some of the wealthiest areas of Washington, DC. And yet it is only a short Metro ride away from downtown DC and all it has to offer. Many students live along the Metro line in Virginia or Maryland. A one-bedroom apartment costs about $1,000, but sharing is the norm and runs about $600 to $700 per person. Cars might come in handy for shoots but are unnecessary. The Metro is reliable, and it's also a good biking town.

## ▶ THE LOWDOWN

About seventy applications are received each year for the MFA. As with most schools, American searches for storytellers but not necessarily those with media experience. Approximately one-half of the students accepted have none. The admissions committee feels that students from a variety of backgrounds enrich the program. Other than the standard statement of purpose and letters of recommendation, there are no creative portfolio requirements. Many students are locally based. Some students come directly from undergrad programs, but half have been out of school for three to five years. Because part-time study is an option, students can take beyond two or three years to complete their thesis. And since full-time is only nine credits, nearly everyone has a part-time job either on or off campus.

You cannot escape the political climate in Washington. American University attracts applicants who tend to be politically savvy and socially conscious, and this climate is exactly what they most enjoy about living here. Students interested in documentary production will not be disappointed. After all, this is home to PBS, the National Geographic Society, National Public Radio, and the Discovery Channel.

Although American has diverse course offerings, not all classes are offered every term or even every year. There are semesters when the pickings are slim and other terms when there is an abundance of interesting courses. Sometimes you have to settle, and other times you will be forced to choose. The end result is you might graduate not having taken all the courses you would have liked to.

The equipment staff is well-liked, but the equipment is not. Because it is shared with undergrads, cameras frequently break, and first-year packages are especially inferior. Grads do get priority over undergrads, and some equipment is reserved for thesis projects, but equipment is also class-specific. Lighting and sound are in better shape, just not quite up to date. In addition to Bolexes and a few Aririflex 16 mm cameras, Panasonic DVX100s and Sony PD170s are available. Many students purchase their own cameras or befriend classmates who have done so. On the upside, there are seven Avid stations and fifteen Final Cut Pro suites that are always available along with a multimedia lab. There are no high-definition cameras owned by the program or any sort of purchase timetable for acquiring them. There is a one hundred–seat theater with quality sound and projection and a small TV studio. The program recognizes some of these shortcomings and is fund-raising to finance a new building equipped with upgraded facilities and soundstages.

Filmmakers in this program have strong opinions and messages to convey. There's real camaraderie in helping one another achieve goals. Students are more competitive with themselves than each other. The documentary instructors are the most respected. Oscar-winner Russell Williams's sound design course is a student favorite. Lower-level classes tend to be taught by less-experienced faculty, and students sometimes feel shortchanged.

*Some of the worst things about the program:* The equipment is hands down the greatest gripe. It needs to be upgraded and better maintained. The lack of structure can be dangerous for the less focused. Sometimes students scatter before they have a chance to bond or form a community. Writing courses tend to be weak. Washington is very serious about permits for any filming. Being stopped by the military or Secret Service is the norm rather than the exception, and carrying ID is a must for every crew member

*Some of the best things about the program:* There is tremendous flexibility for students who know what they want and are self-directed. The university is especially well-connected to the professional media community in Washington, and excellent documentarians teach within the program. The internships are first-rate. If you are a socially conscious filmmaker who wants to be in the mix of current affairs, look no farther.

# ART CENTER COLLEGE OF DESIGN

1700 Lida Street
Pasadena, CA 91103-1924
626-396-2200
www.artcenter.edu/accd/programs/graduate/fgprograms.jsp

| | |
|---|---|
| Tuition: | $27,812 |
| Enrollment: | 4–7 per session, around 15 per year |
| Deadline: | Rolling |
| Focus: | Experimental |

## ▶ THE PROGRAM

Art Center was founded in 1930 by an advertising executive named Tink Adams. He intended the school to train artists to work on commercial projects: industrial design, advertising, and so on. When in the early 1970s the school added a film program, it was specifically to fill the same need for film: to train filmmakers to make short commercial films, especially TV ads and "musically oriented theatrical shorts" (which would a few years later become known as music videos). A number of people who came out of the program in the seventies and eighties gained renown making innovative television commercials and music videos. At that time, however, it was nearly unheard of for a filmmaker to jump from directing commercial shorts into directing features.

So the school was kind of taken by surprise when, starting in the late eighties, some of their alumni, after establishing themselves as commercial filmmakers, began to make the transition into feature filmmaking. Certainly the most financially successful of these graduates is Michael Bay (*Armageddon* [1998] and *Pearl Harbor* [2001]); Tarsem Singh, who gained fame for his video for REM's song "Losing my Religion," has also moved into feature films (*The Cell* [2000]); Roger Avery, cowriter of

*Pulp Fiction* (1994), is an Art Center alumnus. The school responded in the early nineties by adding courses in narrative filmmaking; while students still learn to operate in the world of commercial film, most make narrative thesis films. The result is a somewhat schizophrenic program, where students are taught to be true to their artistic instincts one minute and to be as commercially viable as possible the next.

As of this writing, the faculty tells us they are rebuilding their film program from the ground up; a completely new, innovative program is in the works. However, this restructuring is in progress as we go to press, and we have been unable to obtain details as to the specifics of the new program. But from what we are able to ascertain, it appears that the overall program is not changing a great deal; the major change is that the school is looking for innovative ways to get student-made productions onto television.

So perhaps the program will be different by the time you read this, perhaps not. But here's how the program is now: The graduate program is a two-year, year-round program, with three terms per year. New students are accepted into the program each term; from twenty-five or so applicants, between four and seven new MFA students are accepted. In the undergraduate division, out of about eighty-five applications, the school accepts around thirteen per term.

The first year of the MFA program is pretty rigidly structured; in the first term students take Directing I and Screenwriting I, undergraduate courses that teach the basics of film production and writing for the screen. In Directing II, in the second term, students spend the entire term in a studio working with actors. Students make no films in Directing I or Directing II. It is only in the third term, in Directing III, where graduate students are separated from the undergrads, that students make an entire film. Directing III projects tend to be narratives, shot on video, that run about five minutes.

After the third term most students have decided what they want to do; some focus on cinematography or editing; others continue on as writer-directors. From the fourth term on, there are no specific courses students must take, just a number of course credits they must fill, and students are free to study what interests them. Students take courses in film history and theory—a lot of students are surprised to learn that there are theory classes at Art Center, but we hear these classes are quite good.

In the fourth term many students take the Cine Workshop. This is probably the most unusual film course that Art Center offers, and takes a bit of explanation. Art Center, as we have said, has long been focused on advertising and commercials. A few years ago the school developed a program called Design Matters, where students make public-service films for nonprofits and NGOs, primarily the United Nations, but sometimes other nonprofits like the Red Cross. The program gives students the chance to make commercial films that actually air on television around the world, and the clients get their spots made inexpensively. In the Cine Workshop, students are given subjects on which spots are needed: avian flu, for example, or AIDS awareness. Students develop ideas for public-service spots and pitch them to the clients. Three or four spots are chosen to be produced, and the students are given 35 mm film, processing, and a small budget to make them. After production, students show their cuts to the clients, take comments, and refine their work based on client input. This is the only MFA film program we know of where students can graduate with real-world experience in the advertising industry; many student-made works have won Clio awards.

Because there are no summer breaks, many students take a term off after three or four terms, and just spend the term writing their thesis films. In the fifth term most students begin work on their thesis films, finishing them by the end of the sixth term. Though a few students make documentary films, the majority work in straightforward narrative. Along with the thesis film, each student must present a thirty-page discussion of it. In the end, most students leave the school with a wide variety of completed films, from polished narratives to advertisements and music videos.

The program does not currently have an industry screening of student films. But the school does maintain a large network of alumni who are scattered throughout the advertising and entertainment industries. Students who have a clear vision of the direction they want to take after graduation can ask the school to locate a related internship, and the school will often be able to help out.

### ▶ THE PRICE

| | |
|---|---|
| $27,812 tuition for two years | $55,624 |
| $15,000 per year rent and living expenses for two years | $30,000 |
| $2,000 per year maintenance and insurance on a car for two years | $4,000 |
| Average thesis films cost | $20,000 |
| **Total** | **$109,624** |

Art Center's tuition is pretty high; the one advantage the school offers is speed. Students are out of the program and off into their careers in between two and two and a half years.

The main campus is in Pasadena, in the rolling, wooded hills above the Rose Bowl. It sits in a wealthy neighborhood of family houses, so there are few places for students to live near the campus. Some find rooms to rent in houses near the school, but the vast majority of students live a twenty- or thirty-minute drive away, a little west in Glendale, or east of Pasadena in the San Gabriel Valley. It is not possible to survive here without a car.

## ▶ THE LOWDOWN

Students are free to take classes anywhere in any department of the school and are encouraged to cross-pollinate film with other art forms. Some of the school's classes reflect this cross-pollination; students speak highly of a course in drawing storyboards.

One professor tells us that the hallmark of the program is complete artistic freedom, that even if every professor in the program hates your idea, you're still going to get to do it. Students are expected to pursue their own paths and take their own initiative creatively, but there is an overarching commercial imperative. Students take classes in film theory but also in the business of advertising. We are told that students who want to work on, say, music videos are sometimes discouraged, told that there's no money in music videos, and are encouraged to focus instead in more lucrative areas of filmmaking.

Equipment-wise, the school has mostly gone digital. The school owns 16 mm and 35 mm film equipment, and many students shoot their thesis films on 35 mm, but most everything else is shot on digital video, and all postproduction is done digitally. The school has a few Avids, but many students use the more numerous Final Cut Pro systems—of course many own their own systems, and just edit at home. The sound facilities are quite good, with ProTools editing stations and two mixing stages; the newer of them, installed recently by Skywalker Sound, is a good space for recording ADR and Foley but is dragged down a bit by a dated ProTools system.

One thing most schools provide that Art Center does not is production insurance. Students have to get their own insurance before they can shoot; most will join together into groups and set up limited liability corporations in California, through which they can then get insurance coverage over all of their productions.

*Some of the worst things about the program:* Students say screenwriting is not as strong as the program's other elements. The tuition is high, and the program compressed; many students, when they get to the fifth or sixth term find themselves exhausted and broke, no longer able to make the thesis film they would like to.

*Some of the best things about the program:* A mere two years! Complete artistic freedom! And the ability to make commercial films for actual paying clients. The school is probably best for people who really want to get into commercial filmmaking; because Art Center graduates permeate the advertising world, and the school actively maintains a large alumni network, graduates can find internships at a wide variety of firms to make the transition out of school and into the world of commercial filmmaking.

# BOSTON UNIVERSITY

College of Communication
640 Commonwealth Avenue
Boston, MA 02215-2422
617-353-3481
www.bu.edu/com/ft/film/

| Tuition: | $31,530 |
|---|---|
| Enrollment: | 16 |
| Deadline: | February 1 |
| Focus: | Independent |

## ▶ THE PROGRAM

Boston University is located along the banks of the Charles River, close to the downtown area of one of New England's most historic cities. The school, part of the College of Communication, has offered an MFA in film for over fifty years. Approximately twenty years ago the program evolved from being one purely focused on documentary to one that embraced narrative film in all of its forms. It now produces a mix of documentary and narrative work and offers concentrations in production, film studies, and screenwriting. The production program emphasizes filmmaking principles and aims to graduate technicians who understand the underlying concepts and aesthetics of film.

On the books this is a two-year program. In actuality, students take two years of classes and then begin to work on their thesis. Most complete their thesis films within one or two additional semesters. The good news is that students pay no additional fees or tuition during this time. Special arrangements can also be made to insure that international students, whose student status is normally dependent upon enrollment, can remain in the country to continue to work on their theses without registering for classes and paying tuition.

Production I is the center of the first semester. In this 16 mm course each student produces three silent films that are edited on Steenbecks. Along with this heavy production schedule students must also take Acting, Screenwriting I, and American Masterworks, a cinema studies course.

After just one semester of study, students take Thesis Preparation and begin to think about and prepare for their final film. While they are thinking about their thesis, they work on Production II, in which students collaborate on one short 16 mm project. They make the switch from Steenbecks to Avid editing, which they will continue to use for the remainder of their film postproduction. The first course in directing is also taken at this time with students choosing between Screenwriting II and an elective as their fourth and final second-semester course.

Second-year directors begin to focus on documentary or fiction filmmaking by taking either Line Producing or a documentary practicum respectively in the third semester. With fundamental training out of the way, students are free to explore a bit in year two with three courses of elective credit. One of these must be a film studies course. There are many other electives from which to choose, but students will often find themselves in a mixed population of grads and undergrads for these classes. This is especially true in introductory production courses where the graduate curriculum is not so different from that of the undergraduate.

Thesis Project is the only designated course in the fourth and final semester. The remaining three courses are electives. At thesis level, students have the option of collaborating in a creative capacity as producer, editor, or cinematographer instead of directing for thesis credit. Thesis projects are capped at twenty-eight minutes. Narrative projects shoot on film. Thesis documentaries may be shot on digital video. A thesis review committee is formed, and members work individually as mentors to the student throughout the thesis process. In the near future this is expected to move into more of a portfolio review at the end of the year.

▶ **THE PRICE**

| | |
|---|---|
| $31,530 tuition for two years | $63,060 |
| $9,600 per year rent and living expenses for two and a half years | $24,000 |
| Average film costs | $20,000 |
| **Total** | **$107,060** |

Boston is in the same tuition league as some of the more famous programs, yet there is little financial support other than merit-based scholarships that are awarded during the admissions process.

The program is trying to fund tuition remission packages for its grads, but they have not been successful as yet. Within the College of Communication there is one undergraduate class that typically uses a few graduate teaching assistants from the Graduate Film Program. TAs teach and assist instructors with teaching-related activities. In return they receive partial tuition remission that covers a substantial portion of the first semester at BU. This is a one-time opportunity.

Just about every other course in the Communication Program has a graduate assistant assigned. These are not tuition remission appointments because typically GAs tend to perform simple jobs like getting cable from the stockroom rather than grading papers. These positions pay about $1,000 per course, and most students take on a few of these every term and can supplement incomes by four to five thousand dollars over the year.

The university provides $1,000 toward all thesis projects. There is also a small finishing fund through which select students can get some additional cash for completing thesis projects. Students must apply for this extra assistance.

Most grads submit thesis projects to the annual Redstone Film Festival that screens eight to ten films selected by the faculty to represent the best from the Department of Film and Television. Sponsored by Viacom, this is a bicoastal festival that consists of separate juried screenings in Boston and Los Angeles. The festival is open to both graduate and undergraduate film and TV majors. A total of $5,000 in cash prizes is awarded between both screenings. It is possible to win twice. One recent grad film was awarded $500 in Boston and $1,500 in L.A. (Rumor has it that the L.A. judges are more impressed with high production values, while the East Coast judges favor documentaries.)

The Film and Television Department also sponsors BU Cinematheque, an ongoing series that screens important and innovative films and videos of both established and young and upcoming filmmakers. Guests have included Paul Schrader, Thelma Schoonmaker, Todd Solondz, and Ross McElwee.

The program is especially proud of their Los Angeles internship program for graduate students. Now in its fourth year, this program grew out of a strong West Coast alumni base. Students can participate in their fourth semester or add an additional semester after their two years of course work. Room, board, and tuition are identical to that paid in Boston. The program typically consists of an internship taken along with three elective courses taught by local professionals. The courses and instructors change regularly. The program helps facilitate the internship possibilities, but the onus is on students to secure the positions.

Recently a Boston University student won a television pilot script contest sponsored by mtvU, a TV channel of MTV networks that is broadcast on many college and university campuses across the United States. The student flew to Los Angeles to meet with writers and producers, and mtvU eventually aligned with Boston University to produce the series pilot. In the fall of 2005, a Boston faculty member directed the pilot in high definition. Student and local professional actors performed, and the crew of thirty was comprised of graduate and undergraduate students. The program hopes that this will turn into an annual event for the university.

In 2006, Boston University also launched BUTV, a new student-run cable channel. It broadcasts student films and also offers students the chance to create and direct their own shows.

Boston is a big, progressive college town with an artsy edge. There are lots of theaters. The nearby Harvard Film Archive screens a wide variety of current independent and classic films and often hosts filmmakers. Boston has a strong documentary scene, but not much else in the way of industry production. Permits are a must for city filming, and applying for them gets tiresome. But since there is no soundstage, students have little choice. This is obviously a drawback during those frigid Boston winters. On a recent student film, one student's credit was actually listed as "Snow Shoveler."

Students rarely own cars, because the public transportation is good and parking is expensive. They also find it easy to rent from Zipcar for film shoots. Closer to the campus, a one-bedroom apartment can run about $1,000. Students tend to share off campus for about $400 to $500 each.

## ▶ THE LOWDOWN

The program receives between sixty and one hundred applications each year. The target class size is sixteen, but recent classes have been as large as twenty and as small as nine, depending upon the talent pool. No prior film experience is required, and most accepted students have none. What the admissions board values most are accomplished writers who grasp visual storytelling. Applicants must complete three one thousand–word written assignments. The first is an essay about your life. This should paint a fairly comprehensive picture of both your personal and professional experience. The second essay deals with your current favorite reading material, including periodicals and books. You'll need to explain your choices and specifically discuss your favorite book and author. The third assignment is a short story written in present tense for which you must write only what can be seen and heard. The last piece of the application package is a visual assignment. Using only nine photos, you must tell a short story that illustrates the development of a clearly defined emotion. The quality of the photographs matters less than the storytelling. This exercise is a chance to show just how clever you are as well as to demonstrate your strong visual sense.

Equipment is shared with the undergraduate program. Like most other programs in this situation, crunch times can limit access, and sharing increases wear and tear. The equipment room staff is very accommodating, and repairs are reportedly speedy.

For the most part, narrative graduate work is shot on 16 mm film with Arri SRs and is supported by adequate lighting and sound. Video equipment exists within the Television and Film Department, but it is primarily reserved for the undergraduate program. Grad students can request special permission to shoot digitally, and most documentary directors do so. There's a very small sound booth with two Pro-Tools stations. Grad students rarely use ProTools because few people are familiar with this software. The sound classes that instruct in its use are apparently popular and thus difficult to get into. First-semester projects are edited on Steenbecks. Advanced projects edit on one of fifteen G4s loaded with Avid and Final Cut Pro in a large editing lab.

The program just received a quarter of a million-dollar grant from the Katzenberg family to fund the Emily and Jeffrey Katzenberg High Definition Center. The plans are to lease (as opposed to purchasing) high-definition cameras on an annual basis for ten years so that the center can remain state-of-the-art until the high-definition format is established. The grant will also expand basic production equipment to support the high-end production and install appropriate post facilities. This also means that all thesis projects shot on Super 16 will be able to post in any format.

Professors are accessible and supportive. Sam Kaufman is the much-respected Avid guru. While most instructors are working professionals, the faculty responsible for narrative work tends to be more academic, and those teaching directing are felt to be weak.

**Some of the worst things about the program:** There's no getting around the cost. Since there is little film production going on in Boston, production jobs are rare. Just about everyone settles for becoming a graduate assistant to earn some extra cash.

**Some of the best things about the program:** Students like the flexibility of the program because they feel they graduate as filmmakers who can work in any position on any production. The program boasts some impressive alums like producers Lauren Shuler Donner (*You've Got Mail*) and Richard Gladstein (*Finding Neverland*); and director Gary Fleder (*Runaway Jury* and *Kiss the Girls*) as well as executives in place at HBO, Paramount Classics, 20th Century Fox, and Revolution Studios. They must be doing something right.

# CALIFORNIA INSTITUTE OF THE ARTS

School of Film/Video
24700 McBean Parkway
Valencia, CA 91355-2397
661-255-1050
http://film.calarts.edu

| | |
|---|---|
| Tuition: | $29,300 |
| Enrollment: | Film and Video: 25 |
| | Directing for Film: 8 |
| Deadline: | January 5 |
| Focus: | Film and Video: |
| | Experimental/Documentary |
| | Directing for Film: Narrative |

▶ **THE PROGRAM**

When CalArts opened in 1971, USC and UCLA had been offering film courses for some time. The founders of the film program decided to focus on a kind of filmmaking that other schools were not teaching: experimental film. Students learned to use photographic effects, to use optical printers and stop-motion, and to work directly with the celluloid. Far from teaching students the ins and outs of Hollywood moviemaking, CalArts taught students to think of film the way experimental pioneers Stan Brakhage and Maya Deren did: as a medium for personal expression like clay or paint. As filmmaking becomes more and more digital, CalArts is moving along with it. But students are still encouraged to be experimental, and those who choose to can still work with the film like the experimentalists of old did.

CalArts is well-equipped with both film and digital equipment, and staffed by a large, diverse faculty, many of them working professionals. The film department offers MFAs in three divisions: Experimental Animation, Film and Video (until recently called Live Action), and Film

Directing. A fourth division, Character Animation, is an undergraduate-only division renowned as the starting point for some of the most successful animators of the last two decades.

There are two separate divisions devoted to live-action filmmaking, and their names sound an awful lot alike. Film Directing and Film and Video, though similar in name, are very different programs, which originated in different places and have fundamentally different intents and philosophies.

## Film Directing Program

Film Directing is primarily concerned with narrative filmmaking and devotes a great deal of time to working with actors. Students work in film and video but also spend a great deal of time acting, writing, and directing for theater. The program is less about the technology of film in particular than it is about creating and telling dramatic stories through various media.

A moderately structured two-year program, it begins with acting and directing for the stage; students start off taking courses in acting, then learn to work with actors in a studio, and to direct them in scenes for the stage. They then apply these skills in the staging of dramatic scenes for film. Students take courses in dramatic writing, and in the second semester take a course in film production techniques where each student makes a short film or video.

At the end of first year each student proposes a thesis project to a review committee, which includes the student's mentor plus two other faculty members of the student's choosing. Thesis projects can be films, theater productions, or written projects such as screenplays or stage plays. If the thesis is approved, then the student develops it during second year; each student's second-year curriculum is determined by the review committee to match the requirements of his thesis project. At the end of second year, students present their thesis projects to their review committees. If the thesis is a written piece, it may be completed at this time, and, with all the course work done, the student may make this presentation her graduation review. But for those who intend to make a thesis film, this is the launching point for third year.

In third year, students focus entirely on shooting and completing their thesis projects. Most students have completed their course requirements by this point, but a student's mentor may recommend a student take a specific class if it pertains to that student's thesis project.

## Program in Film and Video

Where the Directing program is primarily about traditional drama, the program in Film and Video focuses on the technical aspects of filmmaking and about using the technology of film and video for personal expression. Narrative films are common, but students also work in experimental and documentary and sometimes create video installations. Many student films combine these elements. Unlike directing for film, this is a largely unstructured program, and students are free to study whatever aspects of film and video interest them.

When students enter at the beginning of first year, they take an elementary technical course called Film Fundamentals. The first two weeks of this course are devoted to determining how much each student knows about the technology and technique of filmmaking. After two weeks, students who are judged to be proficient in filmmaking are dismissed from the class and are allowed to jump into any other classes they like, while the less-experienced students continue on learning the basics for the remainder of the semester.

Beyond that single class, the school has no set structure and no specific course requirements. Instead, each student is assigned a mentor, a faculty member whose responsibility it is to suggest a curriculum of courses that will conform to that student's specific interests and goals. There are some tracks—suggested class lists for students interested in specific areas like narrative filmmaking, lyrical filmmaking, or experimental filmmaking—to follow. But these aren't rigid requirements or concentrations like you'd see at other schools, just road maps for those students who want or need some direction.

The program offers a wide variety of classes, from straightforward writing and production workshops to more offbeat classes such as Video Installations or Video Graphics. Students working in experimental film often hand-process their film; the school has a film processing lab for this purpose. Film students do not have to stick to film classes; the entire school is at their disposal so they can study whatever strikes their fancy, from theater to painting to music to dance.

There is a yearlong Thesis Workshop class to help second- and third-year students prepare and shoot their thesis projects. At the start of this class, students present their thesis ideas and participate in discussions of the films they want to make. By the end of the year many students have shot their films and are ready to screen cuts for the classes. While this class is helpful, it is not a requirement, and some students make their thesis films without taking it. All that is required of students to begin making their thesis films is a mid-residency review, wherein they discuss with their three-member faculty review committee what they have learned in the school so far and what they want to make for a thesis.

While the class credit assignments can be completed in two years, the completion of a thesis always takes three, and most students continue to take classes through their third year, as they work on their thesis films. When students finish their thesis projects, they screen them for their committees and then participate in discussions of their films. No comprehensive exams are required, and no written thesis is required.

## ▶ THE PRICE

| | |
|---|---:|
| $29,300 tuition for three years | $87,900 |
| $15,000 per year rent and living expenses for three years | $45,000 |
| $1,500 per year maintenance and insurance on a car for three years | $4,500 |
| First- and second-year exercise films cost | $2,000 |
| Average thesis film costs | $20,000 |
| **Total** | **$159,400** |

Because the Film and Video program is so unstructured, these amounts are especially unpredictable. Many students work entirely in video and spend very little on film expenses; others work in film and spend more.

Certainly the simplest way to save money is to finish the program in two years. This is possible if you come into first year with a thesis script ready to shoot. If you have a good script at the start, and if your mentor approves, you may shoot the film over the summer after first year and have it finished by the end of second year. You won't learn as much about filmmaking this way, but you'll save a lot of money.

There is little financial aid available. One student per year gets a free ride; a few others get awards that range from $1,000 to $10,000, but none makes much of a dent against the cost of the school. CalArts is a small school, with a total of about a thousand students in all departments, so there is little need for TAs, and little money available to pay for them. The school hires students in work scholarships, glorified work-study positions that pay little more than minimum wage. Many students take these positions to help make ends meet; others work outside of school. There is quite a bit of film production work around, whether nearby in Santa Clarita where a number of television shows are shot or farther away in Los Angeles.

## ▶ THE LOWDOWN

CalArts receives between a hundred and a hundred fifty applications each year for the MFA program in Film and Video, and accepts about fifty, figuring that only twenty-five or thirty of those will actually come to the school.

The admissions board does not look at GREs, but you have to include some written materials and a creative portfolio. The written materials consist of some comments on works (books, films, plays) that you feel have influenced you, and a description of projects that you want to make while at CalArts. The creative portfolio is the most important piece of the application. We are told that, in general, the admissions board looks for something weird. They like to be surprised by an applicant's strange personal vision. Remember that this is an art school, and the admissions board is basically looking not just for film students but for artists. They seek creative, motivated individuals with a strong personal vision. Your portfolio can include up to ten minutes of film or video, writing samples, photographs, slides of artwork in other media, or any other creative work that you feel shows your abilities. Prior experience in film is not required, but those who can send in good film work have an advantage over those who cannot. Every year a number of applicants send in highly polished Hollywood-type film work—computer-generated special effects of planets exploding, well-staged action scenes, and so on—and these applicants are generally knocked out of the running automatically. The school specifically avoids applicants who want to do this kind of work; CalArts has little to offer these filmmakers. There are plenty of other schools that specialize in this kind of thing. The school also decides who gets financial aid based on the portfolios. The school provides less structure than most; it expects students to know what they want to do. So students who can clearly describe in their application the films they plan to make while at CalArts are at a distinct advantage.

CalArts has traditionally focused on experimental film and animation. For most of the seventies and eighties, students of experimental animation coming out of CalArts struggled to find work. But as animation has experienced a renaissance and as computer-generated animation has gained popularity, the studios have looked to techno-savvy CalArts alumni to lead the way. Tim Burton, John Lassiter (*Toy Story*), and Brad Bird (*The Incredibles*) are all graduates of CalArts, and a large portion of the animators at any studio in Hollywood are either CalArts graduates or CalArts dropouts. As a result, a degree from CalArts has a techno-cool aura around it that you can't get from any other school.

The shift to digital technology has divided the faculty somewhat; as the school has added Final Cut Pro and Pro-Tools systems, many of the older professors are resisting the change. Having taught experimental film for decades, many professors are not happy about giving up film for digital technologies. They still encourage students to shoot film and edit their films on flatbed film editing machines, and many students do. But for the students it is just an interesting retro experience; they are more aware than the faculty seem to be that cutting film is already an obsolete skill, one that the students will never use once they finish the program.

Valencia is a strange place for a college. The town itself is a planned community, designed and built up all of a piece in the seventies. It has all the advantages you might expect in a planned community: well-maintained suburban neighborhoods, convenient shopping centers, well-tended bike paths and walkways. But it was not really intended to be a college town, and it has real disadvantages for students. Nearly all of the housing in Valencia is single-family homes. One-bedroom apartments are rare, so students have to make do with other alternatives. Most share large apartments or condos for the first few years; by third or fourth year many have moved to Los Angeles, an hour away, where they can hold jobs while they finish their thesis projects. Commuting from Los Angeles can be a good solution, but it hardly allows you to feel like you are a member of the CalArts community. And when, as happens from time to time, an earthquake knocks down the one freeway that connects L.A. and Valencia, it can be very difficult to get to CalArts at all.

For a long time CalArts sat on a hill surrounded by undeveloped land. In the past few years urban sprawl has surrounded it—shopping centers and housing developments now encroach from all sides—but it still exists largely in isolation from the conservative bedroom community around it. Down the street from CalArts is a community college, College of the Canyons, which has a theater department of its own. When College of the Canyons puts on a stage play, people from the community flock to see it. Yet few people from the community come to see CalArts' productions. This isolation is a cause of frustration for many students, as the creative works they slave over are seen only by a few classmates and family members.

Each of the school's departments puts on its own juried end-of-year show each year in a public space in Los Angeles. While the school offers little official career guidance, there is a large network of CalArts graduates in Hollywood who can help out.

*Some of the worst things about the program:* Valencia itself is a problem; students either have to live in this rather depressing town or commute a long way from someplace more livable. While most students appreciate the freedom the Film and Video program affords, some students get lost.

*Some of the best things about the program:* The small size and the funky attitude. Students tell us the people are the best thing about the program; the students, the faculty, and even the support staff create a great atmosphere in which to be creative. Students with energy and ambition are free to do all kinds of crazy projects. And, with strong programs in such areas as dance, design, and computer animation, CalArts offers students great opportunities to combine filmmaking with other media and disciplines. With unfettered access to facilities and resources, CalArts is a creative candy shop for self-motivated students.

# CHAPMAN UNIVERSITY

Lawrence & Kristina Dodge College of Film and Media Arts
DeMille Hall, Room 127
One University Drive
Orange, CA 92866-1005
714-997-6765
http://ftv.chapman.edu

| | |
|---|---|
| Tuition: | $28,050 |
| Enrollment: | 25 producers |
| | 15 screenwriters |
| | 25 directors |
| | 12 cinematographers |
| | 6–8 editors |
| | 6–8 production designers |
| Deadline: | Priority: February 1 |
| | Regular: May 1 |
| Focus: | Industry |

## ▶ THE PROGRAM

Orange County's Chapman University only began offering film classes in the late nineties. But after a remarkably successful round of fund-raising among the plutocrats of the OC, this very young program has become probably the best-funded and most technologically advanced film school in the country. Only a few years ago students were using broken-down old equipment and taking classes in a converted garage. In 2004 the film school received a multimillion dollar grant, and was christened the Lawrence & Kristina Dodge College of Film and Media Arts. In 2006 the program moved into a brand-new $50 million production facility, the Marion Knott Studio, which, as its name suggests, is more like a movie studio than a film school. The funding stretches far beyond equipment and facilities; the school actually pays for all student films.

The program offers two-year MFA programs in screen-writing, producing, and production design, and a three-year MFA program in film production. Film production is a conservatory-style program, where students choose areas of specialization—cinematography, editing, or directing—and work together as tightly knit teams to make films.

The specializations don't really come into play until the second year. The first year offers a general education in production technique, film history, and basic cinematic storytelling. All production students, including the editors and cinematographers, write and direct films in first year.

When students are accepted into the program, they are given a number of assignments to complete before arriving in the fall: a list of films to watch, a list of books to read, and each student is instructed to create a two-minute video that introduces him to his classmates. After a week of orientation and parties, classes begin. In first semester's Production Workshop, students make short exercise videos based on simple concepts provided by professors; in second semester's Production Workshop II, they make two longer projects. The first is shot on video and is an exercise in sub-text; all students have to use the same page of neutral dialogue, but each student is given different motivations for the actors to pursue. The second project is the first that students write and direct themselves; these projects are shot on 16 mm film. The first-year students also hone their production skills by working as crew on the second-year students' films. This isn't happenstance as at other schools; the faculty assign first-year students to second-year productions, ensuring that all second-year productions have full crews, and all first-year students get a base level of on-set experience before they start making their second-year films.

It is only in the second year that students break off into their chosen areas of specialization. Occasionally, after the first year, one or two students may switch from one specialization to another; the school is open to this, and faculty will from time to time even encourage students to rethink their specializations.

The school forces students to work collaboratively throughout the three years, but the enforced collaboration hits its peak with the second-year "cycle films." These films, generally shot on 16 mm film and running around fifteen minutes, are initiated by the screenwriting students. (One unusual benefit of Chapman's two-year screenwriting program is that all screenwriters are guaranteed to see something they wrote produced.) At the beginning of second year, the screenwriters submit screenplays through the school's website. On an appointed day, these screenplays—most years there are around sixty—are made available to the directing students to download and read. Each director chooses a screenplay he wants to direct, contacts the writer, and asks to be allowed to direct it. If a screenplay sees interest from several directors, negotiations ensue, and the writer decides on a director for his project. Within a day or two all of the writers have chosen their directors, and the writer/director teams begin recruiting the other core crew members; editor, cinematographer, producer, and production designer. Once these core production teams have formed, each team presents its project to the faculty and requests shooting dates and equipment packages. The faculty then work out a production schedule for the entire year, with two projects shooting at a time in two-week windows from October to March. The faculty assign a full production and postproduction schedule to each project that ensures completion and delivery before the end of the year. Each film shoots for six days over two weekends. Directors are forbidden from doing any writing or rewriting of the scripts. Directors may request revisions, but any actual changes to the scripts must be made by the writers. By mid-March all twenty-five students have finished shooting, and by May they have all finished editing.

There is no end-of-year crunch time like you see at most schools, when students compete for equipment in a frantic attempt to finish on time. Because the postproduction schedules are so carefully prescribed—and because students do not have to spend time raising money for their films—the students who shoot in the early fall often finish their films as early as March. So rather than holding one frenzied screening at the end of the year, Chapman has the luxury of holding "crit sessions" every few weeks throughout the winter and spring. In any given session, two or three recently completed student films are screened, and a senior faculty member leads an in-depth discussion of each.

As the second semester progresses, and more and more of the second-year students finish their cycle films, the focus shifts to preparing scripts for their third-year thesis films. A thesis development class allows students to develop their thesis screenplays under the oversight of a faculty advisor. By the end of the semester most have completed their screenplays and are ready to spend the summer preparing to shoot their films in the fall.

The structure of third year is similar to second year. On the thesis films, directors are free to work however they like. Many write their own screenplays; others continue to work as they did on the cycle films, developing and writing ideas in collaboration with screenwriters. At the beginning of the third year, the directing students submit their screenplays through the school's website, and those screenplays are made available to the other students to download and read. The producers, cinematographers, editors, and production designers read the scripts and pitch themselves to the directors. Once the crews have formed, the faculty then assigns production and postproduction schedules. Most students shoot 35 mm film, though some shoot Super 16, and with the school's recent purchase of professional high-definition video cameras, many will soon be shooting HD. The school provides each student with film stock, processing, telecine, and about $20,000 to make these films. Students who want to can raise additional funds to make their films more impressive; however, they can't take additional time to do this; they must complete their films within their assigned schedules. Students are allowed to shoot for ten days over a two-week window on these films. As the year progresses and students complete their thesis films, many have free time and begin working in internships in Hollywood.

At the end of the year the school holds a public screening in the main theater of all of the thesis films. A jury chooses seven or eight of the best, and these are screened for invited industry guests at the Directors Guild in Hollywood. The school also publishes a booklet each year that lists feature-length screenplays written by the screenwriting students, and delivers it to executives in Hollywood. Since students own their films, they do not have to consult with the school before applying to festivals. However, the school has a full-time film festival coordinator on staff, who maintains relationships with programmers at festivals all around the world and helps students to find and apply to appropriate festivals.

▶ **THE PRICE**

| | |
|---|---|
| $28,050 tuition for three years | $84,150 |
| $15,000 per year rent and living expenses for three years | $45,000 |
| $1,500 per year maintenance and insurance on a car for three years | $4,500 |
| Average film costs | N/A |
| **Total** | **$133,650** |

Chapman is a private school, so tuition is fairly high. The two things it really has going for it, price-wise, are promptness—students are out the door and into their careers at the end of third year with no dillydallying around—and the fact that all films are funded by the school.

The City of Orange is surprising; only a few blocks from the Knott Studio are the low brick buildings and tree-lined central square of a late nineteenth-century farming community. It's as if a small town from Kansas had been picked up by a tornado and dropped into the middle of the suburban sprawl of Orange County. It's a surprisingly charming town, reminiscent of Disneyland's Main Street USA, a few miles up Interstate 5. As Chapman University has expanded in recent years, many houses in the historic downtown area have become shared housing for students; large apartment complexes are plentiful another mile or two away, outside of the historic district. Most students live in or around the City of Orange.

## ▶ THE LOWDOWN

Nobody makes documentaries at Chapman. Nobody makes experimental films. Students make straightforward, Hollywood-style narratives with the hope of moving on to careers in the industry after graduation. And everything about the school—its faculty, its curriculum, and its facilities—is directed toward that goal.

Industry schools have traditionally paid for student productions, but there's always been a downside: the schools claimed ownership of all student films. AFI and USC used to work this way; in recent years both have largely stopped funding their students' films, but both continue to claim ownership of all student films. So Chapman's policy comes as a surprise; the school not only funds all student films, it makes no claim of ownership on those films.

We said up top that the Marion Knott Studio is less like a film school than a movie studio. It's practically a factory for short narrative films, with every piece of equipment linked in to every other, and every student project carefully scheduled so that a dozen or so films are completed each month like clockwork for much of the school year.

The Knott Studio itself is a technological wonder. When a student finishes shooting, she'll bring her footage to the data center on the studio's second floor. If the footage is film, the school will telecine it to high-definition video on its Spirit 4k telecine machine; if the footage is digital video, the school will download the footage; either way, the footage winds up stored in digital form on the school's enormous central server. From that point on, the footage is accessible via high-speed network from any machine in the building for any purpose. The student can go to any of the school's 130 Avid editing stations and cut the footage together; she can go to the sound facility and record dialogue or sound effects directly into the project's timeline. When she goes to class, she can pull up the work in progress off of the server and screen it for her classmates. Even the digital projection system in the school's three hundred–seat THX-certified theater is on the network; any student project can in an instant be projected at the highest quality for a large audience. The theater also serves as the school's main sound mixing stage.

That's just the postproduction; the production equipment is no less impressive. The studio houses two large state-of-the-art soundstages and several smaller stages for television production and cinematography work. There is a motion capture stage, for students who want to combine live action with digital effects and animation. The school's Foley stage is a dedicated Foley studio, with sandboxes, water tanks, a wide variety of flooring materials, and racks of shoes and other props. Students are free to shoot DV, 16 mm, Super 16, or 35 mm, and the school recently purchased a Panasonic Varicam high-definition video camera.

Chapman has made a point in the last few years of recruiting professors who have a lifetime's experience in Hollywood. The directing program is headed up by John

Badham, director of *Saturday Night Fever* (1977) and dozens of other films; the producing program by Alex Rose, producer of *Norma Rae* (1979); the screenwriting program by David Ward, Oscar winner for *The Sting* (1973); production design by Lawrence Paull, production designer of *Blade Runner* (1982). One AFI student we spoke with commented that Chapman seemed to be luring away AFI's best professors. Mind you, these professors are figureheads; they are new hires at the school, lured with large paychecks and instant tenure. They don't know as much about the program and don't have as much teaching experience as the many professors who have been working here for years. As a student you shouldn't expect to actually see much of these folks, and you should expect to sense some animosity toward them from the other professors, who do most of the actual work but are unlikely to ever see the same kind of paychecks.

*Some of the worst things about the program:* This isn't a place to make documentaries or experimental films; it's narratives or nothing. It's also not a place for auteurs, since students are forced to embrace the collaborative nature of the medium in everything they do. The school doesn't yet have a reputation in the outside world; it's such a new program that few outside of Orange County have even heard of it, and none of its alumni have yet become famous.

*Some of the best things about the program:* If there's a better-equipped, better-funded film school on the planet, we haven't seen it. And if Chapman doesn't yet have famous alumni to put them on the map, they certainly will before long. Think of it as challenge; you could be to Chapman what George Lucas is to USC.

# CITY COLLEGE OF NEW YORK

Department of Media and Communication Arts
Room 473, Shepherd Hall
138th Street at Convent Avenue
New York, NY 10031-9198
212-650-7235
www1.ccny.cuny.edu

| | |
|---|---|
| Tuition: | Resident: $6,400 |
| | Nonresident: $13,500 |
| Enrollment: | 25 |
| Deadline: | April 1 |
| Focus: | Independent |

## ▶ THE PROGRAM

The Department of Media and Communication Arts at the City College of New York began offering an MFA in Media Arts Production in 1997. City College is part of the City University of New York network that has several locations in the New York area.

This is a compressed, two-year program designed for those with prior experience in film. An undergraduate film degree is preferred. Students may apply in one of the following areas of concentration: Writing and Directing Fiction, Writing and Directing Documentary, Camera, Editing, or Producing/Production Managing.

Four courses are taken during the first semester. A cinema studies course presents a broad survey of independent film and also examines the advent of media arts. Two production courses, Camera I and Digital Production, each require several exercises in both 16 mm and digital filmmaking, essentially filling this semester with nonstop production. The remaining class is either Fiction Screenwriting for narrative filmmakers or Research and Writing for the Documentary Film, for the documentary directors.

Thesis films are developed in both of these classes, and students submit their proposals for review and feedback at the end of the term.

During the second semester in the Camera II class, exercises become increasingly more complex and might involve movement and interfacing with sound. Students learn to work with Avid in Editing I and tackle producing in Media Management. Narrative directors will polish their thesis scripts in Fiction Screenwriting II and direct actors in preexisting screenplays in Directing Fiction. Documentary directors continue working on their thesis projects in Researching and Writing the Documentary II and complete exercises related to their projects in Producing and Directing the Documentary.

At the end of this first year, every directing student must have a thesis production package ready. Theses are presented to the faculty and are green-lighted based on readiness to shoot more than on content. As long as a project can be produced, it will be approved. Faculty will work with directors to get their projects to this point.

Thesis films begin shooting starting in the fall of second year as part of Thesis Project I. There is also an advanced editing class this semester, but attendance is spotty at best, as everyone is in production. During this time the school functions as a studio to ensure that every thesis is shot.

In the spring of the final semester there is a Sound Design class in which several small exercises are completed simultaneously with thesis postproduction in the Thesis Project II course. All directors are required to create a film distribution strategy, and class time is also spent on creating press kits and conducting festival research. A Seminar in Independent Media Arts brings working artists to discuss and evaluate the current state of media arts. Thesis projects are screened at the school's annual Media Arts showcase at the end of the semester.

► **THE PRICE**

| | |
|---|---:|
| $13,500 nonresident tuition for one year | $13,500 |
| $6,400 resident tuition for one year | $6,400 |
| $20,000 per year rent and living expenses for two years | $40,000 |
| Average film costs | $15,000 |
| **Total** | **$74,900** |

New York residents can decrease the above figure by $7,100. After one year of living in New York, any number of documents can be used to prove residency and drop to the lower tuition rate. A driver's license, New York tax return, or even an apartment lease will suffice.

There is strong competition for a small number of merit-based scholarships distributed during the second year of study. The New York in Film & Television Fellowship awards $2,000 toward tuition for a talented woman filmmaker. The Bert Sapperstein Award sponsors two $1,000 awards. The National Board of Review Film Grant offers two $2,000 grants for promising thesis projects, one fiction and one documentary. The Public Media Scholarship awards $4,000 for thesis projects. The faculty selects the recipients or nominates finalists for all of these awards.

There are no teaching assistantships or graduate assistantships available. Most classes are taught during the day, and it is not easy to balance anything other than part-time employment. As with other NYC schools, jobs are plentiful, and the city is so expensive to live in that you must work. And although the degree is billed as "Media Arts," there is little emphasis in this area.

CCNY students live throughout the New York boroughs. The college is located in Spanish Harlem, one of the lone New York neighborhoods that has not been completely snatched up and rehabbed by developers. Although safety has vastly improved in the last few years, there are still some dicey areas in this tightly knit community. Because of this, some of the largest apartments in Manhattan are up for grabs in East Harlem. On Craigslist you still might be able to find a studio sublet for under a thousand dollars. This is a bargain in the out-of-control New York housing market. If you are up to the challenge, you'll be privy to some of best tortas to ever tempt your taste buds, a lively Latin music scene, and flourishing shops and restaurants. Jefferson Park offers some much appreciated green space, and there is finally some new architecture starting to spring up in the area. As of this writing, the school had just broken ground on its first-ever dorm.

The City Visions student festival screens at Lincoln Center for two nights every May. The faculty selects the films for this juried event. Judges from outside of the program award prizes in eight categories. Most of the films tend to be grad theses, but inclusion is paramount for both graduate and undergraduate students, and the awards are highly coveted. It is considered to be a good networking opportunity.

## ▶ THE LOWDOWN

Applicants apply for one the following specific areas of study: Writing and Directing (Documentary or Fiction), Camera, Editing, or Producing. Specific portfolio requirements for each focus are slightly different, but every applicant must submit a fifteen-minute reel of film and/or video work and declare a first- and second-choice area of study. Writer/Directors must also submit a thesis outline/idea including the project's proposed length and budget and format. They must also declare a second technical area of study. The program is looking for twenty-minute thesis films but is open to considering longer projects if a strong case can be made. Screenplays of no more than twenty-five

pages or interactive digital media work are optional portfolio additions. Those with nonfilm creative work will be
considered but will more than likely be required to take
prerequisite undergrad courses in film history and theory,
screenwriting, production, editing, or directing before
they start the program.

107

CCNY's graduate film students tend to be older, aver-
aging around thirty, and have a background in film, either
an undergrad film degree or the equivalent in life experience. Some come from film-related industries but show
promise in their portfolio materials. This can make for a
very competitive, sometimes disconnected group with
varying levels of experience and success. It also means that
a professional editor might wind up suffering through a
required class waiting for editing novices to get up to
speed.

Most students are New York locals from a myriad of
cultures and ethnic backgrounds, but women are definitely in the minority. The program has been known to
upload some students straight from their undergrad film
program, but this is the exception. About one hundred
applications are received for the twenty-four annual openings. There are quite a few who wound up here after not
being accepted into NYU or chose to simply buck the system and eschew the more expensive program.

CCNY searches for independent, self-motivated individuals who are able to be resourceful and arrive ready to
work; with your application you will be required to
describe the thesis film you want to make at CCNY. You
won't be held to it, but they want to know that you have
given it some serious thought and will be capable of shooting something in the second year. They are not interested
in Hollywood knockoffs and try to balance the program
between independent documentary filmmakers and fiction
directors with a smattering of experimental artists. Most
applicants apply with directing as their first choice, so the

odds of acceptance are better in the technical craft areas. Since all applicants are forced to list a second choice, you may wind up being accepted, just not as a director.

The truth is, while students declare an area of focus, the program is really not structured to address all of these individual areas with extensive supporting courses. There isn't enough time. This is really a Writer/Director program, and the few available electives amount to choices between writing and directing documentary or narrative films. Everyone takes the same courses in camera, editing, and producing, and those seeking to specialize in these areas really do so by simply working in these positions on thesis projects.

Directors and producers select whom they want on their teams. All projects are not equal in scope or quality, and problems can arise with the choice productions for those on the craft tracks. A cinematographer or editor might get saddled with a disappointing film to shoot or edit. Sometimes international students choose to shoot in their home countries, leaving their classmates high and dry. One recent cinematographer simply couldn't shoot enough films to fulfill the requirement for her reel. Writer/directors, who get to make their own projects, seem to fare the best.

Thesis films are the priority from day one, so you will have to learn fast and keep on track. Once projects are approved, students must work together to coordinate dates to assure that crews and equipment are available.

There are two Arriflex 16 mm cameras (no Super 16) and a large number of Bolexes. Each year more and more thesis projects are filmed digitally, so there is a need to increase the existing numbers of these cameras (Panasonic DVX100s and Sony PD150s). Many students show up with their own cameras. What's available within the program is grad-only and is well-maintained, although first years get limited lighting and sound. There is a bit of a race to lock down thesis shooting dates in order to confirm equipment availability. When one recent thesis student dropped out, there was a major scramble to snatch his time slot and equipment. There is a shooting studio and a good amount of Mole Richardson lights. For post there is one Steenbeck and five Final Cut Pro stations and one Avid editing station for first years. Thesis projects are assigned individual editing suites that they share with one other student. There is an audio editing room equipped with two ProTools stations, which can be used for ADR and Foley work.

With so few classes taken in year two, training is for the most part completed in the first year. There is little time to experiment outside of classes or take more specific or advanced courses in any area. The first-year films are fairly insignificant in length. And sometimes classes are not structured to address the program's mind-set. The producing class, which is largely disliked, has a strong Hollywood slant that is not in sync with the overall program or the independent filmmakers it grooms. The tech classes are problematic, especially sound, and students sometimes rely on each other for instruction. The theory and history courses, along with cinematography classes, are the most popular. This is a thesis-driven program, and almost every course, even those in first year, is focused on this final project. In general, the faculty is respected and well-liked for bringing life experience into their classrooms and for being dedicated to the students. They often hire students to work with them on their projects. Most instructors work in the independent film world and many have their MFAs from NYU.

*Some of the worst things about the program:* Sometimes classes are taught to the lowest common denominator due to the varying levels of experience. There is a constant push toward the thesis with little time to explore or experiment in other areas. You will live in the shadows of NYU and Columbia.

***Some of the best things about the program:*** CCNY is like the NYU of the proletariat. It's a diverse, international group of students in an inexpensive program in a great independent film city. The faculty is willing to mentor you if you ask for it. It is definitely a writer/director-driven program. But even students not accepted as writer/directors get a great deal of hands-on experience.

# COLUMBIA COLLEGE CHICAGO

Film & Video Department
600 South Michigan Avenue
Chicago, IL 60605-1900
312-344-6701
www.filmatcolumbia.com

| | |
|---|---|
| Tuition: | $16,328 |
| Enrollment: | 12–14 |
| Deadline: | January 3 |
| Focus: | Independent/Documentary |

## ▶ THE PROGRAM

Located in the Loop, in Chicago's urban core, Columbia College offers a moderately priced MFA program that specializes in independent narrative and documentary filmmaking. The program consists of three years of classes followed by an additional year or two of thesis production. Each year of classes is a distinct phase with a distinct set of goals

First year is Phase I. In the first semester students take Production I, a rigorous 16 mm course in basic filmmaking skills. Every student directs their own final project and works on those of their classmates. A directing course gives students time working with actors in a studio setting, and a screenwriting course guides students in the writing of a short narrative screenplay. In the second semester students take a course in film history. But Production II and Editing, where students shoot and edit the films they wrote in Screenwriting I, dominate the semester. At the end of the year students undergo a focus review where they present their finished Production II films, Screenwriting I screenplays, and Film Theory papers to a faculty committee. Most students pass the review, but every year one or two will fail and be asked to leave the program, and a few will receive a conditional pass that requires them to complete additional work over the summer before continuing into Phase II.

In the third semester, Phase II expands into documentary film. In Production III, small documentary and experimental films are produced. Short Forms provides an overview of alternative and experimental approaches to structuring short films as well as a bit of low-budget production methods. During the fourth and fifth semesters, Phase II becomes less strictly structured than Phase I. Students choose to focus on documentary or narrative filmmaking and follow a track of courses that concentrate on that area. They also study creative approaches and expressions that lead to a script idea that may be produced in Directing III. The three remaining courses, taken in the fourth and fifth semesters, can be selected from dozens of electives that complement students' chosen tracks or simply interest them.

Phase III, the final two semesters, is centered on thesis development. The goal is to complete a twenty-minute narrative screenplay or a proposal for a twenty-minute documentary. At the end of the third year, after two semesters of preparation, each student chooses two faculty members to act as thesis advisors. In the months and years following third year, these advisors approve a student's thesis proposal, offer guidance during the project's production and postproduction, and approve the granting of degrees when the project is finished.

Students should be able to finish classes and a thesis in around four years, but some students, as at any other school, can take quite a bit longer. For these students' benefit, the school has a firm limit of seven years after initial enrollment by which a thesis must be completed.

At least seven films will be made in classes during the three years of course work. Course fees and tuition funds cover film and processing costs as determined by the length restrictions set for each film, excluding the thesis. Students routinely use and pay for more film than allotted.

There is a large alumni network in Chicago and an active alumni office on the West Coast. Students have the option of participating in a five-week intensive semester in Los Angeles. More popular with undergrads, the L.A. program has a bungalow on the CBS studio lot where students take sessions like Producing, TV Pilot Development, and Writing the Sitcom and have access to the professionals that teach them.

Columbia College offers more career guidance upon graduation than most film schools. The school has a Portfolio Center that exists solely to help with the post-school transition. There is a film department liaison that works with the center to help students put portfolios together and position them in the industry. The center has an extensive internship program and job placement service along with festival information.

Two nights of thesis screenings are held in the fall. The best films produced within production courses, as judged by students and faculty, are shown at the Take One Festival. Then the best of the advanced undergraduate films and graduate thesis films are shown at the Big Screen Student Film Festival that happens in the spring. About one hundred students vie for one of the eight to ten Big Screen spots chosen by the faculty. Every two years the Big Screen travels west to hold a DGA screening in L.A. for films from the previous two years. A final perk for five or six select students comes in the form of a free trip to attend and screen work at the University Film and Video Association's annual convention.

▶ **THE PRICE**

| | |
|---|---|
| $576 per credit for sixty credits over four years | $34,560 |
| $13,000 per year rent and living expenses for four years | $52,000 |
| Average film costs | $25,000 |
| **Total** | **$111,560** |

Columbia has some funding from an assortment of sources. The Follet Fellowship awards one year of tuition remission to two incoming graduate students. New students can also receive smaller tuition remission assistance through the merit-based Lumiere Award and Department Merit Awards. The program selects winners. Continuing students look to the merit-based Rosebud Award or the one-year Graduate Opportunity Award. The Getz Graduate Award is given to up to eight grad students each semester (fall and spring only). Recipients must demonstrate contributions to the grad program student life or scholarship outside of the classroom.

Most students take advantage of tuition remission awards (formerly called grad assistantships), small tuition waivers for continuing students who provide education/project/research support in their department. There is an enormous undergraduate population of film students, and grads are highly sought after to assist with undergrad courses. Each must take a course in teaching in order to qualify and must be nominated by the department. A great deal of work is expected for minimal money.

Finally, the Production Fund has given as much $100,000 annually to students' film projects. Grads can apply for this after their first three semesters. It's a lengthy application process, but winners can receive up to $4,000 in aid.

There is some student housing near the school, but most graduate students opt to live in the relatively quiet, spacious, and inexpensive outlying areas. For $600 to $800 you can have your own place in accessible areas like the popular artist community of Wicker Park. While the city has pretty good public transportation, it is spread out over a huge area. Generally speaking, students who live close to town can get by without a car and can rent vans when production makes it necessary. But those who live farther out tend to need cars. Since most students live a short train ride from the school, we are not including a car as a necessity.

Columbia College is located in one of the country's largest cities. You will find great theater, music, film, museums, and restaurants. The Illinois Film Office is very helpful. Not a lot of feature-film productions come through town. Chicago is a commercial town, and there are many job opportunities to be had in commercial production, especially post.

▶ **THE LOWDOWN**

Columbia admits fourteen students each year from about a hundred applicants. Incoming students are not required to have a background in film, but the admissions board tends to be most interested in applicants with both interesting life experiences and demonstrated creative talent. You can send a creative portfolio with your application, and doing so will give you an edge, but it is not required. Probably the most important element of the application is the thesis project proposal; if you can clearly describe a compelling thesis film you plan to make while at school, you will be at a significant advantage.

It is difficult to work at all during the first year. Many students cut back on classes starting in the fourth semester in order to work part-time jobs. As a result these students take four years just to complete their classes. Once course work is completed, you can matriculate for the cost of one credit for every semester you work on your thesis. You can even eliminate the one-credit fee by teaching during the thesis stage. If possible, it's a good idea to try not to take classes beyond three years. However, if you choose to lengthen your stay, and things take even longer than you imagined, as long as you are still working productively in the eyes of the faculty, you can petition for an extension beyond the seven-year cutoff.

There is a healthy competitive spark in the program, mostly due to the financial awards. There are a lot of films to be made, so students must depend on each other. As projects increase in size, students gather crew from other years and even the undergraduate program.

There are about thirty full-time faculty members and over one hundred adjunct faculty teaching in the film and video program. Full-time instructors teach both undergrad and grad programs. The faculty is a mix of independent filmmakers and academics. It's a sore point with students that none of the writing staff have ever had scripts produced professionally, but they are fine mentors. There is genuine excitement for a new producing instructor who has well-known Hollywood features under his belt. The Directing III is the strongest of the directing courses. Most of the production instructors are locals who come from commercial backgrounds, but they are highly skilled in their areas and great at motivating and guiding students. Students find it easy to connect with the faculty.

Considering that the equipment is shared with undergrads, it is surprisingly well-maintained. Grads have priority over undergrads, so there are rarely problems with access to the best equipment, especially after the busy first semester. Reservations are made through an online system. Shooting dates are assigned at the beginning of every semester for each course. While things get tight near the end of the semester, planning ahead usually minimizes problems. The Film and Video Department has some of just about every 16 mm camera in existence including Bolex, Arriflex SR, Arriflex BL, Arri S, Aaton XTR, Aaton A-Minima, Eclair, and CP-16 cameras. The Sony PD150s are mostly used for documentaries.

A new audio postproduction facility fills an entire floor. It houses a Foley studio, ADR facilities, two state-of-the-art mixing theaters, ProTools labs, and a dozen or so computers, and individual sound suites.

On another floor, the postproduction center contains four Steenbecks and lots of editing suites with Avid Express and Final Cut Pro connected to a central server. There is even a Bosch telecine for transferring film to video.

**Some of the worst things about the program:** Chicago does not have the bustling independent filmmaking community the way New York, Los Angeles, San Francisco, and Austin do. And in winter Chicago can be trying. Seven years is a heck of a long time to be in school. The school does not have the prestige or name recognition of some others, except for those who confuse it with Columbia University.

**Some of the best things about the program:** This is an intimate program that offers a lot of personal attention. The equipment is good and is fairly available. The instructors are committed. The school puts a heartening emphasis on developing the personal voice. Chicago is a great city.

# COLUMBIA UNIVERSITY

School of the Arts

Film Division

513 Dodge Hall

2960 Broadway

New York, NY 10027-2365

Department: 212-854-2815

Admissions: 212-854-2134

www.columbia.edu/cu/arts/film

| | |
|---|---|
| Tuition: | $35,327 |
| Enrollment: | 65 per year |
| Deadline: | January 4 |
| Focus: | Independent |

## ▶ THE PROGRAM

Columbia University's film program deserves to be better-known than it is. The department has long had a reputation for being a little underfunded and a little short on equipment. And it does not yet have a superstar alumnus—a Coppola or Scorsese or Lucas—to put it on the cultural map. But the faculty is strong, and the focus—on story and performance rather than technical craft—has shown good results in recent years; since 1990, Columbia has been second only to NYU in number of Student Academy Award–winning films.

First year begins with a weeklong orientation, an intense period that introduces the incoming students to one another and to the faculty, and introduces them to the equipment they will be using. Students then start a standard menu of classes in writing, directing, acting, producing, and film history.

The school assumes no prior experience in film, so Directing I starts with the filmmaking basics. Students work with digital video cameras, learning basic technique, and over time shooting a number of short exercises. In Screenwriting I students write silent films, learning to tell stories through action and gesture rather than through dialogue; as the course progresses, students begin writing the scripts for the eight- to twelve-minute films they will make in second semester. Directing the Actor is a workshop where students learn the craft of acting in a studio setting; as the semester progresses, students direct scenes using one another as actors. These classes are pretty intimate; rather than meeting as one large class, these classes are taught in six separate sections, each taught by a different professor, with about twelve students in each. Introduction to Film Studies gives students a basic history of film. Around the middle of the semester, each student begins work on a three- to five-minute video. Students work as crew on one another's shoots; the finished 3-to-5s are screened at the end of the semester.

In December, students submit their pitches for the eight- to twelve-minute screenplays they have been writing in Screenwriting I. The trick with the 8-to-12 is that the school requires every film be written by one student and directed by another. The students read through all of the submitted script ideas, and each student picks a few stories he would like to direct. Negotiations then ensue, with each writer choosing the director he'd like to work with, while also negotiating to direct a screenplay written by another classmate. Once the negotiations are done, everyone is set to write one project and direct another. Over the course of the second semester, the writer-director teams present drafts to class, rehearse scenes with actors, take criticism from faculty and classmates, and repeatedly write and rewrite. While doing this in Directing II, in Screenwriting II students are writing a feature-length screenplay, of which they must complete at least sixty pages by the end of the first year. Students shoot their 8-to-12s during the summer break. As a result, summer is in many ways more hectic than the school year; Columbia is essentially a year-round program for the first two years.

Early in the second year the finished 8-to-12s are screened and discussed in a weeklong event called Crit Week. But beyond that, after the frantic pace of first year, second year is less intense. Each student chooses an area of concentration—Directing, Producing, Screenwriting, or History/Theory/Criticism (HTC for short)—and from there on the concentration dictates who her faculty advisor is, and many of the courses she takes. This is not a terribly dogmatic thing; students may change their concentration later if they like. It is also possible to concentrate in both screenwriting and directing simultaneously. The screenwriting concentration has the benefit of saving time and money; most students can complete the required two feature-length screenplays within three years, graduate, and start paying off their debt, while the directors go on amassing debt for two more years. The producing concentration is an interesting option for those so inclined; fellow classmates' thesis films provide many opportunities to produce, and real-world producers regularly teach classes. Perhaps one or two students a year might go into the HTC concentration.

In the second year, those who choose directing move on into Directing III and Screenwriting III. Directing III is devoted to more advanced directorial technique; students shoot four exercises over the course of the semester. While each exercise is an independent project, the school suggests that students come to the class with a screenplay for a short film with four scenes, and make each of the exercises a scene of the film. This way a student can wind up at the end of the semester with another completed film. This is not a requirement, though, and many students instead shoot scenes from the feature-length screenplays they are writing in Screenwriting III, or work out ideas for their Directing IV films, or their thesis films.

In Directing IV, in the second semester, students again prepare a short film. As with the 8-to-12 in first year, students spend the semester workshopping and rewriting their screenplays. They shoot over the summer and edit into the fall for presentation in Crit Week.

After the end of second year, and the completion of the Directing IV projects in the summer thereafter, things get kind of nebulous. There are no further required classes; students pay around a quarter of the standard tuition to matriculate and continue using school facilities as they work on their final requirements. Those requirements, for the directing concentration, are to finish a feature-length screenplay and to make a thesis film. Students may take one course each semester; many take a course called Revision devoted to helping them rewrite and refine their screenplays in progress.

Students planning to make a thesis film during a given year must get approval from the faculty Production Advisory Board at the beginning of that year. Students may, if they like, make another film before beginning work on their thesis films. This film is called the nonthesis; it is bound by most of the same regulations as the thesis film—it must be approved by the Production Advisory Board before it can proceed to production, and requires the oversight of a faculty advisor—but it does not carry the weight of the thesis film. While not required, many students choose to make a nonthesis film. Since all first- and second-year projects are shot on video, some students use the nonthesis as a chance to work with film once before it really counts on the thesis film. Some just want to direct something during the months and years it takes to prepare a complex thesis project. Others want to use the school's facilities to try their hand at a different kind of film—documentary, for example—before launching into their final projects. The nonthesis is basically one more chance to make a movie; some students are happy for the opportunity, while others

121

just want to get on with the thesis so they can get out into the world and start paying off their student loans.

Students must finish both the thesis film and feature screenplay by the end of the fifth year; the school is pretty hard-nosed about getting people out within five years these days.

Each spring the school features student work in a week-long film festival. It begins with a night of the best of the 3-to-5 and 8-to-12 video projects, as chosen by the faculty. A night of readings from student screenplays is followed by screenings of nonthesis and thesis films. Agents and industry representatives are invited. The last night of the festival is "Faculty Selects"; ten or so films the faculty likes the best are screened, and awards are presented. While students are allowed to make films of any length, only films twenty-seven minutes or shorter are eligible to screen in the festival. Some students wind up making two separate cuts of their films: a twenty-seven-minute version to screen in the festival and a longer version for the rest of the world to see.

In June, the Faculty Selects films are screened in Los Angeles. The administration has been working hard in recent years to raise Columbia's profile in Hollywood, not just with these screenings, but also by introducing graduating filmmakers to Columbia alumni in the industry.

## ▶ THE PRICE

| | |
|---|---|
| $35,327 tuition for two years | $70,654 |
| $8,000 matriculation for two additional years | $16,000 |
| $20,000 per year rent and living expenses for four years | $80,000 |
| Average film costs | $30,000 |
| **Total** | **$196,654** |

Gulp. You sort of have to wonder where all that money is going; we know it's not being spent on equipment. And while there are a few grants and fellowships, none comes close to covering the full cost of the school. So, unless you are very rich, be prepared to take on a lot of debt.

A smattering of grants that range from $1,000 to $5,000 are available to first-year students; a $10,000 award sponsored by HBO is available for one student's thesis film. For students above first year there are around twenty fellowships—service fellowships, teaching assistantships, and department research assistantships—that provide compensation of up to half the total tuition. Service assistantships are generally preferred; students who don't get those apply for teaching assistantships. Because there is no undergraduate film production program at Columbia, there are fewer of these to go around than at most schools.

New York is one of the most expensive places in the country to live. Finding an apartment in New York can be a nightmare; living in one once you've found it can be worse. You'll generally have to give up something you currently think of as a necessity in order to afford an apartment; space, privacy, quiet, a sink in the bathroom, a window, all of these are things that will potentially be lacking in the apartments you can afford. A one-room studio apartment is liable to cost $2,500 a month or more.

Many students choose to live in Columbia's graduate student housing. The apartments are right by campus and are less expensive than most for the area, but Columbia is a pretty brutal landlord. The second you are no longer matriculated they'll throw you out on the street. Students have been known to hold off on finishing their thesis films just to hang on to their apartments a little longer. International House, an independent dormitory affiliated with, but not run by, the school is worth looking into. This multicultural city within the city is a short walk from the campus and is a fascinating place to live. The rooms are small, and the bathroom is down the hall, but you get privacy and a view.

It is not possible to hold a job during the first two years. But by third year most students are so deeply into debt that they have to find some kind of gainful employment. While New York is a media center, and there are many opportunities to work in film and television production, the fact that Columbia students don't get a lot of technical training is a bit of a handicap. Students are more likely to find work at production company offices than on film or television shoots.

## ▶ THE LOWDOWN

In years past, Columbia's relatively scant equipment was often cause for embarrassment, but it now seems to be kind of a point of pride. The faculty's approach now is, *You don't want to get tied up in technical issues like cameras and lenses and film stock—just hire someone to do that for you. We're going to teach you how to write stories, and how to tell those stories visually.* And, in a way, the scarcity of expensive film equipment has proven to be an advantage; because the school did not have a lot of money invested in film equipment, it moved easily into the era of digital video and nonlinear postproduction. Students write and direct numerous projects in the first two years of the program, working entirely in digital video. When they get to their thesis films, the students who choose to shoot on film generally hire outside professionals—or NYU students—to handle the technical aspects. The resulting films are often quite good; better-written, better-directed, better-acted—and often better-shot—than films that come out of a lot of other programs.

Columbia is fundamentally about writing. While this may have started out of necessity, in the digital video era writing has become its identity. If your primary interest is writing straightforward narratives for the screen, then Columbia would be a great place for you. If your interests are more in the technical details of filmmaking, then it is probably not the place for you. Columbia is also not a great place to make experimental or documentary films. Not that anyone objects if you try, and students often do. There's just not a lot of expertise in those areas among the faculty, and for these prices you kind of want some expertise.

In the application process, Columbia looks primarily for writing talent. The school does not require previous experience in film, so it is a good place for people new to film. But students who arrive with experience in film, or who studied film as undergraduates, sometimes find the first year frustratingly basic.

As mentioned above, students mostly shoot on digital video, on standard NTSC cameras such as the Canon GL-1, and on 24p cameras like the Panasonic DVX100A. While the school does own an Arri SR 16 mm camera, it seems that students don't use it much; by this point they are used to watching video monitors while they shoot, and find the lack of a video tap on the school camera a real problem. So students generally go to rental houses to rent cameras with video taps.

Students we spoke with are enthusiastic about many members of the faculty. The core courses, such as Directing I and Screenwriting I, are taught in separate sections of a dozen or so students, so for each class you can choose between three different professors. Students quickly determine for themselves who are the best professors, and competition can be tough to get into the sections taught by those professors. Richard Pena, the director of the Film Society at Lincoln Center and the director of the New York Film Festival, teaches the first-year HTC course and frequent courses in International Cinema; James Schamus, cowriter and producer of all of Ang Lee's films, also teaches history and criticism courses and producing courses. Legendary film critic Andrew Sarris and noted independent producer Ira Deutchman are also full-time faculty members.

*Some of the worst things about the program:* One thing looms above all others: the staggering cost and for many students the resulting years of crushing debt.

*Some of the best things about the program:* The acting workshops are a good addition; Columbia students really learn how to communicate with actors in their language. And New York is an exciting place to be a filmmaker. But the best thing about the program is the in-depth training in how to tell a story.

# FLORIDA STATE UNIVERSITY

Film School
University Center 3100A
Tallahassee, FL 32306-2350
850-644-7728
www.fsu.edu/~film

| Tuition: | Resident: $ 9,054 |
| | Nonresident: $33,108 |
| Enrollment: | 30 |
| Deadline: | December 15 |
| Focus: | Industry |

## ▶ THE PROGRAM

The Film School at Florida State University was created by the state in 1989 in order to attract feature film production into the area. It is a heavily funded state-of-the-art school with facilities that often equal industry standards. The focus is on Hollywood filmmaking. Documentary film work is not even an option. All FSU projects adhere to SAG and IATSE regulations.

Twenty-four production track and six writing students are accepted each year. (Professional Writing was added as a designated major in 2004 and graduated its first class in 2006.) The students that make the cut are an energetic group. And energy is something that is needed to survive this two-year, year-round conservatory. The interaction between class years and the workshop training atmosphere on major productions make this program less about classes and more about learning through hands-on experience. All film costs, save some props for short class projects, are covered by the school. A budget is provided for every film. Students will not pay one cent toward film stock, processing, most production costs, or postproduction work for any film produced while in the program. Since projects are funded entirely by the school, the school owns them.

Like most schools, there's instruction in the main production disciplines of writing, directing, editing, cinematography, producing, and sound, and the appropriate in-class exercises that accompany each. Unlike most schools, at FSU these exercises amount to a great deal of film production shared between classes. Production and Professional Writing students follow the same intense first-semester production curriculum.

Prior to the beginning of the first semester, incoming students meet as a group for a two-week crash course that covers industry practices and protocol, set operations, and equipment training. They learn the basics necessary to rotate crew positions on their own first-year Directing I projects and the second-year Directing III projects. This interaction allows first-year students to progress with more hands-on training, while second-year students are supplied with the crew support necessary to create a more advanced film.

Once the program begins, the first four weeks of the semester cover filmmaking principles, craft, and theory in classroom and practicum settings. By the time first years are catapulted into production for Directing I projects, they'll have discussed all aspects of their individual film with writing, cinematography, production design, directing, editing, producing, and sound-recording instructors. In week five, classes halt for six weeks for the second-year film crew rotations. As soon as first-year students finish crewing for these Directing III projects, they immediately shoot their own five-minute Directing I projects. Each student is assigned a one-day shoot date and receives one thousand feet of film stock for this film. The last two weeks of the term are spent in postproduction for the Directing I films.

At the end of the first semester, the five-minute Directing I projects are completed with each student having written and directed her own project and crewed once in every key position on classmates' films. Online evaluations are completed. Directing I students rate the performance of their classmates on Directing I films, and the second-year students for whom they worked on Directing III projects. Second-year students rate the first years' performances on their Directing III crews. These evaluations are important both as assessment tools for students and faculty and because they resurface during second year and can affect a student's chance to direct a thesis. Everyone then attends the thesis pitches, which occur immediately following the end of the semester.

With the start of the second semester, Professional Writing students switch from the production track and branch off to focus on courses that deal exclusively with writing. In spring they write and produce ten-minute one-act plays. During the summer they concentrate on screen/TV writing. There's a course on character development and a second course that varies in subject each year. In the past this course has included a visiting television writer instructing in comedic episodic television or adapting novels for the screen. In fall of the second year, writing students return to the theater school to concentrate on writing full-length plays. In spring of the second year, students return to the film school and work on developing feature-film scripts for their thesis films. They also take a course on either novel or short story writing taught within the English department. During the summer of their final semester, students polish their thesis scripts (feature-length screenplay or full-length stage play) and take the same industry class as the production students.

For production students, the first-year second-semester classes and structure are similar to their first semester. The big change is experiencing their first thesis cycle. Like their second-year counterparts, first-year production students choose films they are interested working on. They then must interview with the directors and producers (whom they already know from the Directing III projects) for below-the-line positions on thesis films. By the third week of February, the thesis projects are in production, and first-year students spend the rest of the second term crewing on two to three projects. Thesis films are allotted nine principal production days and three days for pickups after the faculty has reviewed a first cut. After working on the thesis films, first-year students return to classes.

The focus shifts back to directing in the intermediate summer term when first-year students shoot their Directing II projects. During the first weeks of class, students meet with instructors to plan their project. Then as in the first semester, students again support one another by rotating crew positions for these two-day shoots. The amount of film stock is increased to 1,200 feet for this seven-minute film. At the end of the summer, first-year students have explored all the different crew positions and can meet with the faculty for their first-year review. It also means Directing III projects are right around the corner.

For production majors, the second-year fall semester is often viewed as the most stressful. The first draft of each Directing III screenplay must be ready by the first week of class.

As in the summer session, during the first weeks students will meet with instructors in workshops and classes to rewrite and polish the script and plan their projects. Directing IIIs begin production in late September or early October, each shot in three twelve-hour days. Two thousand feet of film stock is provided. Those who have decided directing is not their calling may skip directing this film altogether and specialize in another area. A student who wants to produce or shoot or edit may work on more than one Directing III project. In other words, every student has the option to work in each major position once, but it is not required. And any student who elects not to direct can apply the money assigned for her Directing III to enhance the budget of the project they do produce or edit or shoot. This might allow a Directing III to shoot on 35 mm. No student can direct more than one Directing III.

By the end of the fall term, Directing IIIs have been completed. Everyone then takes an advanced producing course on developing a feature film. During the last five weeks of the fall semester, second-year students who choose to pitch to direct a thesis will attend workshops, led by a pair of instructors, and geared toward developing thesis scripts/pitches. Students workshop a minimum of nine ideas. After three weeks of workshops, students are encouraged to further develop three ideas of their own. After the final workshops, the faculty recommend two of the three ideas. Each student then chooses one of her preapproved ideas to pitch, or workshop each other's ideas, or pull from a pool of scripts submitted by writing students.

Pitches occur right before Christmas. Anyone who refrains from competing to direct is guaranteed a key crew position. Only two or three students take this option, usually cinematographers and editors. Director/producer teams pitch one of the already approved projects to the faculty. Pitches are always lavish presentations with music and artwork. Costumes and props are not unheard of. Students go all out to demonstrate their talent and connection with a project. From these pitches the faculty selects four to six producer/director teams. The rest of the second year students interview with the chosen producer/directors for the remainder of the above-the-line positions. By the end of the week, those have been filled, and the first-year students interview for their spots early in January. Student thesis producers are assigned their budgets (somewhere in the area of $30,000) and proceed to plan the entire shoot. Theses can be shot in Super 16 mm or 35 mm. The Super 16 films are blown up to 35 mm at the end. Most choose to shoot the less expensive Super 16.

In late February the thesis films enter production. They shoot in two-week cycles. As each film finishes, editors immediately begin the post work that will usually carry through the summer. Finished films range between eight and twenty minutes long.

Summer of the second year is addressed on a student-by-student basis. Editors are still working on films. Some students line up internships. Most years there are opportunities to work on a feature film. Producers are supposed to follow their films through to completion. They can take an additional class or, with school permission, a nonconflicting internship. Serious cinematographers can take advantage of an advanced 35 mm cinematography course so that they may gain 35 mm experience and obtain footage for their reels. Students might request permission to take a visual effects course or propose an independent study as long as a faculty member will act as the instructor of record. Independent studies can be in almost anything. In the past, students have taken studies in writing coverage or storyboarding in addition to the expected writing, editing, and cinematography. Many students take a feature screenwriting class. All students take a class in industry practices taught via teleconference by an alumnus who brings in industry professionals to guest-lecture.

By the time they graduate, every student will have had the opportunity to write and direct three films and will have worked in creative positions on twelve others. And although the school owns the films, there is festival/publicity coordinator who will promote them and pay festival entry fees, with thesis films being given the greatest push.

A public screening is held for family and friends at the end of the semester. The faculty selects five hours of what they consider to be the best films and sends them off for a formal review by the alumni council. The council numerically rates each project, and the films with the highest scores are presented at a well-publicized two-hour thesis film screening at the DGA in Los Angeles and the Angelika theater in New York.

## ▶ THE PRICE

**Resident**

| | |
|---|---|
| $9,054 tuition per year for two years | $18,108 |
| $9,600 per year rent and living expenses for two years | $19,200 |
| $1,200 per year maintenance and insurance on a car for two years in Tallahassee | $2,400 |
| Average film costs | $1,500 |
| **Total** | **$41,208** |

**Nonresident**

| | |
|---|---|
| $33,108 tuition per year for two years | $66,216 |
| $9,600 per year rent and living expenses for two years | $19,200 |
| $1,200 per year maintenance and insurance on a car for two years in Tallahassee | $2,400 |
| Average film costs | $1,500 |
| **Total** | **$89,316** |

Residents can't beat this deal. In order to establish residency, a person must live in and collect a paycheck in the state for one year. Work-study or school-supported employment does not fulfill the requirement. Residents who live in the Academic Common Market, of which Florida is a member, may qualify for in-state tuition. This market is currently comprised of Alabama, Arkansas, Delaware, Florida, Georgia, Kentucky, Louisiana, Maryland, Mississippi, North Carolina, Oklahoma, South Carolina, Tennessee, Texas, Virginia, and West Virginia.

Time constraints make it nearly impossible to have any sort of part-time job, and technically, no one is allowed to work during the first year. Determined or desperate students have been known to tempt fate and pursue some minimal job on the sly in order to cash in on the lower tuition by second year, but nonresidents will more than likely pay the higher fee for both years.

134    A very few graduate assistantships are available and are awarded on the basis of need and/or achievement. A small number are awarded to incoming students, and there is opportunity to apply again in second year. Stipends for these positions average just under $1,500 per semester. If the funds are available, some tuition fee waivers might accompany the cash, but it is not guaranteed, and the amounts depend upon residency status. If available, waivers will range from $900 to $6,000. Responsibilities also vary but can involve work like driving the grip trucks or assisting in the equipment room.

Florida State has an agreement with the Screen Actors Guild and often features SAG actors in Directing II and thesis projects. There is a casting office that coordinates talent searches. Local auditions are held at the beginning of fall and spring. For thesis films it is common for filmmakers to travel to Los Angeles, Austin, Orlando, Toronto, or New York and record auditions through different casting agencies.

There are very strong alumni bases in Los Angeles and New York. An alumni coordinator contacts alums and matches them with a current student to mentor. Once everyone is matched, the school pays to fly the current students out to L.A. to meet their mentors and participate in workshops and roundtable discussions. The coordinator also publishes weekly reports on film events in and out of school, and festival and alumni updates.

Tallahassee is a large, industrial burg with lots of lawyers but little culture. An international student who had lived in many cities proclaimed Pittsburgh to be more exciting. You know you're in trouble when the local rock-climbing gym is cited as one of the best local attractions. Grads do not live on campus. Most feel a car is a necessity not just for the never-ending production but also so that you can live wherever you want and escape for some R & R if you ever have any spare time. First-year students wondered how the one student without a car managed to survive. A nice one-bedroom falls in the $500 price range. Two bedrooms go for around $800.

## ▶ THE LOWDOWN

Three hundred applications are received each year. An exceptional applicant might get accepted straight from undergrad, but those who have more life experience are preferred. Ideally, applicants have careers somehow connected to film and possess an appreciation for the craft of filmmaking in addition to the art. And because collaboration is at the very heart of what they teach, they really scrutinize your essay to see if you have a team mentality. Everything you submit is evaluated and given a numerical score: your GRE and GPA, letters of recommendation, your previous experience, and your individual statement of purpose. Based upon these scores, ninety applicants are invited to visit the campus for mandatory thirty-minute interviews. Applicants will first meet individually with the committee and then be part of a second group interview. Every attempt is made to match a class as a whole and make sure that applicants fit in with the school's Hollywood paradigm. Enrollment for accepted international students is delayed until fall of the following year in order to provide time for documentation of sufficient funding to complete the program and obtain visas. Accepted students are usually in their late twenties.

The program thinks of itself as a "story school," not a film school. During the first year, a team bond is forged through all the production and work that takes over your life. There's no time for egos. Alas, the claws come out second year when the star players steal the show. The Directing III film critiques can turn downright ugly prior to thesis pitching as everyone tries to knock classmates out of the running for the five director slots. There is no way to escape the inevitable disappointment for some. On the other hand, those not interested in directing are elated to have the chance to add one more film, and a high-end one at that, to their résumé.

The faculty is not star-studded, but they do boast Academy Award–winning sound recordist Richard Portman. Most of the faculty continue to work or had successful industry careers before arriving at FSU. Some are not as strong in the classroom as they are on the set, but all are accessible and are willing to help, and students have mostly good reports about them all. The director of the program, Reb Braddock, is also an alumnus. (His thesis film, developed by Quentin Tarantino into the feature film *Curdled*, was released in 1996.) Braddock is extremely well-liked as a teacher and was described by one student as "the spine of the program."

Equipment is partially shared with the undergraduate program, but since the production schedules are well-established and some equipment is reserved just for grads, there are no conflicts. First-year grads use a dozen or so CP-16s. There are ten Arri SRs for second years. And there's a Panavision 35 mm camera for select students. Standard issue are Panther dollies, jibs, cranes, generators, Steadicams, and large lighting packages that come with several HMI Pars. High-quality hard drive sound packages and loaded grip trucks are provided for Directing III and thesis projects. Equipment is in a constant maintenance cycle. At any given time two cameras are being refurbished at Arriflex.

There's a production design facility for building sets. All post is digital and tapeless and supported by many editing stations equipped with Avid and Final Cut Pro. There's a large mixing theater with an acoustically centered mix board and seating for 140 and two smaller mixing stages. There's an ADR/Foley room. Sound Stage A is a 3,000-

square-foot space with remote-control grid lighting. Sound Stage B is about half that size. There's a twenty-four-hour writing lab with ten to twelve Macintosh computers loaded with Final Draft Screenwriting and Movie Magic budgeting software. This lab is open to the entire school. There's a video library with over five thousand movie titles.

*Some of the worst things about the program:* The consecutive year-round training can be exhausting. Students long for more time to write scripts. Production takes precedence over everything, especially theory, which is seriously short-changed. Film allotments must be strictly adhered to. There's no guarantee to direct a thesis film. This creates a great deal of stress around Directing III projects. And there's always some bitterness after the selection of thesis producers and directors. Because so much assistance is given, students might not be prepared for the guerilla tactics paramount in pursuing independent filmmaking once they are in the real world.

*Some of the best things about the program:* Students get a lot for their money and even more with the school's money. Everyone can write and direct something, and can depart with employable technical skills. You will know production inside and out and will have credits on upward of twelve films. The first-year students learn a great deal working with the second-year students. Even those who don't direct thesis films could have a strong showpiece in the Directing III film. Without a budget variable, the student playing field is really level. Aspiring cinematographers, producers, editors, and sound recordists will have a great experience. The equipment is plentiful, well-organized, and up-to-date. The classes are tight-knit. The post-school network is extremely active and supportive. Almost everyone goes to Los Angeles after they graduate. The graduate employment rate is very high.

# MIAMI INTERNATIONAL UNIVERSITY OF ART & DESIGN

1501 Biscayne Boulevard, Suite 100
Miami, FL 33132-1418
800-225-9023
www.artinstitutes.edu/miami

| | |
|---|---|
| Tuition: | $23,760 |
| Enrollment: | 12–20 |
| Deadline: | Fall: Early October |
| | Spring: Mid-March |
| Focus: | Independent |

## ▶ THE PROGRAM

The Miami International University of Art and Design is part of the Art Institute system that consists of thirty-two schools spread across the nation. This is the only school within the system that awards a master of fine arts degree in film. The MFA has been available just since 2003, making it the newest program on the market. It can also be one of the shortest. Those who already have undergraduate film degrees attend year-round classes for just eighteen months. In that time, they earn ninety course credits and depart having directed three films. Those without a BA in film must take five undergraduate prerequisites prior to starting the program. This increases the program length to two years total.

The program is focused on narrative filmmaking, but a student interested in documentary would certainly be permitted to follow this path. A few professors do have documentary experience; it's just that at present there are no courses that specifically instruct in this genre. In fact, the curriculum is one of the most structured of all programs, with literally no elective options included. There simply isn't time. Every student takes exactly the same basic production and craft courses, a bit of theory, and some cinema studies, and winds up with just enough time to produce a thesis. Unlike some of the other shorter programs that are accelerated in terms of pace and production, AiMIU is less about film output and more about an overall foundation in filmmaking. This is not to say that it is not production-oriented, but rather that it tends to be more even-keeled in terms of production. One of the reasons for this is that the first two films directed are only five minutes each and are, more or less, extended exercises. The thesis is the only complete film students make, and students have three quarters to make it.

Essentially, the first half of the program, consisting of the first three quarters, is about learning to write, shoot, and edit. The first quarter is basically a preparation for the film that will be produced during the second quarter. A script is written in Fundamentals of Screenwriting. Then shooting aesthetics and technical skills are reviewed in the cinematography class. Motion Picture Post Production I is an Avid training course. Film Genres is exactly what the title implies, a comparative course on film styles. By the end of this first quarter students have viewed some films, learned to shoot and edit a film, and written a film script. This five-minute script is then shot in one day in Narrative Motion Picture Production I and edited in Motion Picture Post Production II during the second quarter. The university provides a set amount of stock and processing for all productions, but does not restrict students from adding to the amounts provided. In the third quarter, a second five-minute film is written and produced. Post Production this round focuses on sound design. Producing fundamentals are taught in Production Management.

The final half of the program begins with the fourth quarter. Other than editing the second narrative film in the fall, these final three quarters are mainly for thesis preproduction, production, and postproduction. Only two classes are taken in addition to the thesis course each term. These include one course that instructs in teaching methodologies and another that deals with business practices in film. There are also specialized workshops where local professionals guest-lecture. But mainly, it's thesis time. Scripts for films are written in the Master's Thesis I in the fall. Usually thesis scripts aim for a length of twenty minutes. Then the script, a preproduction book, and a portfolio are submitted to a thesis committee for approval. The committee consists of three faculty members, generally the department chair and the thesis preproduction, production, and post instructors who will oversee the project from screenwriting through post. Once greenlighted, the script is shot over three days in Master's Thesis II during the winter and finished in Master's Thesis III the last spring quarter. Thesis films can be shot on video if a student so desires, but 1,600 feet of 16 mm stock and processing is budgeted for every project. Students do have the option of writing a narrative feature script in lieu of making a thesis film.

At the end of every quarter, both grads and undergrads screen their films. A major screening of thesis projects is held off campus in the spring. The program also pays the entry fees for fifteen festivals each year. This could be for one film or several films. The faculty makes this decision. A career services department exists and is supposed to assist students upon graduation, but they prefer to deal with undergraduates and are not very helpful to grad students.

## ▶ THE PRICE

| | |
|---|---|
| $528 per credit for ninety credits | $47,520 |
| Rent and living expenses for eighteen months | $19,800 |
| Car insurance and maintenance for eighteen months | $2,500 |
| Average film costs | $5,000 |
| **Total** | **$74,820** |

This may be a short program, but it is certainly not one of the cheapest. Unfortunately, standard financial aid is the only available assistance that students receive. There are work-study positions, but no grants or fellowships or grad assistantships exist.

AiMIU is located in the heart of downtown Miami. Large populations of Latin Americans and Caribbean natives have had a real impact on the local culture and neighborhoods. English is often the second language. The immediate area surrounding the university is a bit run-down, but no more so than other urban schools. And most of those schools are not a ten-minute drive to South Beach, one of the nicest, albeit touristy, areas in Florida. The weather is great for shooting, but be prepared: it rains a good deal, and more so than ever, tropical storms can be an issue. A car is advisable. The Metrorail and the Metromover have limited stops within the city and don't even run late at night. The buses are unreliable and best avoided. Miami is a flashy town with active art and music scenes, and a small film community. A one-bedroom apartment will run about $800.

▶ **THE LOWDOWN**

Incoming class sizes at AiMIU have been as small as three or as large as eight.

The program prefers applicants who have a BA in film and who want to learn a diverse set of production skills. But if you lack a degree, they will consider your professional experience. Right now half of the current students have film BAs and half do not. If you are a film rookie, you can still attend, but the cost and program length will increase depending on the number of prerequisites you will have to take. The application process is fairly standard, with no special requirements or program-specific assignments to complete. This means that your essay is heavily weighted. You will also be interviewed in person or over the phone to assess your skills in correlation to the program offerings. Because it is so new, only twenty-five applications are received annually. That makes your odds of acceptance very good.

If you do get in, the program is so small that you are sure to get tons of individualized attention. Granted, three of the five full-time instructors are graduates of Florida State University, so their perspectives might not be all that diverse. But it also means the instructors are relatively young, current, and active in their careers. The faculty is really involved with students but can be a bit lenient as far as worthwhile criticism goes. And some instructors have the degree and experience but are just not organized or effective in the classroom. Students find the technical courses, specifically the post classes, are the most useful. Each year dozens of student computer animators or graphic designers or fashion designers informally collaborate with film students on projects. On the downside, you can never take a course with any of these folks because you get no electives. But you will depart with a solid overview of film production and a film under your belt. The thesis film is the crowning achievement.

Many classes are taught in the evening, so it is easy to work part-time during the day. Many commercials are shot in Miami. And features do come through, so it is production-friendly, but the biggest source of production work is in post for Latino and Spanish networks. Students sometimes land these jobs. Speaking Spanish comes in handy.

Equipment is shared with undergrads. Sometimes it gets stretched, but generally speaking, there are no major problems. There are six assorted Arriflex cameras, three of which are grad-restricted Super 16. Video cameras exist but are not usually used for grad projects. The lighting and sound packages are fairly extensive. Students sometimes rent supplementary equipment like prime lenses or more sophisticated dollies. Recently some students have started to rent high-def cameras for thesis projects. There's no screening room, but a green screen studio and ADR recording studio are available. There are sixteen editing stations with Avid and Final Cut Pro. The real production issue is the difficulty in crewing your projects. With so few people in the class, it's a given that you will have to search outside of it to fill many positions. It's not unheard of for students to hire professional cinematographers or sound recordists.

*Some of the worst things about the program:* In only eighteen months you will barely scratch the surface in many areas and will not be able to seriously focus on any one craft. With class sizes of three or four, try avoiding someone you don't like. It can't be done! The small numbers also guarantee that you will scramble for crew at some point. You don't make many films. The lack of financial support could be a deal-breaker. It is not extremely challenging.

*Some of the best things about the program:* You will graduate in just eighteen months. This is the only program we cover in which you can direct a film, get your MFA, and join the workforce in less than two years. The small class size and nurturing environment really make this one of the most relaxed programs out there. The equipment is accessible and up-to-date.

AiMIU is still in its infancy. We think it is safe to say that this program will continue to grow and evolve. While the overall goal of a broadly focused program that leads to a thesis might remain the same, the courses and structure and even boundaries between the undergraduate and graduate programs will no doubt be tweaked after a few years of trial and error.

## MONTANA STATE UNIVERSITY

Department of Media & Theatre Arts

P.O. Box 173350

Visual Communications

Building #227

Bozeman, MT 59717-3350

406-994-5884

http://mta.montana.edu

| | |
|---|---|
| Tuition: | Resident: $4,900 |
| | Nonresident: $9,800 |
| Enrollment: | 15 |
| Deadline: | March 1 |
| Focus: | Documentary/Scientific |

## ▶ THE PROGRAM

In the heart of the northern Rocky Mountains sits idyllic Bozeman, Montana, home to serious skiing, Hollywood transplants, and the world's only MFA in Science and Natural History Filmmaking.

Founded in 2000, this young program is unique and well-financed. Fifteen students are annually accepted into its three years of study and are expected to complete the course and defend a thesis film within four years total. Applicants ideally have degrees in the physical sciences, but students are admitted with degrees or at the very least minors in social science, engineering, or technology. The mission is to teach scientists to tell their own stories through film.

Students are not required to have prior film training. Year one addresses this with a balance of production and survey courses, specific to scientific filmmaking. The first semester delivers courses in Documentary Studies, Survey of Science and Natural Filmmaking, Production Technique I, and Sound. Spring moves onto Production Technique II, non-fiction writing, production management, and Critical

Approaches in Science and Natural History Filmmaking. Five short documentaries will be made during the first year.

During the second year students make only one film: "a film with significant usage." This translates into a professional film used in the real world in a meaningful way. This can mean anything from films broadcast on the Discovery Channel or National Geographic or *60 Minutes* to creating projects for nonprofit groups, like the World Wildlife Fund. Other films might be made for federal agencies such as NASA. Films range in length from 15 to 30 minutes. Organizations and agencies contact the school about specific projects, and the school matches students with the projects.

The big news is that the organizations pay the film costs. In truth, almost every student brings additional science grants to the table, but no money for these projects comes directly out of students' pockets. Budgets have ranged from $2,500 to $110,000 with the average around $15,000 to $25,000. The few classes offered during the second year are geared specifically to producing this film.

During third year, all attention turns to thesis projects. The idea is to apply the professional skills learned during second year to a project for which students now have total creative control. Second-year films are about pleasing a client. Third-year films are about making a film that is important to you. Students are encouraged to experiment and work outside the system. This time they are not permitted to accept financing from any outside source that might influence them or their film. Understandably, budgets are a fraction of the second-year films. However, students do earn money to help defray third-year costs, as most are hired as crew on the second-year films.

Although summer courses are optional and cost extra, they tend to be advanced-level technical workshops that students appreciate. The faculty does not teach these courses. Industry professionals are instead brought in to teach in their areas of expertise. The High Definition

Qualification workshop is only offered in the summer, as is the underwater cinematography workshop to certify students as licensed underwater technicians.

## ▶ THE PRICE

| | |
|---|---:|
| $9,800 nonresident tuition for one year | $9,800 |
| $4,900 resident tuition for two years | $9,800 |
| $7,200 per year rent and living expenses for three years | $21,600 |
| $1,000 per year maintenance and insurance on a car in Bozeman for three years | $3,000 |
| Average thesis film costs | $2,000 |
| **Total** | **$46,200** |

Financial support is limited. About $60,000 in scholarships is available only for the first-year class and is given in amounts as low as $1,000. Teaching assistantships exist, but do not provide tuition waivers. Students are allowed to accept assistantships for stipends, and usually half of the incoming first-year class does so in other departments. All third-year students get paid for working on the second-year films, and some are hired for one of a handful of teaching assistantships available within the department in the equipment checkout or as monitors for the graduate edit bay. To date virtually every student has successfully obtained funding for his or her second-year work. Many students tend to fare well in national scholarship competitions. Montana students have won the Goddard Space Fellowship of $40,000 four years running. Several other scholarships from the federal sector also seem to favor Montana students.

For those who hike, climb, or ski, Bozeman is Mecca. Yellowstone is only one hundred miles away, and in just five minutes the wilderness of the nearby Gallatin National Forest is free to explore. The winters are rough, the summers utopian—again only for those who crave fresh air, clean water, and CGI-like sunsets. Students keep busy bonding with nature inside and outside of the program. And those who enjoy occasional run-ins with Hollywood celebrities will also find a fair share of those, as many directors, producers, and actors have second homes in the area.

The town of Bozeman has a population of around 30,000 with about 70,000 living in the extended county. This is not necessarily small-town life in the traditional sense, but it can be quaint. A favorite faculty pastime is reading the local crime reports. A typical day might include the threat of "A dog reported running inside a business on Main Street" or every citizen's deepest fear, "Kids reported to be throwing rocks at people from behind a business on Main Street: One was warned."

Bozeman has a more active art scene than you might expect, with numerous art galleries and restaurants. The cost of living is very low, but the quality of life is high in Bozeman.

Students interested in the very inexpensive graduate housing ($250 a month) have to apply early as the spaces fill up quickly. However, it would get lonely on campus, as grad film students mostly share off-campus houses for about fifty dollars more per month. Students with families have been known to actually buy inexpensive homes for the duration of their stay. If you live in town, prices are higher, and a car is not necessary. Live outside of town, and you save on rent, but the car is a necessity.

On the festival front, there's the Element, the university's annual scientific film festival (previously the Rocky Mountain Science and Natural History Festival). Students also submit to the Jackson Hole Wildlife Film Festival and Hatch Fest, the newest local festival, now in its fourth year.

▶ **THE LOWDOWN**

Applicants will submit a résumé, essay, and letters of recommendation. Additional materials are optional, and you can submit anything you deem relevant to making your case. Photos or videos reflective of your talent can only help. The bottom line is that Bozeman is extremely selective. Remember, you're dealing with scientists here. The admissions board cares about your analytical side and expects letters of recommendation to be from people who really know you well and can specifically comment on these skills as well as your creativity. If you plan to submit the same generic letters to Montana and USC, you are on the wrong path. Do not underestimate the importance of the essay. Reviewers are not interested in how you and your dad bonded over *NOVA* or even how *March of the Penguins* rocked your world. Knowledge, intelligence, and the ability to communicate are just as important, maybe even more so, than your passion for film. Your verbal GRE scores must be over 500. If your score is below 500, you had better have an explanation for it. And if that's not enough, you can be certain that the scientists on the review committee will also evaluate the quality of your education based upon your undergrad school, the courses you took, and how well you performed.

The greatest competition you will encounter is getting into the program. Eighty applications are received for the fifteen slots. If you do make the cut, you'll find that everyone is highly educated and ambitious and that camaraderie replaces the competitiveness that permeates some schools. There doesn't appear to be a typical age for students in this program. You will find a few straight out of undergraduate universities; many already have advanced degrees in a variety of areas including medicine and law. This means the youngest are in their early twenties, while the oldest can be well into their fifties.

The Discovery Channel originally endowed the program. The two parted ways when the cable network caught on to the fact that Montana wasn't necessarily trying to emulate their model. Faculty are more interested in exploring the way information is translated and want to focus on science education through film in different platforms like museums, classrooms, and the Internet. The Media and Theatre Arts department, where the MFA is located, recently launched *TERRA: The Nature of Our World* podcast. Ninety percent of the content is Montana student films. *TERRA* is podcast through Montana PBS, which is part of the department. *TERRA KIDS*, a weekly show, is in the works for the near future.

A lot of ground is covered training students to play multiple roles, with directing and producing at the forefront. First years are not permitted to attend part-time, and it is fairly impossible to work during this busy period. One student tried to manage just fifteen weekly work hours and had to quit her part-time job. In fact, it is tough to work part-time in the final years unless you drop to part-time classes. Dropping to part-time, you will not be able to get through in three years. Second and third years are very self-driven, and attending part-time creates additional production issues. The program is so young that it is still developing and experiencing growing pains. The continuous tweaking and revising can be a source of frustration, and it will probably continue for a few more years.

The faculty of fifteen full-time instructors is very committed and is comprised mostly of producers and directors. You'll find a mix of Hollywood veterans, TV writers, and some academics. If an instructor isn't up to snuff, students make it known, and she doesn't last very long. Classes are a mixture of theory and workshops. Instructors don't skimp on the academic side. There is a good deal of reading and writing, including a written thesis as well as a thesis film.

There is an extensive inventory of equipment, and access is never a problem. The graduate program of fifty students has as much equipment as the entire undergrad program of five hundred. There are two cameras for every student. Students work only in video, but because second years work in the professional arena, cameras are broadcast quality. There are two Sony HDW-700A high-definition packages and an assortment of fifteen high-end video cameras including Sony DSR-570s, Sony DSR-250s, and Sony PD170s. There is one 16 mm Aaton, but it goes unused for the most part. There are also several Amphibico underwater housing packages. A special deal with Fujinon provides top-of-the-line lenses for both HD and SD cameras. Only select cameras can be taken out of the country. Graduates have their own editing bay. The three stations are equipped with Final Cut Pro and ProTools. During the busiest times, the stations are scheduled to keep things fair. A laptop is almost a necessity during crunch times.

The department is located in the Visual Communications Building, where undergrads share the two large soundstages, a fifty-five-seat theater, and extensive edit bays. Construction is slated to begin on a 200-seat theater in 2006.

Networking is a priority, and Bozeman is aggressive in terms of establishing contacts through visiting filmmakers. The students essentially own all visitors who come to campus. Faculty are hands-off as students coordinate everything from the airport pickup to one-on-one sessions and even dinners. The agencies that students work with second year are invaluable resources for job opportunities.

*Some of the worst things about the program:* They are still a few years away from working out the kinks, and you will be a part of this process. There isn't much financial support and working outside of the program is tough. That's OK, because Bozeman sure is pretty, but it offers nothing in the way of production outside of the university. As nice a place as it is to live, most students leave the area upon graduation.

*Some of the best things about the program:* The contacts. If you play your cards right, you can meet industry people to help you on your way after graduating. The support from faculty and camaraderie among students makes for a pleasant learning environment. Montana is changing the way scientists are involved in the filmmaking process. Their graduates might be able to alter the face of this entire genre and give more mainstream technicians a run for their money.

# NEW YORK UNIVERSITY

Maurice Kanbar Institute of Film & Television
721 Broadway, 10th Floor
New York, NY 10003-6807
212-998-1780
http://filmtv.tisch.nyu.edu

| | |
|---|---|
| Tuition: | $34,788 |
| Enrollment: | 36 |
| Deadline: | December 1 |
| Focus: | Independent |

## ▶ THE PROGRAM

New York University is a big school in Greenwich Village, the crowded heart of America's most famous city. The Graduate Division of the Maurice Kanbar Institute of Film and Television feels small by comparison. Only thirty-six students are invited to enter its doors each year. This is an expensive and demanding program. Students take three full years of classes, then spend a fourth—and often a fifth—year making their thesis films. The school works to provide students with a realistic vision of the field they have chosen and turn out employable graduates who can pay back those student loans (of which there will be plenty) in film-related positions after school.

Every student follows the same curriculum for the first year, taking the Actor's Craft, Aesthetics of Silent Film, directing, editing, motion picture camera techniques, production management, and location sound. Most of the courses are production-oriented, except for the Directors Series, which takes place three nights a week. This series screens features followed by hosted discussions with guest filmmakers. Guests are both alumni and nonalums and have included some heavy-hitting cinematographers, directors, writers, and producers.

The same eight courses are taken over two semesters, but the semesters are broken into blocks. Students have six weeks of classes during the first semester. During this time short scripts are written in the silent film course. Then every student produces a four-minute black-and-white silent 16 mm film during a designated production week. Some film and processing is provided, but everyone adds to this allotment. The last four weeks of the semester are spent editing this film and studying documentary film. The films are reviewed in December, at the end of the semester.

Over the winter break and in the beginning of the spring term, students have another production period. This time they shoot a documentary on digital video. An $800 budget is provided. In the third week of the spring semester, while they are editing their documentary, they begin to write a five-minute adaptation project where the focus is working with actors. Once again there are six weeks of classes, a four-week production period for these projects, and two weeks of editing. This system allows every student to direct three films within the first year. During the summer students write a ten-minute narrative film. This film is viewed as sort of a "prethesis." Students arrive back to campus one week early to take part in a five-day writing boot camp in order to polish the summer scripts and have them ready to go the first week of school.

In fall of the second year, the classes are advanced versions of those from the first year. This round, there are seven weeks of classes, but the focus is on preproduction and workshopping the script. A three-month production period begins in the last week of October and ends last week of January. During this time, every student is given one week to direct her ten-minute film and then work as crew on the films of her classmates. Four teams shoot each week until all of the films are completed.

When they return in February, there are some classes that students might still be involved in, like Editing and

Directing, and most take at least one or two electives, like Advanced Cinematography or Marketing and Distribution for Short Films, but for the most part everyone is busy with postproduction until the end of the term. Second-year films are evaluated in March and followed by another six weeks of classes, where the focus shifts into sound design and advanced post, with instruction in After Effects and ProTools.

The directing and writing classes of third year are geared toward the thesis project. Thesis scripts are evaluated in November, and there is a formal table reading with actors. The remaining courses are all electives that should move students in the direction of their areas of interest in directing, producing, cinematography, writing, or editing. Courses might include directing the actor, producing the low-budget feature, advanced cinematography, comedy writing, or learning Avid Media Composer. There's even a third-year course on directing commercials. Select students also might get one-on-one advising from Spike Lee. After Hurricane Katrina, students were invited to work with him on his documentary about New Orleans.

As of fall 2006, the program is introducing a documentary track for third year. This is designed for students who want to do a documentary for their thesis. The plans are to make a short documentary in the fall and then begin a longer documentary, possibly a feature, in the spring. This will dovetail into the documentary class taught by Sheila Nevins, the president of Documentary and Family Programming for HBO.

Finally, the inevitable fourth year is more of a "post–third year." It used to be that after third year, students were on their own. Now a real attempt is being made to continue support beyond the classroom: to monitor students' progress and keep them connected to the school while they complete their thesis films. Faculty are assigned to work with students past their third year on completing their theses and writing feature-length screenplays.

There has been a real push of late for greater interdisciplinary synergy. In spring of their third year, students have the opportunity to collaborate with Tisch students outside of the Graduate Film Program in specialized classes that provide $1,000 in funding to create a short film. For instance, a director might be paired up with a dramatic writing student. Other partners have included graduate acting and design for stage students. Every third-year student gets to participate in one of these collaborations. Even cinematographers and editors might work on these projects as part of their other classes. A recent film produced in this class was accepted at Cannes.

The program has also teamed up with NYU's Stern Business School in creating Promotion Pictures. This is an extracurricular opportunity that finds clients to do "branded entertainment." The client gives a presentation, and Stern and grad film students put together a proposal. Each project is then given a $40,000 grant to do a five- to seven-minute "movie" to show off the brand for clients like Verizon broadband and Heineken beer.

Another big initiative is finding groups who want to finance student feature films. John Tintori, the department chair, is especially interested in bringing greater focus to feature filmmaking within the program. Already in place is the Richard Vague Production Award that supports two annual awards of $100,000 and $75,000 for alumni of the graduate and the undergraduate Department of Film & Television respectively. This is intended to be the seed money for a first feature film. Applicants must have graduated within five years of the current award year. Thirty to forty students apply for this every year.

There are several weekly opportunities to hobnob with filmmakers. The largest is the previously discussed Directors Series. The Contact Series is an informal one-hour lunch where thirty-five students relate on a more personal level with film and television professionals. Everyone brings their lunch and listens while the guest discusses her role in the industry. Reservations are required for this weekly get-together. John Tintori also hosts The Chair's Workshop, another informal, intimate gathering every Wednesday night. About twenty students show up to have a discussion with actors, directors, and producers invited by Tintori.

The first-ever Graduate Thesis Film Marathon premiered in 2006. This is mainly a celebratory screening for casts and crews. Seventeen students showed their films at the eight-hour session. The more publicized event is the weeklong First Run Film Festival showcasing over 150 films from the undergraduate and graduate divisions. To make time for them all, each day of the festival begins about noon and ends about one in the morning. Few come to see the films shown before six, and few wait to see the films that begin after ten. Few people come on Monday or Tuesday night, but Wednesday and Thursday the crowd grows. Friday is the big night; the one everyone wants her film to screen on.

The best undergraduate and graduate films are selected. More than $50,000 in cash prizes is awarded, in amounts ranging from $2,000 to $10,000. A two and a half hour program of the winning films goes to Los Angeles to be screened as the Haig Manoogian Screenings at the Directors Guild of America.

▶ **THE PRICE**

| | |
|---|---|
| $34,780 tuition for three years | $104,340 |
| $1,200 matriculation for at least two semesters | $2,400 |
| $20,000 per year rent and living expenses for four years | $80,000 |
| Average film costs | $30,000 |
| **Total** | **$216,740** |

Only Columbia University charges more tuition than NYU. However, roughly $230,000 in scholarship money is divided in varying amounts among the thirty-six incoming first-year students. Three of these students also receive the Dean's Fellowship, which provides full tuition remission. Second-year students are usually partially supported through outside grants that total around $100,000. Everyone gets a little something, but for most this is not nearly enough relative to the cost. In the past, many third-year students simply ran out of money. At this point the school has succeeded in providing full tuition for half of the third-year class. There are six graduate assistantships available in the third year. These provide full tuition remission and a $14,000 stipend. The GAs are hired to assist with tech classes; three for camera, two for editing, and one for sound. The remaining financial support comes through departmental awards. Although the matriculation fee is reasonable and does postpone repayment of student loans, the reason most students don't graduate within fours years is financial. After handing over a hundred thousand dollars in tuition, after paying to make a number of films in first and second years, and after shelling out to live in overpriced apartments in New York for three years, few students have $20,000 left with which to make a thesis film.

Such is the price to live in the cultural capital of the world. New York pulsates with an energy not found anywhere else. The museum, performance, and music scenes are unrivaled, and for filmmakers there is something to be said for seeing the world on foot. Different perspectives that often elude those in cars await the streetwise New Yorker. Manhattan is home to a large population of artists and independent filmmakers. It is a tight-knit, supportive environment that respects individualism, and the food ain't bad either. Every ethnic community imaginable has a neighborhood filled with local eateries. These perks almost outweigh the absurd rents. Almost.

As at Columbia, students contend with exorbitant New York rents. Those coming in from out of state will be tempted to apply for university housing. Don't. Rents are outrageous (over $1,000 per month) to share a one-room apartment with a total stranger. International students often fall victim to university housing. The Off-Campus Housing Office has an extensive database of apartments and shares. Check it frequently, as it is updated on a regular basis, and the good listings don't last. Craigslist is also useful. Luckily, a car is not necessary and would pose more of a problem than anything else.

► **THE LOWDOWN**

Upwards of eight hundred applicants vie for those thirty-six openings each year. NYU does not look for people straight out of undergrad. They prefer students who have some life experience. The application can be daunting. You will have to submit a script for a completely silent four-minute film (no music or voice-over), a two-person, two-page dialogue scene, a one-page treatment for a feature-length script, and some kind of visual work. You need to demonstrate an ability to perform in an academic environment, have stories to tell, and show a strong visual sense. It is best to submit a portfolio that exhibits originality. With so much competition, your application will have to really stand out to get noticed.

Once you're in, you had better keep getting noticed to have even a long shot at the coveted GA slots. And that's not the only area where you will run into stiff competition. With so many high achievers working so closely under such stress, it can't help but breed competition. Everyone wants to be the best. Everyone wants to get screened in Los Angeles. With so few getting the opportunity, resentment is natural. It doesn't help that the faculty select the First Run Festival Wasserman Award winners, the ones who get the cash and the trip to Los Angeles. Without a professor fighting for you, you don't stand a chance.

If you are involved in a relationship, you can pretty much kiss it good-bye, as you will have little or no life outside of NYU during the first two years. Although necessity forces some to try to work, it is not recommended, will certainly complicate production, and will add to your level of stress. This is not good news in a town where simply putting a roof over your head comes as a challenge.

The interdisciplinary production courses expand opportunities and provide some very useful experience that students are happy about. The aesthetics courses are a highlight for many. Some students pointed out that although the school is very concerned with storytelling, they are less effective in instructing in the craft of writing.

The faculty is accomplished and appreciated, but sometimes the best professionals are not necessarily the best teachers and vice versa. In-class critiques can be harsh, so you will need a tough shell. There are mentoring possibilities, but it doesn't work out for everyone. There is not a heck of a lot of diversity on the faculty. Currently the Directing Masters class instructors are all middle-aged white guys. The school is aware of this, and as the old-timers retire, more current, active, and hopefully diverse instructors will join the ranks. The conscious effort to bring in outside guests on a weekly basis gives students great exposure to various industry perspectives.

Although students complain, the equipment is very good and well-maintained. Students are taught to handle and use the equipment carefully, so it remains in pretty good condition. Eleven full-time staff members and over fifty work-studies keep things running smoothly, including on-site film and video repair. Because production dates are reserved in advance, each class is assigned the correct number of complete packages tailored for that particular level of production. Faculty and students decide shooting dates within the preassigned schedule. Because the equipment is in such good shape and each identical package is available when needed, there is no panic about getting a troublesome rig or no camera at all when needed. While the schedule evens the playing field during production, it makes it hard to get cameras outside of one's scheduled time for tests or experimentation. But then again, the schedule is such that who has the time?

There are two dozen grad-only Arriflex SRs, one Arriflex 35 mm, and dozens of digital cameras, including Panasonic DVX100s and Sony PD150s. Cameras for the first-year silent projects are of the Arriflex S variety. First-year documentaries shoot on digital, with the ten-minute prethesis films working with Arriflex 16SRs. Some of these cameras are being converted to Super 16 for fall 2006. Theses are split about evenly between digital and 16 mm formats with some students choosing to shoot on the 35 mm camera reserved for thesis projects. The film camera lenses vary from good to great. Second- and third-year shoots are provided with just enough lighting and grip equipment to light a medium-sized room. Second-year and thesis students often rent lenses, filters, and lights. The sound recording equipment is good. Shortly, Panasonic HVX200 high-def cameras will be introduced along with the post to support the format.

The tenth floor of 712 Broadway is the grad film hub. The post situation is reevaluated annually to keep current. There is an editing lab with twelve Final Cut Pro stations for first years. Second-year students work in two eight-station Avid DV Pro labs. Third years move on to Avid Media Composer and Symphony in six private rooms. A new eight-station producing lab loaded with Movie Magic scheduling and budgeting software was added fall 2006. On the eleventh floor are the ADR Foley and mixing stage. There are also a large soundstage, recording studios, and two large state-of-the-art theaters.

The financial burden of paying for film is enormous, but each student owns her own films when she is finished and is free to do with them as she pleases. Most enter their films in festivals and competitions, and some even get distribution deals. While the financial return is never enough to recoup the original expense, it is always nice to see some money for all that effort, and the exposure that festival and distribution provide can help to make contacts and even lead to being befriended by agents and producers.

Keeping one's head on straight is the first way to make the most of NYU. Some students are really full of themselves the first year. They seem to think, *If I got into NYU, then I must be really hot!* People tend to calm down pretty fast, especially once production kicks in. Then students are too stressed to worry about how "hot" they are. And since everyone works for everyone else, everyone has a stake in everyone else's success.

**Some of the worst things about the program:** The bill. You will sink an obscene amount of money into your education. Just how obscene doesn't really click until after you graduate, and those loan payments come due.

**Some of the best things about the program:** NYU embodies the spirit of independent filmmaking. As for technology and facilities, NYU can hang with the best of them. There is tons of hands-on experience and the equipment is really good. Most students now leave with a feature screenplay. Living in New York can be a life-altering experience. There are real efforts being made to graduate employable students with marketable skills. And although it helps to have a great film, a degree from NYU is very prestigious. Many people will agree to meet a graduate based solely upon that association. The festival and DGA screenings can both be real stepping-stones for the chosen few.

# OHIO UNIVERSITY

School of Film
Lindley Hall 378
Athens, OH 45701-2979
740-593-1323
www.finearts.ohio.edu/film

| | |
|---|---|
| Tuition: | Resident: $8,586 |
| | Nonresident: $16,578 |
| Enrollment: | 12 |
| Deadline: | January 15 |
| Focus: | Independent |

## ▶ THE PROGRAM

Founded in 1804, Ohio University is a picturesque school around which a town grew up. Most students live within walking distance of its quaint brick buildings and streets. The three-year MFA film program was established in 1973. In addition to a directing track, the school offers tracks in screenwriting, cinematography, and postproduction

The first year is very structured. It involves the most intensive course work of the program and is required of all students. Students can expect to be busy all the time. Over three quarters twelve different foundation courses are taken in sequential progression each term. In Filmmaking I students make a 16 mm silent film. In Filmmaking II another 16 mm project is completed, and sound is introduced. In Filmmaking III a short digital documentary is produced. A short narrative screenplay is written in Screenwriting I. In Screenwriting II students create another narrative script that will be filmed during their second year. There are two film studies courses, a sound course, and Digital Editing I & II.

Finally, there's first-year practicum; the course that helps students prepare for their end-of-year review. Practicum students meet as a group and individually with two faculty members, each mentoring six students. At the end of the first year each student must create and present a first-year portfolio of creative work. This portfolio includes all the projects produced during the first year: two 16 mm narrative films, one digital video documentary, and directing and editing exercises. Students rarely fail the reviews, because if there are problems, advisors work with the student to solve them.

The second year is much simpler in terms of requirements. Students choose specialization classes offered in the various crafts. In second year Production I, II, and III, students work on creating second-year projects for the portfolio review. Students take another editing course, crew for classmates (eight credits), select two electives (called *cognates* here) and choose a film history and theory course. At the end of the second year students can commit to the nondirecting tracks. Everyone submits a second-year portfolio that should include two creative projects, one of which must be a film or video.

The final year can be spent directing a thesis or fulfilling requirements for the nondirecting thesis tracks. Each of these tracks requires specific classes and separate thesis requirements. Cinematographers must shoot four films, including a thesis, and write a research paper. Screenwriters complete a feature-length screenplay and choose two of the following: one adaptation, one teleplay, one produced thesis film, and two produced second-year films. Students who take the post-production track must complete all post on two thesis projects and mix five second-year films.

—

## ► THE PRICE

| | |
|---|---|
| $16,578 nonresident tuition for one year | $16,578 |
| $8,586 resident tuition for two years | $17,172 |
| $7,200 per year rent and living expenses for three years | $21,600 |
| $1,200 per year maintenance and insurance on a car in Athens for three years | $ 3,600 |
| Average film costs | $15,000 |
| **Total** | **$73,950** |

Actually, you can subtract $33,000 from this amount; the school provides funding, through grants and assistantships, which pays for all tuition, plus a small stipend, for all MFA students. The also provides free film for first-year projects.

The school offers students only a handful or small cash awards, but what with the free tuition and everything else, students don't mind.

Several hundred dollars are available to help with festival submissions. Director Betty Thomas has endowed a $2,500 production grant that students can apply for at the end of their second year. Sometimes this is divided among a few students. There is a $500 grant provided by another donor, and there are also small university-wide grants for which film students can apply. Students still manage to run short on funds and have been known to take a quarter off and work full-time for a quarter in order to finance their thesis film.

In the fall, honors films are screened in weekend screenings for the students. In the winter, the previous year's completed second-year films are screened. But these are internal to the film program. The school does not hold a public festival of students films as most schools do. Students will sometimes put together their own screenings, but without the school's backing and promotion, interest is tepid and audiences are small. Athens is host to an established annual festival of short films, the Athens Internal Film and Video Festival. Students like to screen there, but they have to compete for entry with short films from all over the world.

The acting pool is generally limited to the theater department, and students find it frustrating to juggle both departments' class schedules and coordinate film shoots. Local community theaters are the only other talent source. It is especially difficult to cast for the young and elderly.

▶ **THE LOWDOWN**

The program receives between 100 and 150 applications for twelve spaces each year. Two or three of those twelve openings might be filled by undergrads that come directly through the university's Honors Tutorial College. With so few spots, the competition is stiff. A DV portfolio is required from all applicants. Almost everyone who applies has at least one film under her belt. Those interested in screenwriting can send in a script. Most send two to three samples of creative work and have been out of school for three to four years. An art background carries a lot of weight. The school looks not so much for a polished project or technical skills but rather the creative spark.

The six schools that make up the college of communications boast a large international student population. Luckily, international students seem to adapt easily to the rural existence of Athens. Americans have a harder time adjusting. That said, Athens is a good place to reside and focus on work. The community is slow-paced, and there isn't the pressure prevalent at some of the larger institutions. There are very few distractions—unless you count the endless bars in the center of town. Frequenting these is a regular pasttime for the undergrad imbibers. There's a decent live music scene and numerous, but few good, restaurants. There are three movie theaters and lots of video stores, but it is not an artistic community in any sense of the word.

It's very inexpensive to live in Athens. There are lots of apartments to choose from. Almost all students share apartments and pay as little as $300 a month. The environment is apparently ripe for romance as a good number of third-year students wind up sharing housing as couples instead of roommates. Living in town won't necessitate a car, but there's no way to get out of town without one. Cincinnati is three hours away; Columbus (and the nearest airport) is a ninety-minute drive. A car comes in handy on film shoots.

The program lacks Hollywood or industry representation. Instructors are disconnected from what's going on in the current film scene. Students expressed disappointment in the directing and producing instructor. On the other hand, the post staff scores high marks, and students are very pleased with the production courses. Although the program is supposedly open to all filmmaking, narrative is not as well-supported as documentary work. There is a strong experimental filmmaker on staff, but fewer students pursue this genre.

The equipment is shared with undergraduates with certain cameras and accessories reserved just for grads. It is well maintained, and access is never a problem. On the film end there is one Arriflex SR2, six Arriflex SRs, ten Bolexes, and a dozen or so mini DV cameras. After first year, most students shoot on video. The Peterson Sound Studio offers a soundproof room, Foley capabilities, mixers, and a Pro-Tools station. For postproduction, a lone Steenbeck suffices for the first film project, and two digital editing labs take care of the rest. There are fourteen Avid Express bays and a Media Composer.

Surviving the first year intact is every student's goal. It can be tough, and some wind up quitting early due to the pressure. The school is small enough that everyone can really get to know one another. In your classmates you will find a real sense of solidarity and creativity that might be missing from classes. The Athens Film Festival welcomes volunteers, and students who participate speak highly of the experience. Push your professors to give you more. The good teachers can be very good and can really help you. This is especially true of the production and post staff.

*Some of the worst things about the program:* The remote location limits your exposure to culture. If you are not small-town material, you may go out of your mind. If you don't connect with the faculty, you might miss out. If you have Hollywood aspirations, you are on your own.

*Some of the best things about the program:* Self-motivated individuals can shape the program to suit their needs. The Athens Festival is well-established and respected and offers a chance to mingle with lots of independent filmmakers. If you want to work locally or teach, the faculty is very helpful. You can't argue with the price.

# SAVANNAH COLLEGE OF ART AND DESIGN

Admission Department

22 East Lathrop Avenue

Savannah, GA 31415-2105

404-253-2700

www.scad.edu/academic/majors/film

| | |
|---|---|
| Tuition: | $23,400 |
| Enrollment: | 100 total |
| Deadlines: | February 15, May 1, June 1, July 1 |
| Focus: | Independent |

## ► THE PROGRAM

The Savannah College of Art and Design has only been around since 1978. The Film and Television program started out as an MFA in video in 1985 and has gone through a number of revisions over the years. This latest incarnation has been in place since 2004.

Technically it is a two-year program, but finishing in that time frame is only possible for the most experienced of students who manage to work at the fastest pace. Based upon portfolio reviews, the faculty determines necessary prerequisite courses that must be completed prior to beginning the MFA. These courses are introductory undergraduate-level courses in production and postproduction and consist of subjects like introduction to film and video, preproduction, scheduling and budgeting, and Avid postproduction. Students who must take these courses can graduate in a little over two years. Three years is more common, and four years is not unheard of.

The school operates on a rolling admission system; students can apply to enter in any quarter of the year. Most apply for fall, taking necessary prerequisites in the summer before they begin. There is no cap on the number of students admitted each term. Instead, the school aims for a total program size of one hundred and admits students accordingly. Usually thirty-five students are accepted over the course of a year. About 10 percent of those are international students. Just about everybody is in their midtwenties, and rarely is anyone over age thirty.

Once the provisional courses have been completed, students must take ninety hours of graduate-level study, twenty of which are electives taken within or outside of the department. Each course is five credits, for a total of eighteen classes taken from start to finish. This amounts to three to four classes each quarter during the traditional school year and two classes if you attend the summer session. The summer session is notoriously light on courses, so some students choose to take the term off. The program has a narrative film focus, but a small percentage of students work in documentary. Art installations are acceptable as theses.

It is up to students to schedule all of their classes. There is no established sequence in which to fulfill the requirements of contemporary art, art criticism, producing for film and television, sound design, directing for film and television, writing for the screen, cinematography, postproduction, field production, and thesis courses or any elective credits. And since some grad courses are only available every other quarter, students hoping to graduate on any sort of specific time frame need to keep tabs on when required courses are offered. Undergraduate courses are acceptable as electives, but students are encouraged to stick to graduate-level courses. Graduate classes are taught at a faster pace and with more intellectually challenging standards than similar undergrad offerings. Some graduate elective classes also instruct in the operation of advanced equipment like the Steadicam and Panther dolly.

Graduate students can pursue a specific discipline and choose elective courses that support it. For instance, all students take writing for the screen. Those who choose to focus on writing can take classes in writing the short film, writing for television or drama or comedy, as well as special topics and seminar classes with a writing focus. There is enough wiggle room through elective credits to explore and really figure out what you want to do. It is not unusual for someone to arrive intending to be a director and then by year two decide to switch to cinematography or editing or any other area.

At some point students must complete an internship in teaching or production. Teaching is performed within the college, but not in the graduate film program. Production-wise, Savannah has had a slight escalation in locally shot feature films with one coming to town every few years or so. The school has an internship coordinator to assist students in locating production opportunities.

After arriving at the halfway mark of forty-five credits, there is a faculty review. Prior to this review students must fulfill three support positions, other than production assistant, on thesis films. Most choose to work on four or five films. This work is in addition to crewing on the short group projects produced in classes typically taken during the first year. For the review, students gather their best work along with an artistic statement that explains what they have accomplished thus far, what they still aspire to, and a detailed thesis proposal. A committee of three faculty members evaluates this portfolio. A student may fail this review if the artistic statement and thesis proposal aren't in sync. Recently a student was asked to make a new film and rewrite her artistic statement to bring her closer to what her reviewers felt was a more achievable thesis. The committee feels obligated to do everything they can to position students for successful final projects and will not green-light anything they deem below par.

Once the thesis is approved, students take the thesis pre-production course, in which they must pitch their project before all faculty and classmates and assemble a crew. The pitches often define the best- and worst-prepared students, and crews divide along these lines. Crewing is crucial, as every thesis candidate must fulfill primary and secondary work on a thesis. Primary positions are that of writer, producer, director, cinematographer, and editor. Secondary positions are any of the below-the-line positions such as sound recordist, gaffer, or grip. This means each student will graduate with key credits on at least two thesis films. It also means that students fully grasp the collaborative nature of film.

Students are required to screen film work publicly at the end of every quarter, and there is a faculty-juried show at the end of the year. Plans are in place to also screen the juried winners at the College of Art and Design Atlanta campus in the future. The relatively new Savannah Film Festival occurs every fall. The program cancels classes during festival week so that students can attend all of the festival screenings and discussions.

## ▶ THE PRICE

| | |
|---|---|
| $23,400 tuition for three years | $70,200 |
| $9,600 per year rent and living expenses for three years | $28,800 |
| Average film costs | $20,000 |
| **Total** | **$119,000** |

There is little in the way of financial support outside of government loans and grants. A few teaching assistantships are awarded to the academically best of the incoming graduate class across the college. A select number of partial scholarships and fellowships that pay one-quarter to one-half of tuition are awarded based upon high GRE scores or outstanding creative portfolios. Students apply for the talent-based awards on their own, and they can receive both academic and talent scholarships. There are no Film and

Television teaching assistantships, as the program insists faculty teach all of its courses. Students cover all film costs, except for those of the Field Production course, for which some stock is provided.

Savannah is a charming city, and the college is located in its historic district. Gorgeous buildings from the 1800s have been restored and remodeled by the college's architecture department. Some students live near the school where the apartments are pricey compared to the city at large. A one-bedroom can cost around $1,000. Other students share one of the many large Southern homes. These can be had for as little as $300 to $500 per person when shared with several classmates. The beach is nearby, and you can count on nice weather for nine months of the year. This is, however, the Deep South, and beyond the campus community there are significantly less affluent neighborhoods and some that are downright poverty-stricken. You must be careful, because this can vary street by street. A wrong turn around a corner can have dire consequences. It is imperative that you explore the city, preferably with a local, prior to settling in and definitely before committing to an apartment. Otherwise you might set yourself up to be a crime statistic.

The town shuts down early, and those accustomed to an active social life might experience a bit of culture shock. Outside of the university there is little in the way of a film industry, and theaters and video stores are scarce. It can take a long time for smaller, independent films to screen in the area—if ever. A car is not strictly necessary—most students get by with bikes—but it is helpful, especially when you need to visit the solo downtown grocery store. The college operates buses that go just about everywhere. Residents still exhibit the famous Southern hospitality, but as the program has grown and the number of students has increased, they are starting to get a little burnt out on student productions. The city is usually helpful with film permits. Casting locally is problematic. Few trained actors exist outside of the school's small performing arts program. Be prepared to travel to another city to find your talent.

About half of the students are funded by their families and don't need to work. This is just as well, as it is really hard to find the time. Those who must work take part-time jobs. Many work at local television stations. Some work in nearby stores and restaurants.

▶ **THE LOWDOWN**

GPAs count on the Savannah application. And although the GRE is optional, applicants should remember that there are scholarships available for applicants with higher scores. Those with art backgrounds tend to win the few college-wide fellowships. Students will need the usual letters of recommendation and a statement of intent, along with a portfolio and résumé, in order to apply. The statement is extremely important. Applicants should use it to illustrate their artistic identity. Screenwriters should submit a script. Cinematographers should submit a reel that showcases digital video, 16 mm, and 35 mm film if possible.

As the program has increased in size, so has its competitive side. The independent spirit on which it was built is becoming increasingly more Hollywood. Although the school boasts about its diversity, there are few international students relative to other film schools.

Savannah is focused on production. Students have told us the program is lacking in courses on film theory and criticism.

The ten-week quarters can be brutal. Try writing a feature and simultaneously producing two short films in ten weeks. Savannah students do just that. The faculty has a great deal to accomplish, and students need to keep pace. The workload is huge, and you can overload if you are not smart. You can breathe a bit easier during second year, and slow down if you feel the need, but even while shooting your thesis you will still be taking classes. Students sometimes take years to complete their thesis films, and there are always a few students who simply don't finish the program. Sometimes they land jobs; other times they just run out of time or money.

The technical courses get high grades from students, especially the postproduction classes. Sound courses are a problem, as the sound department is not part of the program and is located in a separate building. In the past these courses were more academic than production-based, and students found them disappointing. Hopes now rest with a newly arrived instructor with more industry experience.

The faculty is a strong contingent of experienced TV writer/producers. Instructors are big on mentoring, and students find them to be very helpful and knowledgeable. However, none of them are tenured, so turnover can be high. The upside of that is a constant flux of fresh faces and talents and the enthusiastic energy and optimism that only comes with being new on the job.

All equipment is shared with the undergrad program, but there is a lot of it, and grads get preference. Despite being well cared for, the recent increase in student numbers is starting to take its toll on the equipment. Lately there is frequent downtime for repairs, and the equipment room is cracking down on the culprits. You will be charged if anything is returned damaged. Crews must be trained on specific cameras in order to use them.

Film-wise, there are Bolexes and plenty of Arriflex 16 mm cameras, a few of which are Super 16, some Aaton Minimas, and one 35 mm Panavision camera available for instructional purposes. On the video end are Cine-altas, Varicams, some Sony DVC Pro cameras, and many Panasonic DVX100s. Savannah also has three high-definition cameras. The majority of students are now using the high-definition cameras for their thesis films. The department is also home to a green screen studio and three soundstages.

Students edit films on Avid Express and have two grad-designated ProTools stations, four Adrenalines, and one Symphony. There is a full sound design department in a new building separate from the program. In those labs students can work with ProTools, and do ADR and Foley work. With training, students can also check out a Steadicam and a Panther dolly. There are also opportunities to collaborate on special effects with students in the school of Digital Media.

*Some of the worst things about the program:* Ten week-long quarters pose difficulties for such a production-oriented program. Students constantly work under extreme pressure. The program is growing very fast and courses are becoming crowded, and equipment is wearing down as a result. The prerequisites add to the price tag and length of your stay.

*Some of the best things about the program:* The equipment, faculty support, and mentorship help make a crazy schedule more bearable. The school strives to be state-of-the-art, so equipment is regularly updated.

# SAN FRANCISCO ART INSTITUTE

800 Chestnut Street
San Francisco, CA 94133-2206
415-749-4577
http://sfai.edu

| | |
|---|---|
| Tuition: | $27,400 |
| Enrollment: | 3-4 |
| Deadline: | January 15 |
| Focus: | Experimental |

## ▶ THE PROGRAM

The San Francisco Art Institute was founded in 1871; it began offering courses in film in the 1940s and focused from the start on avant-garde filmmaking. Like many art schools that added film to their curricula, the Art Institute treats film as a medium for personal expression, more as another visual medium like painting or photography than as a form of entertainment. This isn't a place to learn how to shoot a narrative film with a crew of thirty people; it's a place where artists work directly with the medium of film; most shoot footage by themselves, and many process their own film on campus. And as new variations of video technology appear, students work with these technologies in a similar way, testing their limitations and manipulating them toward an expressive end.

The school is very much about individual work—students largely work alone—and there are no specific films to be made—no first-year film or second-year film like you see at other schools. Students are only expected to assemble a body of work over the course of their time here that shows their growth as artists.

The graduate program is centered around two courses, Graduate Critique Seminar and Graduate Tutorial, which students take repeatedly throughout their time at the school. Graduate Critique Seminar consists of one-on-one meetings with faculty members, held three or four times each semester. Graduate Tutorial also meets three or four times, sometimes as a group of students and faculty members, sometimes as individual consultation with professors. Students round out their course work with undergraduate film history and technology courses or with courses in other arts. Each student must also serve as TA for two semesters.

At the end of each semester, the faculty holds resident reviews with each student. The review committee consists of two faculty members from within the film department, one professor from another department, and one visiting faculty member—students may choose to invite an additional faculty member. As at many art schools, this review is a serious business; if the committee feels a student is not progressing as an artist, he may be told to repeat his work and go through the review again at a later date, or, in rare cases, even be tossed out of the school.

The annual Master of Fine Arts Graduate Exhibition of SFAI student works is held at Fort Mason each May and is a popular event in San Francisco's vibrant art scene. Unfortunately, film students' works are not featured there; instead, films are screened separately in a room at the Yerba Buena Center for the Arts in downtown San Francisco, at the same time as the opening reception at Fort Mason, so turnout tends to be kind of low for the films.

▶ **THE PRICE**

| | |
|---|---|
| $27,400 tuition for two years | $54,800 |
| $15,000 per year rent and living for three years | $45,000 |
| Average film costs | $10,000 |
| **Total** | **$109,800** |

San Francisco is a fun, livable, obscenely expensive city. The Art Institute is a cloisterlike structure located on Russian Hill with breathtaking views of San Francisco Bay. Housing in this very desirable part of town is rare and expensive; most students wind up living in the Mission, a relatively inexpensive neighborhood of artists a few miles south of campus. Few students have cars; they're difficult to keep in the city and not really necessary, given the city's excellent public transportation. San Francisco has car-share programs, which are a good, inexpensive alternative to owning a car for people who only need a car to move equipment around once or twice a month.

▶ **THE LOWDOWN**

Experimental film has always been about working directly with the medium, finding its limits, and seeing if those limits can't be pushed a little further. In the sixties and seventies, this meant manipulating the actual film directly: drawing or painting directly onto acetate, hand-processing exposed film to achieve certain effects. And this sort of filmmaking is still done at the Art Institute; students still shoot Super 8 and 16 mm film and hand-process their footage with the school's film processing equipment. But the school is doing a good job of keeping up with new technologies; the school has 24p video cameras and recently added an HDCAM high-definition video camera. But students aren't racing out to make reality TV shows with the new video equipment. They are treating this new technology the same way they treated film; experimenting with it, pushing it to its limits, finding how it reacts to different treatments, and then using the results for personal expression. Many students are finding ways to combine film and video in their projects.

Narrative films are fairly rare here. Students will sometimes make documentaries, but they tend to be what are often termed experimental documentaries: intimate films where a filmmaker explores personal issues and emotions, often in unusual and opaque ways.

One thing the professors like to do is take courses that are typically taught as theory courses, and make studio courses out of them. So, for instance, in a course about personal essay films, students will listen to lectures and watch numerous examples of such films by filmmakers such as Chris Marker, but they will also make their own personal essay films using the techniques and concepts they've learned and screen these films in class.

Like the technology, the faculty are a mixture of the old and new. All are working artists; a number of professors have been working in experimental film since the sixties, while new faculty members specialize in digital media. Legendary experimental filmmaker George Kuchar is on the faculty; his course, AC/DC Psychotronic Teleplays, is not to be missed. We're told that the old-timers are surprisingly open to the new technologies and do not force students to work in outdated film technologies when they don't want to, as happens at some other old-school experimental schools.

Successful alumni are largely in the experimental world, so you probably wouldn't have heard of them. One you may have heard of is cinematographer Lance Acord, who has shot numerous films, including Spike Jonze's *Adaptation* (2002) and Sofia Coppola's *Lost in Translation* (2003).

*Some of the worst things about the program:* There's little overarching structure here, nobody telling you what to do and when to do it. If you are not self-motivated to explore film and video as a medium of personal expression, you will sink quickly. Many students feel the film department is the neglected younger sibling of the school, receiving less attention and support from the school than the fine arts departments.

*Some of the best things about the program:* Everyone should live in San Francisco at some point, and the Art Institute is one of the nicest places to spend time in this city. Students are encouraged to take risks. They are free to work at their own pace and follow their own interests. Access to equipment is by and large unlimited.

# SAN FRANCISCO STATE UNIVERSITY

Cinema Department
1600 Holloway Avenue
San Francisco, CA 94132-1722
415-338-1629
www.cinema.sfsu.edu

| | |
|---|---|
| Tuition: | Resident: $3,710 |
| | Nonresident: $7,778 |
| Enrollment: | 15 |
| Deadline: | May 1 |
| Focus: | Independent/Experimental |

## ▶ THE PROGRAM

San Francisco State has been offering courses in film since the 1960s, an MFA since the early 1990s. Its traditional area of expertise is experimental film, and like many experimental programs, it is having some difficulty making the transition to the new technologies and new realities of film.

The overall arc of the program is straightforward; first year is devoted to the creation and completion of a single five-minute 16 mm film. Second year is devoted to preparing a presentation of a thesis project to a faculty committee. At the end of second year, after students' faculty committees have given their approval on the thesis projects, students spend third year making those projects.

For many students the program begins even before the first day of first year. New students have to show that they have already taken courses in film theory and history prior to starting SFSU; those who are deemed to have insufficient knowledge in this area (as much as a third of each new class) are required to take a class in the school's summer session prior to the start of first year.

In the first semester, the primary course is called Creative Process. Students start out by pitching ideas for five-minute films and spend the semester incrementally fleshing those ideas out into synopses, then into treatments, then into screenplays. Students also take a course in theory and in sound and postproduction. Cinematography is actually more about basic production techniques—about how to work as a team on a set—than about the specifics of cinematography. At the end of the semester each student presents her project to a faculty committee and receives approval to continue; this is kind of a trial run for the procedure leading up to the thesis project. Students shoot these films over the winter break. In the spring semester the course load is lighter, allowing students the time to edit these films. Students take a course in editing, where they screen cuts of their five-minute films as they work on them, and another course in film theory.

These first-year films are shot on 16 mm film, and students are required to complete them—to take them all the way to answer print—before they can continue on to second year. Of course, 16 mm film is expensive and students typically spend between $7,000 and $10,000 on these simple films. Many students continue working on these films through the summer and only complete them in time for the fall semester.

In second year the primary course is called Writing and Directing, yet we are told it is kind of short on both. Much of the course, which meets in six-hour sessions, is spent working with actors from the undergraduate theater department. Students are encouraged to make a film as part of this course; however, the course does not provide access to equipment, so that's not so easily done. Advanced Cinematography continues on in the same vein from first-year Cinematography, with much of the time spent working as crew members shooting exercises. In a theory class, each student is expected to lead one entire class meeting as teacher.

Students spend much of second year preparing to present their thesis projects to their faculty committees. Each student is expected to present a complete package at the end of the year, including a screenplay, an analytical essay about the project, budget, schedule, and any other pertinent paperwork.

Students are encouraged to teach. All students are asked to TA a course for no pay for one semester; after that they can apply for the few available paying TA-ships. Paying TA-ships do not pay much—they only provide remission of some of the school's negligible tuition—so a TA at SFSU doesn't get a free ride for a year the way TAs at some other schools do. But it's a good opportunity for those who want to build teaching experience.

### ▶ THE PRICE

| | |
|---|---:|
| $7,778 per year nonresident tuition for one year (est.) | $7,778 |
| $3,710 per year resident tuition for one year | $3,710 |
| $15,000 per year rent and living expenses for three years | $45,000 |
| First-year films costs | $7,000 |
| Average thesis film costs | $20,000 |
| **Total** | **$83,488** |

Nonresident students pay resident tuition plus an additional $339 per unit; we assumed twelve units here, but that could vary. If you're already a California resident, just subtract about $4,000 from the total.

The good news is the tuition is incredibly low. The bad news is everything else in San Francisco is pretty expensive. The cost of living is high here; one-bedroom apartments in the city are more expensive than most students can afford, so just about everyone winds up sharing two- or three-bedroom apartments with other students. Shares like this cost each person $600 or $700 a month.

There are few ways of getting around these costs. The few grants the school gives out are for $1,000 or less, which doesn't go very far against the cost of 16 mm film. First year is too intensive to allow for employment outside of school, but from second year on, most students work to pay their bills and production costs.

A car is neither necessary nor even a good idea in San Francisco. Few apartments have garages, and street parking is scarce. Most students find it best to befriend people who have cars and borrow those cars when necessary or to just rent vehicles. Public transportation in San Francisco and the Bay Area is very good, so when students are not in production, they get along perfectly well without cars. If you want to be everyone's best friend, though, bring a van.

Most everyone works in 16 mm film in first and third year. These films by necessity cost $8,000 or more to complete; there's not much flexibility when you're working with 16 mm film. Students can shoot on video, though the professors don't encourage it.

There is one film processing laboratory in town: Monaco. Since it has a monopoly, Monaco is fairly expensive, but it is fast and very convenient. Monaco only processes color film, so students who shoot black-and-white have to send their footage off to labs in Los Angeles or Seattle for processing. Some students band together into large groups and negotiate volume discounts with Monaco.

## ▶ THE LOWDOWN

San Francisco State receives about two hundred applications each year, from which no more than fifteen new students are accepted. The faculty are picky about who they accept, and will accept fewer than fifteen when there aren't fifteen that they feel are up to their standards.

With your application you will be asked to send a résumé, a personal statement, an example of academic writing, two letters of recommendation, and a portfolio of creative work. Applicants who send films or videos have an advantage over those who don't, but the school will consider applicants with no experience in film if they show both an ability to write and a strong visual sense. At the same time, this is still a school rooted in experimental film, and someone who sends in a Hollywood-style narrative short film is likely to be rejected as too mainstream. Students who have both film production courses and film theory courses in their transcripts are at a distinct advantage. GREs are not required.

The program is currently a little schizophrenic. It has, for decades, been known as an experimental program, and many of the professors have dedicated their lives to 16 mm experimental film. But few students are interested in working in experimental these days; almost all of the students want to make traditional narrative films, and many want to work in digital video. So students and professors sometimes seem to be working at cross purposes; the professors are intent on making everyone shoot 16 mm and edit on flatbeds, but the students are aware that this is both expensive and a largely useless skill in the outside world. One student tells us he feels that the school has all the elements to be a great program—good facilities and some excellent teachers—but it currently doesn't have a clear direction.

The school is also schizophrenic in that it goes from rigid structure to complete lack of structure. For the first two years, the class of fifteen students is herded through every class and every project together as a group, yet once the thesis films are approved at the end of second year, students are essentially cut loose and expected to arrange the production, postproduction, and final screenings of their thesis films on their own.

California's state university system is perennially under-funded, so the equipment and facilities are hit-or-miss. About ten years ago the film department got a new building, with a 2,500-square-foot soundstage, a 150-seat screening room, editing rooms, animation studios, and audio recording and mixing studios. There are animation stands, computer graphics workstations, and an optical printer. But most of the school's production equipment is rather dated. The school now has an Arriflex SR-I 16 mm camera and a Panasonic DVX100-A 24p video camera for thesis projects. But for other projects, the school provides only older Eclair NPRs or CP-16s. The school reportedly owns the camera Maya Deren shot her experimental films with in the early forties—and it's still being used to shoot student films. The school maintains flatbed editing machines for students to cut 16 mm film on, but most students cut on Final Cut Pro.

To supplement the school's facilities, most students join the Film Arts Foundation. FAF, located a few miles away from SFSU in the South of Market area, rents production and postproduction equipment to members at very low rates. Though intended as a resource for all independent filmmakers in the Bay Area, Film Arts at times can seem like an extension of San Francisco State's film program. In some ways Film Arts is the savior of SFSU; without the equipment Film Arts provides, SFSU students would sometimes be hard-pressed to complete their projects.

One unusual course the school offers is in film festival management. Students learn the ins and outs of running film festivals, and at the end of every year the students of this class arrange the end-of-year screenings of student films.

San Francisco is a nice town with pleasant weather and beautiful surroundings that provide a wide variety of locations. There is an established independent filmmaking community here—especially documentary filmmaking—

and the town as a whole is very cinema-literate. There are a number of great repertory cinemas scattered around the city, and even the local public television station runs uninterrupted classic films every Saturday night.

*Some of the worst things about the program:* Probably the single worst thing about the program is the perennially destitute state of the California state university system. Students and faculty argue that it builds character; by making films with minimal equipment and money, students get a good idea of what life will be like as independent filmmakers after graduation. But it is also true that sooner or later everyone despairs at having to fight for even the smallest amounts of money or equipment.

*Some of the best things about the program:* Perhaps the best thing about SF State is that you get to live in San Francisco. And, for all the problems, the students and alumni we spoke with were genuinely fond of the place.

# SOUTHERN ILLINOIS UNIVERSITY CARBONDALE

Department of Cinema & Photography
College of Mass Communication and Media Arts
Communications Room 1101, Mailcode 6610
1100 Lincoln Drive
Carbondale, IL 62901-4306
618-453-2365
http://cp.siu.edu/

| | |
|---|---|
| Tuition: | Resident: $4,632 |
| | Nonresident: $10,099 |
| Enrollment: | 6 |
| Deadline: | January 2 |
| Focus: | Experimental |

## ▶ THE PROGRAM

Carbondale has offered a film program since the late seventies. Since 2006, the MFA degree has been housed in Communication and Media Arts. Artistic development is the goal, and all forms of media, including film, video, sound, and new media, can be used to accomplish it. The number of applicants admitted fluctuates between six and eight per year for this three-year program. Carbondale's focus is on experimental and documentary film.

There's a core of thirty-six credits of required courses. Students usually take three to four classes a semester. Each student takes MFA Studio Arts Practice twice. This is a survey of various media forms. MFA Studio Critique is co-taught by three instructors. This class is taken five times and provides a forum for students to talk about or present their work for feedback. There are media arts theory and history courses, a critical research class, and a seminar for which the topics change each semester. Outside of these core classes, students take eighteen credits of electives either inside or outside of the department and six credits of Final Creative Project, which is the thesis prep course. Some courses are taken with upper-level undergraduates. Independent studies are very popular, because students can do whatever they want as long as an instructor signs on to supervise. Taking four or five of these is perfectly acceptable. For the most part, the education will be as specific and individual as each student.

189

Typically, students take Studio Arts Practices, Studio Critique, and History of Media Arts and Culture two times each over the first two semesters. In the second year, Critical Research Methods, Studio Critique, and an elective are taken in the fall; History and Theory, Media Arts, another studio critique, and an elective are taken in the spring. Year three consists of one final Studio Critique, three electives, and Final Creative Project taken twice. First-year students are assigned a faculty mentor.

On average, each student makes four films within the program. The program has a strong commitment to film, and while students still shoot 16 mm, projects are usually completed on video these days. Students pay for all of their own stock and processing.

At the end of first year, each student is reviewed by a committee of faculty representatives of the various media arts disciplines in the college. Students who fail this review are asked to leave. Students who receive a conditional pass will be reviewed again the next semester, at which time they might pass or fail. Failure of a second review results in automatic dismissal from the program.

At the end of the second year, students assemble a three-person MFA committee to review thesis work. A thesis plan is approved by the committee and filed with the director of graduate studies. Once approved, there are no restrictions on a thesis project other than that it must be presented or screened when complete. Many students show a retrospective of all of their graduate films along with their thesis films. There are small screenings at the beginning and end of every semester.

For those few who dare to tackle a narrative piece, casting locally is extremely difficult. Talent is usually imported from Chicago or found within the university theater department.

The biggest film event, held every spring, is the Big Muddy Film Festival, the largest and oldest student-run festival in the United States. Two graduate students always fill the director and assistant director roles with the help of a faculty advisor. There is a full-time staff member who works with students to find grants and expand the scope of the festival. Hundreds of films are screened over ten days, and well-known filmmakers visit with their projects. Carbondale students are dissuaded from entering Big Muddy, since the school runs the festival.

## ▶ THE PRICE

| | |
|---|---:|
| $10,099 nonresident tuition for one year | $10,099 |
| $4,632 resident tuition for two years | $9,264 |
| $9,000 per year rent and living expenses for three years | $27,000 |
| $1,200 per year maintenance and insurance on a car in Carbondale for three years | $3,600 |
| Average film costs | $15,000 |
| **Total** | **$64,963** |

Ignore these figures. No student will pay these tuition fees. Every single graduate student is funded at Carbondale from day one until the end of his three years. This is why they limit the number of admissions. But in order to encourage students to graduate on time, at the end of three years all funding ceases.

Funding is provided through half-time graduate assistantships. Assistants work about twenty hours a week and receive full tuition remission and a monthly stipend of $1,100 for nine months of the year. During the summer the stipend shrinks to $400 for the semester, but classes are still free. There is also a Kodak grant awarded on a competitive basis and some nominal production awards to help in varying capacities.

Carbondale is a scenic, rural community bordering the Shawnee National Forest. The nearest cities are Chicago, a mere six-hour commute by car, and St. Louis, just a two-hour drive. There is little in the way of decent film or art or culture of any kind outside of the school. Some students don't even like to shoot there. A group of students recently joined forces to improve the situation by creating Cinema Under the Ground, an informal assembly of student shorts that are screened once a week. Of course, the lack of distraction means students put exceptional amounts of time into their films. There is little else to do. It's easy to get almost anywhere in town on foot. For those who live outside of town, the bus system is terrible, and a car is a necessity. A car would also be nice for those cold production days or sanity-preserving weekend getaways.

One-bedroom apartments are a steal at around $400. A share can be had for as little as $100. Though rents are cheap, the job market is minimal, so students try to get more than one assistantship rather than seek employment outside of the university.

▶ **THE LOWDOWN**

Forty people apply for Carbondale's six openings. A couple of students might come directly from an undergraduate program, but the admissions board prefers students that have been out in the world for three to five years. Those accepted tend to have degrees in media, but the program is not exclusive to those who don't. The school is often willing to take a chance on people with minimal technical skills, but only for applicants whose portfolios offer proof of exceptional talent potential in one or two media areas. Your personal statement should describe what you plan to achieve at Carbondale that goes beyond your current professional or artistic experience.

Both the town and the school are very laid back. This is about as far away from Hollywood filmmaking as you can get. Competition between students is unheard of, even the healthy kind. This friendly atmosphere can prove lethal for some. When everyone's nice and helpful and you set your own pace and you can choose whatever courses you want, you can slide by with the bare minimum of work. You must supply your own inspiration and set your own deadlines.

The faculty is heavy in the experimental realm, but there is no pressure to impose this genre on students. They are student-centered and will try to train you to master the total process of filmmaking as opposed to focusing on one area. Equal emphasis is placed upon research and writing and production, so you need to be prepared to budget time accordingly. Other than the seminars and MFA-specific courses, the remaining classes are taken with undergraduates. You may wind up teaching students one day and sharing notes with them the next. If you are willing to seek them out, mentors are available.

There are ten Bolexes, a large assortment of Arriflex sync cameras, a CP-16, and an Arriflex SR, and even some Super 8 cameras. All but the Arriflex SR and one Bolex are shared with the undergrads. Steenbecks, which few if any touch anymore, are also available. There's a rarely used Oxberry animation stand. On the digital end, there are Canon XLs and Sony PD 170s. A Sony F900 HD camera and editing system were just acquired through a recent grant. There's plenty of light and sound gear. Reservations can be made two weeks in advance, and equipment can be checked out for twenty-four hours during the week and for weekends. With faculty approval, extended shoots can be arranged providing no one else is waiting in the wings. Checkout is via the honor system. Graduate students have keys to the equipment room, so they can take equipment whenever they want.

Avid editing is available, but you will also find Final Cut Pro editing stations. Three classrooms are dedicated to new media. There's a small screening room, interlock projection, and a new digital recording and mixing to picture studio with ProTools. The college is in the midst of a large renovation. The basement has already been gutted and is in the process of being transformed into a dozen graduate studio spaces. There is a sixty-by-forty-foot soundstage that contains track lighting and a dolly. Although this space is normally used as a classroom, student projects override all other uses. The stage is also used for Foley and ADR work and recording.

There's no staff in place to maintain equipment. They have been lucky thus far, and no one reports ever encountering any difficulty getting what they need. This is good, because in the middle of Illinois there's no place to rent. If you elect to shoot somewhere else and need to rent, be advised the school does not have an insurance policy, so you will have to cover that yourself.

Carbondale is best for students who have a need to make small, personal films and are sufficiently responsible to finish them before funding runs out. Make as many films as possible. This is also a great place to cut your teaching teeth if that is a path you are considering. Most graduates depart with extensive teaching experience and move on to careers in academia. It would help to have some savings in place to cover film costs before beginning.

**Some of the worst things about the program:** "You went where?" Despite being ranked in the top fifteen best graduate programs in America by *U.S. News & World Report*, no one has heard of this small school (until *you*, of course, put it on the map). But then again, experimental filmmakers are not featured on *E!* Students seeking a hip, exciting learning environment will be greatly disappointed in the town. Of course, this leaves plenty of time to heighten self-speculation and awareness. Some students find it annoy-

193

ing that the graduate department is not really separated from the undergraduate. Others worry that the relaxed atmosphere and lack of exposure for films places too much onus on students to forge their own path. Carbondale is not a haven for narrative filmmakers.

*Some of the best things about the program:* No tuition. The interdisciplinary nature. You'll have a chance to impact your art in new ways. A degree in Communication and Media Arts can position you for more teaching opportunities than just film. You will depart with significant training in both research and teaching. Experimental and documentary filmmakers might enjoy the less-structured, personal nature of the program. The Big Muddy Festival brings the independent film industry up close and personal.

# STANFORD UNIVERSITY

Department of Art & Art History

Nathan Cummings Art Building

Main Office—Room 101

Stanford, CA 94305-2018

650-723-3404

http://art.stanford.edu

| | |
|---|---|
| Tuition: | $32,994 |
| Enrollment: | 8 |
| Deadline: | January 17 |
| Focus: | Documentary |

## ▶ THE PROGRAM

Stanford University has offered an MA in documentary film through its Communications Department since the late 1970s. At the start it was more of a journalism program, teaching students to make segments for television news. But over time the program came to focus on documentary filmmaking as a medium separate from television and news; in 2005 the school finally shut down the MA program in Communications, and in 2006 reopened it as an MFA program within the Department of Art. Most of the facilities and equipment are the same, and the two-year structure of the program remains largely unchanged. The only real difference is the addition of a number of courses in film history and criticism, courses that would not have had a place in the Communications Department but that fit right in over in the Art Department.

In each quarter of first year, students make a documentary film. At the beginning of each quarter, students first talk privately with the professors about ideas they would like to pursue, and the professors help each student pick one idea to make into a film during that quarter. Students then pitch their films to the class as a whole; classmates ask questions and provide feedback, helping to narrow and shape the films before shooting begins. Students are not allowed to choose their own crew; the crew for each film is assigned by the faculty. Much of the program is designed to make students understand the value of a shot and to make them choose what they shoot carefully; the faculty prescribes for each film how much film or tape each student will be allowed to shoot. At the end of each quarter students screen their finished films. Even on the most basic of these films, students are expected to attain clearances for any music or video material that appears, and consent forms from any people who appear.

In the first quarter, students work entirely in 16 mm film. They make exercise films starting almost immediately upon arrival and work up to the fall film, a three- to four-minute documentary shot on black-and-white 16 mm film. These films are shot using windup Bolex cameras; as late as 2006 these films were still being edited on flatbed editing machines, but under the new program the film is now telecined to video, and students edit in Final Cut Pro. In the winter quarter, students work in pairs on their winter projects. These documentaries, which generally run around ten minutes, are shot on digital video; students may shoot no more than two hours of video for these projects. On the spring film, in the third quarter, the eight students are broken up into two groups of four, and each student shoots for two days, using the other three as crew. These films are shot on color 16 mm negative film and again edited in Final Cut Pro; each student can only shoot forty minutes of footage; the finished spring films tend to run around seven or eight minutes.

The quarter system really compresses time. Each of these films has to be approved, shot, edited, and completed in a ten-week period. As a result, by the end of first year, most students are exhausted; some find jobs during the summer, but many just want to rest. There are no classes to take, but students generally spend the time developing ideas for the thesis films they'll make in second year.

Second year revolves around the thesis films. Students again discuss ideas with the faculty and then pitch their chosen ideas to the class. Students are expected to prepare a great deal of documentation on these films—detailed schedules, budgets, and funding proposals—and present them to the faculty. They are also expected to raise their own funds; students learn to find appropriate sources of grants for their films and to apply for them, and to raise their budgets in other ways. Students present their packages to the faculty at the end of the first quarter and must receive faculty approval before they can proceed to production. When a project is not approved, it is usually because it is deemed too ambitious considering the funds raised. The school only has two thesis-quality video cameras—Sony DSR-570 DVCAM cameras as of this writing, though the school plans to move into high definition in the near future—so students have to schedule their shoots in advance. Each student's crew is again assigned by the faculty, though for this film the faculty will take into account requests by the filmmakers to work with specific classmates. The only limitation on the thesis film is that students cannot shoot more than ten days. The thesis films must be completed by the end of the year; a screening of the finished thesis films is held the day before graduation. In extreme circumstances, if a student cannot finish her film before graduation, the school will allow her to matriculate for one additional quarter free of charge in order to finish the work. But this is very rare; almost all students adhere to the program's two-year time frame, finish in time to screen with their classmates, and head off into the wide world of documentary filmmaking after graduation the next day.

197

▶ **THE PRICE**

| | |
|---|---|
| $32,994 tuition for two years | $65,988 |
| $15,000 per year rent and living expenses for two years | $30,000 |
| $1,500 per year maintenance and insurance on a car | $3,000 |
| Average film costs | $10,000 |
| **Total** | **$108,988** |

Stanford does not have an undergraduate film production program, so there are not many assistantships available to graduate students. But at the same time there are not many graduate students. In recent years every student has received research assistantships and work-study for part of the first year, amounting to one free quarter's tuition. This probably isn't going to change for the MFA program, so you can strike $10,000 off of the above number. Under the MA program, the course load was so light in second year that students were classified as part-time students and paid less tuition for that year. However, that discount will likely go away with the additional courses of the MFA program. Stanford has an undergraduate program in cinema studies; now that the graduate students will be taking history and theory courses under the MFA program, some will probably begin helping to teach those courses. But at this writing no students have actually started the MFA program, so that still has to be determined. The work is so intense throughout both years that it is not possible to work outside of school at all.

Students are responsible for the budgets of their own films. However, the school provides a great deal of training in raising funds. Students apply for grants, seek fiscal sponsorships, hold fund-raising parties, and raise funds in numerous other creative ways. Most manage to raise more than half of their budgets before they begin production.

A car is necessary. Most students live within a few miles of the school. Students will sometimes live in San Francisco and commute to Palo Alto, where Stanford is, but this is not a good idea. The program is so grueling, especially in the first year, that you'll want the trip home at the end of the school day to be as brief as possible.

▶ **THE LOWDOWN**

Out of about ninety applicants per year the school admits only eight new students. GREs are required, but they don't have to be stellar; much more important is the sample of work and statement of purpose. The faculty also seems to pick people by personality; they seem to look for people who will work well together as teams. While fewer people apply to this program, competition is still very tough. The people who apply tend to already know a lot about the program and tend to be well-qualified for it. It's not like USC or NYU, where hundreds of people apply who have no real sense of whether the program is appropriate for them. This is a program for people who know they want to be making documentaries. But a background in documentary is not required; most people who are accepted have experience in other professional fields, but not specifically in documentary filmmaking.

The program is small and specialized and has never really advertised itself, so not that many prospective students even know that it exists. The place where the program is most conspicuous is in the annual Student Academy Awards. Since 1990 Stanford films have won thirteen Student Academy Awards in the documentary category; not bad for a program that only admits eight students a year. No other school comes close to this number in the category. By contrast, USC, with one hundred new graduate students per year and a strong documentary program, has taken five documentary awards in the same period. Temple and UT

Austin, each with a well-regarded documentary program, have each taken only one such award.

When asked why this might be, students seem to agree that the faculty is especially strong at story—at finding a compelling story in a concept before production begins, and at editing it down, sometimes brutally, to its most concentrated form in postproduction.

It is largely because of Stanford's high tuition that the program is structured to make students finish in two years. Under the old MA program, students completed most of their course requirements in the first year, freeing them to travel a great deal in pursuit of their thesis documentaries in the second. The new MFA program, with its additional courses in film history and theory, requires students to spend more time in classrooms in the second year. Students will be much less free to travel as a result, and it is expected that students will make more documentaries on subjects local to California.

There are no specific courses in technical aspects of film; no courses in cinematography or lighting, for instance. And students are not allowed to specialize in any one technical area; the faculty assigns students to crew on one another's films, so no one student can become, say, the cinematographer on all of his classmates' films as happens at many schools. Every student comes out of the program fully capable of filling any position on any shoot.

The students we spoke with are extremely enthusiastic about the program. With only two professors overseeing eight students per year, Stanford offers a rare level of intimacy and collaboration between students and faculty. Students work together closely and form bonds that last long past graduation. The term *Stanford Mafia* is used in reference to the small but tightly knit ranks of the program's graduates. Because there are so few, alumni of the documentary program feel an unusually close bond. Alumni who are making films will often recruit interns and assistants from the school, either by contacting the faculty or via the program's e-mail Listserv. Many students go from graduation directly into working relationships with older alumni who are already established documentary filmmakers. This isn't something that the school arranges or has to arrange; the Mafia looks after its own.

*Some of the worst things about the program:* With only two professors in the department, students don't get a lot of training in the more technical aspects of filmmaking. They get enough cinematography, but students sometimes find themselves adrift when confronted with the most technical aspects of postproduction—online editing, mixing, and color correction—on their finished projects.

*Some of the best things about the program:* Stanford is about documentary and nothing else. If you want to learn to make documentaries and establish a lasting career as a documentarian, there are few better places.

# SYRACUSE UNIVERSITY

Department of Transmedia

College of Visual and Performing Arts

102 Shaffer Art

Syracuse, NY 13224-1210

315-443-1033

http://ams.syr.edu

| | |
|---|---|
| Tuition: | $20,880 |
| Enrollment: | 5 |
| Deadline: | February 1 |
| Focus: | Independent |

## ▶ THE PROGRAM

The MFA degree in Film at Syracuse University has been available since 1976. The program is part of the Department of Transmedia in the College of Visual and Performing Arts. It is a very small program that admits five students annually.

Syracuse offers a good deal of flexibility in its courses. Students work with an academic advisor to structure an individual plan of study that fulfills all of the requirements and also serves their individual goals. Students take twenty-seven credits in film production and film studies over three years. Students also take nine additional credits of film history/theory electives, three credits of graduate seminar, and eighteen credits of studio and academic electives. Studio electives are usually taken within the College of Visual and Performing Arts in areas like video, photography, computer art, sound, animation, or even creative writing. Academic electives are normally taken outside of the college in areas like philosophy, anthropology, foreign languages, or psychology. Everyone takes Problems of Film Perception, the introductory film theory research course. Everyone also takes two 16 mm film-making courses during each of the first two years.

The school makes few requirements regarding students' films. They can be any length, they can cover any subject matter, and they can be any genre. And students incur all costs. However, there is one rule about the first-year project. The program requires that this be a "narrative film." By narrative they don't mean "Hollywood" or even "conventional." They only mean that the first-year film should tell a story, should use actors, and should make use of a full crew.

The first-year film is expected to be in the can by the end of the fall semester. Students edit it in the spring semester while continuing to take three or four classes. All first-year films must be completed by the end of the spring semester when each student's work is evaluated by the faculty. Second year is similarly structured. There are no restrictions at all on the second-year films; they can be in any genre and on any subject. Third year follows the same pattern as second. Students take three or four classes and complete their thesis film by the end of the year. Each student must also complete a written thesis statement to accompany his thesis film project. During the last semester of study, a three-credit class, Final Presentation, is taken to assist in this preparation. The school does not tolerate long postproduction periods. Students who are not finished with their thesis by the end of the third year are allowed to stay through the summer to complete it. But at the end of the summer they are cut off from the school and its equipment. When a student's thesis is finished, Syracuse becomes very academic. Finishing the MFA here is like finishing a PhD program elsewhere. Students choose a five-member evaluation committee, including one professor from outside the program. The thesis is screened for the committee, and the student presents a paper that discusses and defends the thesis. Every student then has to go through an extended oral defense of the thesis, fielding questions and challenges from the five committee members.

204

There is a screening of all graduate films at the end of the year. The best films are also shown at the Carol North Schmuckler New Filmmakers' Showcase and at Universal Studios. Outside of the university the Syracuse International Film Festival screens over 120 films each April. Students can attend panels and discussions and have direct contact with working filmmakers from across the world.

## ▶ THE PRICE

| | |
|---|---:|
| $20,880 tuition for three years | $62,640 |
| $9,600 per year rent and living expenses for three years | $28,800 |
| $1,500 per year maintenance and insurance on a car in Syracuse for three years | $4,500 |
| Average film costs | $8,000 |
| **Total** | **$103,940** |

The university has limited funding. There are a few TA-ships, each of which gives full tuition remission and a stipend of $9,683. Usually these are split in half by the film program (half a year's tuition and a stipend of $4,841) in order to fund more students. About four students receive half assistantships. Students may also find TA-ships in the university outside of the film department. There are some tuition-remission-only scholarships. The department receives a set number of these per year and then makes recommendations on which students should receive the scholarships and how many remission credits each student gets. These can vary from three to nine credits per student. There is a very competitive university-wide fellowship that provides a full ride. First-year students rarely receive any financial assistance outside of standard grants and loans. Work-study jobs exists for those students who receive no TA-ships.

Life at Syracuse is inexpensive. Rents are about $500 a month off-campus for a small house or large one-bedroom apartment. There are some good and not-so-good areas. It's still a city, and you need to have some street smarts. A car is definitely necessary for moving equipment, cast, and crew around on shoots.

Syracuse is a prime example of the crash of American industry. There are an abundance of vacant warehouses and factories in Armory Square, a nineteenth-century warehouse district slowly transforming into a hub for students and tourists. The university recently renovated one such warehouse and it is now home to several colleges, including two programs for the College of Visual and Performing Arts. A project is under way to connect the university to Amory Square via a new "cultural corridor." In the last ten years the city has seen a real growth in the arts. There is a surprising number of theaters, several of which show independent films. In fact, there is more culture than you might imagine in this largely collegiate town. Syracuse has a symphony orchestra, several new art galleries, and a decent visual arts scene. It doesn't hurt that the Finger Lakes are nearby. While they attract more snow in the winter, the region is a naturally beautiful distraction to the city. Shooting is a breeze, and locals are still friendly and open to filmmakers.

## ▶ THE LOWDOWN

The program receives between forty-five and sixty applications. Since only five slots are available, a portion of qualified students are usually wait-listed. Along with your application and transcripts, you will need letters of recommendation. The school will not consider any applicant with an undergraduate GPA below 3.0. They look for creative people who write well and already possess basic technical skills. A creative portfolio is mandatory. Without previous film or video experience, you have no chance of acceptance. If you really want to go to Syracuse, you might want to go to a local college or art school right now, take some courses in film, and make a short to send with your application. The faculty clearly aims to assemble an interesting mixture of people. Special attention is paid to the personal statement. You must convey a clear understanding of the Syracuse program and strong reasons for wanting to attend.

The school is very strict about how long students can stay. It is a three-year program, and you can stay only three years, plus the summer after your third year if you absolutely need it to finish your thesis film. Completing the program in less than three years is not possible, and staying for more than three years is not allowed.

Syracuse is very strong in film theory and somewhat weaker on technical filmmaking. It is very much an art department with a film component. While there is no specific focus, experimental films are more the norm. No one here is concerned with Hollywood or the latest blockbuster.

There are three full-time faculty members. Students find Owen Shapiro, the director of the program since its beginning, to be more of an academic these days. Both Shapiro and Miso Suchy, the resident documentary filmmaker, are known for not pulling punches when instructing or critiquing work. Some find them downright mean. But both are viewed as upholding professional standards.

Film is still the medium of choice at Syracuse, but the school has gradually been moving away from 16 mm to Super 16 and now has twenty-four reasonably good 16 mm camera packages including Aaton and Arriflex SR 2 Super 16 cameras along with Arriflex BLs, CP-16s, Eclairs, and a large number of Bolexes. Some of the equipment is shared with undergrads. One exception is the grad-reserved Super 16 cameras. But graduate students try to work out schedules among themselves so that there are no issues. There are ten digital cameras: five Panasonic DVX100s and five Sony HDV cameras. The Panasonics are more popular than the Sonys, as editing HDV video presents technical obstacles. The hope is that students will combine and experiment with all formats. Syracuse is one of the few schools that still relies on flatbeds. First-year films are all edited on Steenbecks. There are seven Final Cut Pro stations. Sound packages are a bit outdated, with no harddrive based recorders. There is a lighting studio, animation studio, and a sound studio for mixing, dubbing, and recording music. The film studies library has over 3,000 titles available for student viewing. There are no film processing labs close to Syracuse.

Syracuse is ideal for those who prefer a slower pace but are comfortable with their choices and confident about the types of films they want to make. You will need to stay focused and on schedule in order to complete your thesis in the time allotted.

*Some of the worst things about the program:* There are no connections to working professionals. If you need a January reshoot, you might have to wait until the spring thaw. On the other hand, in the words of one student, "If you don't mind the snow, it's fine."

*Some of the best things about the program:* This is a very small program, making it easy for students to work closely with professors and other students. Syracuse provides a solid education, with an especially strong foundation in theory. Students are free to make any type of film.

# TEMPLE UNIVERSITY

Department of Film and Media Arts
School of Communications and Theater
Annenberg Hall, Room 120
2020 North 13th Street
Philadelphia, PA 19122-6005
215-204-3859
www.temple.edu/fma

| | |
|---|---|
| Tuition: | Resident: $11,592 |
| | Nonresident: $16,896 |
| Enrollment: | 12–15 |
| Deadline: | January 15 U.S. |
| | December 15 International |
| Focus: | Independent |

## ▶ THE PROGRAM

Temple University is a well-funded, reasonably priced school in the heart of Philadelphia. The first graduate class was admitted in 1969. The program started out with a documentary focus, then in 1980 expanded to include narrative films. While it is still best-known for its documentary filmmaking program, in recent years students have also made good narrative and experimental films. Twelve students are accepted each fall. The group is usually equally spilt among those straight from undergrad programs, a group in their mid-twenties, and professionals in their thirties or forties who are interested in taking their lives in a new direction.

Temple is a three-year program than can take as long as five years to complete. It is a conservatory environment in which students are expected to produce a work of significance each semester or at the very least, every year. Student interest is divided just about in half between documentary and narrative film with a very small percentage working in experimental and new media. There are two annual reviews conducted to insure that students are producing satisfactory work and are on schedule for graduation and comprehensive exams just prior to beginning thesis work.

There are only eight required courses for the entire program: Cinematography Workshop, Videography, Writing for Media I, Film History, and Theory are taken during the first year; MFA Colloquium can be take almost any semester; Critical Methods and Advanced Problems are third-year courses. Colloquium is a one-credit course of screenings, guest lectures, and discussions that must be taken twice. Beyond these courses, students tailor the program to their own needs, including taking courses outside the department.

Twelve credits are taken each semester of first year. There are only two technical classes: Cinematography Workshop, which students take in the fall of their first year, and Videography, which they take in the spring. Every technical aspect of filmmaking and video is jammed into these two classes, including cinematography, lighting design, sound recording, editing, sound editing, and sound mixing. It's a lot of work.

That's because the first year is filled with film exercises. Five projects are shot in Cinematography Workshop alone. The largest of these is the final film, which can be fifteen minutes long. Another large video project of similar length is shot during second semester in Videography. During the middle of the second semester, the first-year reviews take place. At that time students present current work and receive faculty feedback.

During the second year the number of required credits drops to nine per semester. At this time students begin to set their own pace and decide which direction to follow. There are dozens of film electives to choose from, including directing, animation, and advanced-level courses in documentary or fiction filmmaking, writing, and theory. Some people take courses to pick up some technical skills in Avid, for instance. The second-year review has two parts and takes place in late November. First, students meet one-on-one with their advisor to review course credits and again make sure that they are on track. Then a public screening of work the student completed during the second year follows in the spring.

Credits drop to six a semester during third year. The remaining required courses, Critical Methods and Advanced Problems, are taken during the fall of this year. The first is a prep course for comprehensive exams; the second is a prep course for thesis.

Students complete forty-two credits before taking the required comprehensive exams. At that point each student registers for Critical Methods and chooses three faculty members to serve as her exam committee. She prepares and researches eight questions with committee guidance. The written exam is administered during the final week of Critical Methods and consists of four of these questions that deal with the student's own creative work as well as pedagogical issues associated with media production and studies and theoretical/critical or historical issues pertinent to film. Each answer will be seven to ten pages long, and students have three days in which to answer them. A student cannot begin thesis production without successfully passing the comprehensive exam.

In the fall of the third year, students register for Advanced Problems and another three-member committee is again formed for thesis. This time the student has the option of requesting someone outside of the university. Every thesis has to be formally proposed to and approved by the committee. If approved, a student is expected to finish her thesis by August of the third year. Once the thesis is completed it must be submitted a final time to the committee. Every thesis, regardless of format, must also include a Production Notebook that chronicles the work involved in completing the thesis. If the project passes, a student is recommended for graduation. If it does not pass, graduation will be postponed.

The Diamond Screen is Temple's annual spring film festival that showcases the best of undergraduate and graduate work. The faculty selects the films that screen over several nights on campus and then travel to local independent theaters including the newly established Bryn Mawr Film Institute. It is a juried competition with cash prizes. Every two years or so these winning films are also screened on the West Coast at the Directors Guild of America or on the Warner Brothers lot. Temple is also home to the Next Frame Film Festival, an international touring student film festival run by Temple graduate students and cosponsored by the University Film and Video Association. Another outlet is The Philadelphia Film Festival, which runs over two weeks each April. Students might not get accepted, but they can certainly check out lots of excellent films and attend the many filmmaker discussions and events.

## ▶ THE PRICE

| | |
|---|---|
| $704 nonresident for twenty-four credits (first year of course work) | $16,896 |
| $483 resident for thirty credits (two years of course work) | $14,490 |
| $483 matriculation for two semesters | $966 |
| $16,000 per year rent and living expenses for three years | $48,000 |
| Average film costs | $15,000 |
| **Total** | **$95,352** |

These prices mean little, as it is almost impossible not to get additional funding from Temple at some point. And for Pennsylvania residents, the first-year tab would be $5,304 less than the above-listed figure.

All incoming applicants are considered for fellowships. These are based on academic, creative, and professional credentials. Presidential fellowships include three years of support in the form of a $20,000 stipend, full tuition remission, and health insurance. The film program averages two to three of these each year. Seven current Film and Media Arts students receive university fellowships. These offer the same benefits, but a lesser stipend of $14,000. Future faculty fellows receive the same benefits as the university fellows. These fellowships are available for students of color who have expressed interest in college-level teaching. Four FMA students currently receive this package.

Other than the fellowships, there is no additional funding for first-year students. But the school is working to fully fund every second-year student. Right now each is awarded a graduate assistantship. Thirteen receive full assistantships that deliver a $14,000 annual stipend, tuition remission, and health insurance benefits in return for teaching or assisting with two classes each semester. A few get half assistantships that provide the same benefits, excluding the health insurance. Adjunct teaching positions are available for those not on fellowships or in teaching assistantships, most typically in the third year and beyond. Adjuncts earn about $4,500 per course. The program even manages to fund some third years or exceptional first years by taking funds not needed by second-year fellowship students and shifting them to other students!

Production classes are partially subsidized. This amounts to about $300 in film and processing for the cinematography class, $200 in cash for video work, and $3,000 for thesis projects. Students always add significantly to these budgets. There are also two types of completion grants available for film students. Both are very competitive, and the faculty chooses recipients.

The department has $15,000 in Film and Media Arts Awards that is distributed annually in varying amounts.

Nonthesis films can receive up to $1,000; thesis projects can be awarded up to $2,000. The University Completion Grant is available for the completion of MFA projects. In order to qualify, a student must have completed all course work and comprehensive exams. Recipients receive a $3,000 cash stipend. Finally, students can apply for $500 in funding from the School of Communications for travel to festivals and conferences.

The City of Brotherly Love has much to offer. *National Geographic Traveler* recently listed it as "The Next Great City." The number of restaurants has more than tripled since 1992, and we're not talking cheese steaks here. There's a thriving art scene, great theater, music, and film, and new construction in most neighborhoods. It is even slated to be one of the nation's first Wi-Fi cities. And if you need a break from city life, Fairmount Park offers miles of great biking and walking trails. In a nutshell, there's a lot going on. Alas, not much of it surrounds Temple. Temple University is basically a commuter school, and most of the students hail from the Philadelphia area and wouldn't dream of living on campus. Neither should a grad film student. Although it's probably just a matter of time until the gentrification reaches Temple's borders, for now it is smack in the middle of one of the worst crime areas of the city. However, campus security is good, and the actual buildings and intermediate streets are safe. Students should join the commuter ranks and drive or take public transportation to school. Don't despair, because there is affordable housing available in many safe areas. Philadelphia is in the midst of an astounding revitalization of neighborhoods. Apartments can be had in funky South Philly or trendy Manayunk, or up-and-coming Fishtown to which area artists flock for still-affordable lofts. A one-bedroom can be had for as little as $600 or more than double that amount, depending on the area and amenities. The bus service is not the best, but the subway, elevated trains, and regional rail are reliable. This is also a bike-friendly city. Cars are available from Philly Car Share when absolutely needed. New York City is a short train ride away.

▶ **THE LOWDOWN**

Each year Temple gets between eight hundred and one thousand inquiries about its program. The admissions board does all that they can to discourage all but the most serious from applying. One way they accomplish this is by stressing the importance of a desire to do socially conscious work. They honestly are not interested in anyone who wants to pursue film purely as entertainment. This pre-screening process brings the actual number of applicants down to around two hundred. Those who apply submit an essay, letters of recommendation, and a creative portfolio. You will not be accepted solely because of a stellar GRE, but you might be rejected for a poor one. It is helpful to be involved in the arts, but not necessarily in film. Temple looks for content and strong opinions, not so much for experience in the technique of filmmaking. The admissions board wants people who have things to say about the world and a strong drive to say them through the medium of film. You will be at an advantage if you demonstrate some sort of aptitude for socially conscious films.

One student described his first year as ranging from "busy to mind-blowing," with the first semester almost "ridiculous" in the amount of work expected. Students must reach advanced levels very quickly. It can be a steep learning curve that is often overwhelming, especially for those with little production experience. Working on four films in addition to your own is not uncommon. One student worked on seven. None found time to work outside of the school. Students report that it is the support they find from their classmates that helps them make it through. Part of this is due to the very personal nature of projects students create. Films tend to be very different from student to student. Often they blur the boundaries between narrative and experimental. No one at Temple is looking to make a splash in the industry.

Locals are receptive to student filmmakers. People are still excited about seeing films made and will often give locations and assistance for free. The Greater Philadelphia Film Office can be very helpful and will go so far as to shut down streets for a student film. In the last few years the city has become busy with film and television production. M. Night Shyamalan shoots all of his films locally. There are at least two casting agencies that will assist filmmakers and lots of talented actors, some of whom are grads in Temple's very own theater program. Every year the school hosts a huge casting call where actors from around the region audition for student directors.

Most of the faculty still work as filmmakers, with the majority in documentary. There is exposure to new technology as some instructors are interested in nonlinear work through installations and media for performance. And although students lament over the amount of work involved in the cinematography course, in hindsight most reflect upon it as a standout. The animation class is one of the most popular. Most appreciated is the balance of theory and production that every student cites as an integral part of the program. Temple students transition well into dual careers as independent filmmakers and academics, much like their faculty. They graduate with extensive teaching experience.

Students have access to a great deal of equipment. There are several varieties of Arriflex and Aaton 16 mm and Super 16 cameras, a few dozen Bolexes, a dozen or so high-definition cameras, and well over thirty digital cameras, including Panasonic DVX100As, Canon XL2s, and Sony TRV900s. There's also a Steadicam flyer, several dollies, and expansive lighting and sound packages. Film shoots can be approved for as long as four weeks, and students can keep equipment for the duration. Granted, there is a very large undergrad population with which equipment is shared, but for the most part there is only a month or so each semester when sharing poses real problems. And the equipment room staff tries to keep cameras well-maintained and makes sure that students get what they need. Recently a camera went down during the end of semester crunch time, and the program actually rented a replacement until it was back online.

In 2005 Temple opened a 75,000-square-foot, state-of-the-art technology center with 700 computers. The center is open 24-7 and contains seventeen Avid and Final Cut Pro high-definition editing stations. Within the School of Communications there is a graduate editing lab with four Avid and Final Cut Pro workstations and a larger lab of eighteen Avid workstations shared with the undergraduates. There are also ProTools and Graphics workstations.

*Some of the worst things about the program:* Almost every student bemoans the bureaucracy. The school is resistant to any changes in policy, and trying to implement them is guaranteed to mire you in red tape. Apparently this is a source of frustration for students and faculty alike.

*Some of the best things about the program:* Every student we spoke to mentioned their classmates as one of the things they liked best about the program. The conservatory approach provides real creative freedom. Those interested in academia will be well-positioned for employment after they depart.

# UNIVERSITY OF CALIFORNIA, LOS ANGELES

School of Theater, Film and Television
102 East Melnitz Hall
Box 951622
Los Angeles, CA 90095-1622
310-825-5761
www.filmtv.ucla.edu

| | |
|---|---|
| Tuition: | Resident: $8,110 |
| | Nonresident: $23,071 |
| Enrollment: | directors: 21 |
| | screenwriters: 20 |
| | producers: 12 |
| Deadline: | November 1 |
| Focus: | Independent |

## ▶ THE PROGRAM

UCLA's School of Theater, Film and Television offers MFAs in directing, screenwriting, and producing. The department as a whole is very large, including hundreds of undergraduates, and graduate students in film theory, film preservation, animation, and new media.

### Directing

UCLA's directing program is firmly in the independent camp and is similar in many ways to NYU's program. Students take three years of classes, making several short films in first year, one more complicated film in second year (the advanced project), and a thesis film through third year and into at least a fourth. The school makes students work together so closely for the first year that they bond as a group and work as tightly knit teams through the remainder of film school and into the real world afterward. Because of the school's proximity to Hollywood, directors, producers, and other industry professionals frequently stop by to give lectures—some teach entire courses—so students are able to pick up a pretty good knowledge of how to get by in the industry. A large and diverse faculty provides specialized courses in many kinds of filmmaking and in many aspects of history and criticism.

Because the school assumes no previous experience in film, the first quarter is devoted to intensive studio courses in the basics of filmmaking—writing, directing, and camera—that ensure all students have a base level of filmmaking knowledge. The first year begins with a weeklong orientation/bonding ritual called boot camp. Students meet on one of the schools' soundstages, where they break the ice by doing actors' warm-up exercises and learn how to use the equipment they will be using to make films in the first quarter. There's a barbecue at a faculty member's house one evening. And at the end of the week every student has to present an idea for a two-minute-long film he'd like to make in the first quarter. After boot camp, when classes begin, students are surprised to find that classes are not terribly different from boot camp; the pace is still hectic, the flow of information is still enormous, and it's still the exact same twenty-one people in every class every day.

For the two-minute films, the class is broken up into three groups of seven people, who work as teams making seven films in a single week, each directed by one student. The restrictions on the two-minute film are severe; over the course of one week, each person gets one 400-foot roll of film (about eleven minutes' worth), and is allowed to shoot for no more than four hours. After these films are shot, students edit for two weeks; all of the two-minute films are screened at the end of the quarter.

Winter and spring quarter are devoted to the six-minute film. At the beginning of the winter quarter, students are again divided into groups of seven (different groups from the fall semester), but this time the shooting lasts for seven weeks, with each student shooting Thursday through Sunday of one week. No classes are held during these seven frenzied weeks. Students rotate through the positions of the crew; everybody gets to be director one week, but also boom operator, gaffer, cinematographer, assistant director, and sound mixer in the other weeks. By the end of production of the six-minute films, every student has worked in all of the major positions of a film shoot. Students spend the spring quarter editing their films. These films have to be completed by the end of first year; students are not permitted to start work on their second-year films without first finishing these films.

Second year is less rigidly structured than first year. Students are required to take courses in writing, directing, and film theory and criticism, but otherwise they are allowed to choose their own directions. Having learned the basics of film production in the first year, students are encouraged to explore different facets of filmmaking in the second. Students choose an area of filmmaking that interests them: narrative, documentary, experimental, television, new media, even directing for theater. Once a student has chosen an area of study, a faculty advisor who specializes in that area is assigned to her. This faculty member then acts as mentor, advising the student, and guiding the student through the production of her second-year project, the advanced project.

Advanced projects tend to run between fifteen and twenty minutes. The school does not allow students to find outside talent to work on advanced projects; students may only recruit crew members from within the program. While the advanced project is usually a narrative film, it can be a television production, a short documentary, or any number of other creative projects. The students who make films shoot them in the winter quarter and work on them through the fall of their third year. Officially, students are not allowed to begin work on their thesis films until they have finished their advanced projects. But in fact many students give up on their advanced projects to save time and money, and focus instead on their thesis films.

Classes continue on through to the end of third year. Each student must come up with a thesis project and present it to a three-member faculty committee. Once this committee has allowed a student to advance, she has a few quarters in which to make it. Thesis projects are generally shot in the winter or spring quarter of third year, and students do postproduction on them in fourth year. Thesis projects have only one restriction on them; narrative films may not exceed thirty minutes, while documentary films may not exceed fifty-six minutes. Other than that, they can be in any medium, and can be made by any crew: student, professional, or otherwise. Most students make narrative films for their thesis projects; out of any class of twenty-one, two or three are likely to make documentaries

## Screenwriting

The screenwriting MFA program is a two-year program, which accepts twenty students each year. One of the screenwriting program's distinguishing features is its faculty; most of the teachers in any year are working screenwriters from the industry, who come to the school to teach for a quarter or two at a time. This makes for exciting classes for the students, as the teachers tend to have up-to-date knowledge and are rarely burnt out on teaching.

The course requirements are pretty straightforward; in the first quarter everyone takes 431, Introduction to Screenwriting, where they learn the basics of dramatic writing and screenplay structure and write the first act of a screenplay. Each quarter after that, every student takes 434, Advanced Screenwriting, where the requirement is to complete a feature-length screenplay. Students generally leave the program with five completed screenplays; those who wish to can continue on in the program for a third year and write three more. Students must also take two critical studies courses of their picking, and one additional elective. Students are free to take courses in other areas, including the directing and producing programs. However, competition to get into those classes is tough.

Screenwriting students often take classes with the producing students. There is a course in Development where screenwriters and producers pair up, and each pair must, over the course of four weeks, develop a ten-minute pitch for a film. After they have done this once, they do it a second time, but swap positions. So the producer has the experience of writing and rewriting based on someone else's notes, and the writer gets the experience of analyzing a pitch and giving notes to improve it.

## Producing

The producing program is a two-year program that accepts twelve new students per year. Its focus is on creative producing for independent film; where AFI's producing program is largely about the minutiae of managing productions, and USC's Stark program largely prepares students to work within the studio system, UCLA's program is angled toward the conception, creation, and completion of independent films. It is a program for creative producers who aren't interested in becoming studio executives.

First-year courses cover the business of producing but also delve into aspects of story and the elements that make films memorable. Business-related courses cover the ins and outs of distribution, how to raise funds and negotiate contracts, how to cobble together advance money from distributors in other countries to finance a production. About half of the program is devoted to story. In the first year students take a full-year course devoted to story, to recognizing stories that are suitable for the screen and to developing those stories into screenplays. In the third quarter, each producer works with a screenwriter from the screenwriting department to develop pitches (as described in the screenwriting section above).

As in the screenwriting program, many of the courses are taught by successful professionals, including well-known producers Barbara Boyle, who currently is the chair of the film school, and Peter Guber. Guber teaches several courses per year: a general course on producing, where he brings in people from different disciplines of Hollywood to talk to students and answer questions, and a course on new media, where he covers new aspects of the entertainment business, such as content for mobile devices, digital downloads, or distribution of entertainment over the Internet. He tells students that a producer is a *creative entrepreneur*, and students say that's a good description of the overall view of producers in this program.

In the last semester of first year, students decide on two projects—a primary and a secondary—they would like to make as thesis projects in second year. The primary has to be a feature-length screenplay; the secondary is often a television project or a documentary. In the summer after first year, almost everyone takes an internship in Hollywood.

In the fall quarter of second year, there are fewer course requirements, so students can work on their thesis projects. Students develop their screenplays in conjunction with their screenwriters over the course of the year and also work up marketing materials—a log line, a selling hook for the project, a full synopsis, a full budget, a full schedule, a distribution and marketing plan, and an in-depth report on a strategy for selling the project. Students present these thick binders to a faculty committee midway through the year and take comments and suggestions on them. They continue working on their binders throughout the year, and at the end of the year officially present the projects to their committees. After that each student then presents his project to a panel of producers brought in from Hollywood; he does a five-minute pitch of the project and then discusses it with the panel.

Like USC's Stark program, students are encouraged to take internships in the industry while they are in the program. Most classes meet at night, between 7:00 and 10:00, so students are free to work during the day. The school facilitates this by seeking out internships for its students.

► **THE PRICE**

| | |
|---|---:|
| $23,071 nonresident tuition for one year | $23,071 |
| $8,110 resident tuition for two years | $16,220 |
| $15,000 per year rent and living expenses for four years | $60,000 |
| $2,000 per year maintenance and insurance on a car for four years | $8,000 |
| Average first-year film costs | $3,000 |
| Average second-year film costs | $8,000 |
| Average thesis film costs | $20,000 |
| **Total** | **$138,291** |

Screenwriting and Producing are two-year programs and don't have any major film expenses; look for those to cost around $65,000 total.

We assume out-of-state tuition for only one year, which is easily doable. If you come to UCLA from out of state, be sure to move to Los Angeles about a month before registration, get a place to live, open a bank account, and get a California driver's license. To be eligible for in-state tuition, you have to be able to prove you've been a California resident for more than one year as of the day of registration. So at the beginning of second year, if you can't prove that you were a resident prior to registration first year, you will be stuck paying nonresident tuition for at least an additional quarter, a needless waste of a few thousand dollars.

While the amount is typical of what students spend overall, most students get TA-ships or grants from the school that cover some of this expense. UCLA is well-endowed with grants and fellowships; about $300,000 worth are distributed to students each winter. Most students get some sort of assistance for their second- and third-year films, but it is far from uniform; in any given year some students will get most of the money they need to make their projects while a few will get very little. There is one enormous grant, the Bridges Larson foundation grant. This $25,000 grant, given out every year, is the holy grail of grants at UCLA. The school plays this grant out for maximum entertainment value, first announcing a few finalists, and then making everyone wait to hear which of the finalists gets it. The proverbial second prize is the Lew Wasserman award, which gives around $6,000 per year (it varies from year to year) to several students making thesis films. The school also has a small fund of unrestricted money that makes small grants to students who can make a case that they need it.

Because UCLA has a large undergraduate population, there are a lot of teaching assistantships. Forty TA-ships are given out each year to graduate film students. First year students are not allowed to have TA-ships, so most of the second- and third-year graduate students get TA-ships of some sort, which provide either 25 percent or 50 percent discounts on tuition, depending on hours worked.

There are inexpensive ways to satisfy the requirements of the program. Second-year projects may be made on video or may be feature-length screenplays. Some students do very small second-year projects to conserve their resources and energy for their thesis films. The school pays for tape for television projects shot in one of the school's three television studios, so it is possible to come out of second year with a good-looking video project that cost very little.

A car is absolutely necessary. Unfortunately, car insurance in Los Angeles is exorbitant; basic insurance runs from $1,200 to $2,000 per year even on a run-down old wreck. One-bedroom apartments near campus are scarce, and the few that exist are pretty expensive. But a mile or so away in West L.A. one bedrooms can be found for around $800 a month. Most UCLA students find it worthwhile to share larger apartments than rent one-bedroom apartments by themselves.

225

▶ **THE LOWDOWN**

For your application to be considered you have to have a bachelor's degree, and you have to send the following supporting materials: a statement of purpose, a two- or three-page description of a project you would like to make while at UCLA, and three letters of recommendation. GRE scores are not required. The school does not look at portfolios or reels of past work at this stage. Like most schools, UCLA is looking for articulate people with things to say, and though these materials they ask for are scant, they are your only chance to show that you have these qualities.

The school receives about eight hundred applications each year. Of these, the admissions committee chooses fifty or sixty applicants in each area with whom to conduct personal interviews. If you make it to this stage, you will be asked to bring a reel or portfolio of work to the interviews. Your portfolio need not include films or videos; the school is not looking specifically for people who have made films in the past, and a large portion of the applicants who are accepted into the program in any given year are likely to come from law or business, or from other fields that have nothing to do with film. Your portfolio should include creative work that shows you have ideas and an ability to express them. When interviewing applicants, the faculty is not only thinking about finding interesting individuals; they are also thinking about putting together an ensemble. With each class they try to assemble a group of people who not only work well, but who will work well together and will learn from one another. Clearly this is something you can't have any control over in your application, but it might help to suppress any antisocial or sociopathic tendencies you might have.

The school has ample film equipment, including good-quality 16 mm and Super 16 film cameras. More and more student films are being shot on video, and the school has ample equipment for this as well. The school has Avids, Final Cut Pro stations, and ProTools stations for audio work. While the school has mixing facilities, it doesn't have the staff to accommodate all of the students who need sound mixes, so many students pay to have their mixes done outside the school. The school has a huge stock of lighting and grip equipment, including three capacious soundstages and three television studios. It even has a remote television truck.

This is not to say that students have free access to the equipment; this is a large program, so the time students get with this equipment is strictly controlled. The faculty determines how much time each student needs with the equipment based on the size and complexity of their projects. While the time allotted is usually enough, some students wish there were more flexibility.

The school also has a new media lab where students can use a handful of multimedia computers to experiment with programs like Photoshop or Flash. While the school's hope is that students will use the lab to create interactive projects and experiment with new forms of media, so far students mainly use the studio to supplement the old media; they create promotional materials for their films, whip up simple special effects or titles for their films, or create websites to promote their films.

One advantage the school offers is the James Bridges Theater, a large and well-appointed theater that screens a wide variety of films ranging from rare items out of UCLA's large film archive to contemporary films. Students in the middle of editing their films can take a break, go downstairs to the Bridges and watch a movie, and then return to editing.

Probably UCLA's greatest advantage is its location. Because it is near all of the major studios, well-known filmmakers visit UCLA's classes and share their experiences with students regularly. Because it is near Hollywood's equipment rental houses, film processing laboratories, sound mixing houses, and so on, whatever limitations UCLA's facilities have can easily be surmounted. And the sun shines all year round.

During first year, students often find the restrictions on their films frustrating. For example, on the two-minute film you can't shoot for one minute over the allotted four hours, and to many students this seems arbitrary and unfair. Some feel that if they had another fifteen minutes they could get one more crucial shot that would make their films work. But older students, looking back at first year, tend to recognize that the point of these exercises is not to make the best movies possible but to learn how to work as a team and make a film under difficult circumstances. And for that purpose the restrictions placed on the two-minute and six-minute films work exceptionally well.

In the first year, students work together closely and develop a sense of camaraderie. But in second and third year, when the school offers plum awards and fellowships, the competition to get them can turn the first-year friendships a little sour. Students frequently complain of favoritism in the granting of these awards, that every year a small handful of students who have forged friendships with faculty will get both the best assistantships and the largest awards for their films, regardless of the quality of their work.

UCLA works harder than most schools to promote student works. The school holds a widely publicized public screening of student films every year at the Directors Guild Theater, and has an office devoted to putting student works into film festivals around the world. The promotion seems to work better here than at most schools; some of the fourth-year students we spoke with were already getting paid directing jobs while completing their thesis films. But that may have nothing to do with the school's efforts and may just be because by the end of their time here the students are themselves well connected to the industry.

*Some of the worst things about the program:* After an invigorating first year, the program begins to lose some focus in second year, and students can fall into political battles for grants and awards.

*Some of the best things about the program:* By any measure, UCLA is one of the best film schools in the country. But of the most famous film schools, UCLA is the only public university, and is thus by far the least expensive. Situated at the edge of Beverly Hills and only a few minutes away from both Twentieth Century Fox and Sony Pictures, UCLA is closer to the industry than any other school. This makes for great educational opportunities during school as working professionals stop by to teach classes, and often makes for great employment opportunities afterward. The equipment is top-notch, and the school gives out an unusually large amount of money to students to help them make their films every year. Students come out at the end with quite a few films under their belt and often some professional credits to their name. Students have a good track record of finding work in the industry soon after graduation. UCLA's e-mail Listserv is a vital resource for students and alumni; all manner of job postings, internships, events, items for sale, and other opportunities are posted there.

# UNIVERSITY OF IOWA

Department of Cinema & Comparative Literature
E 210 Adler Journalism Building
Iowa City, IA 52242-2004
319-335-0330
www.uiowa.edu/~ccl/mfafilmvideo.shtml

| | |
|---|---|
| Tuition: | Resident: $6,959 |
| Enrollment: | 4 |
| Deadline: | January 15 |
| Focus: | Experimental |

## ▶ THE PROGRAM

The University of Iowa MFA in Film Production has existed since 1994. It is a three-year program designed to prepare students for dual careers in academia and film.

There are some basic requirements, but as in some other experimental programs, the filmmaking is very personal, and students choose classes and a structure that best suits their interests and needs. Many classes are taken with undergraduates. Students generally take three courses, or nine credits, each semester. One of these courses is usually a production course. At least six credits must be taken outside of the department, and students have to write papers about why they chose the outside courses they did and what the experience was like. Nine to twelve advanced production credits, in 16 mm or video, must be taken at some point during the first two years. Film stock is subsidized, but students pay for their own processing. Another required course is Graduate Colloquium, a production workshop for which the topic changes every time it is taught. Past topics have included Collage Films, Portraiture, and Fantasy Writing. Colloquium must be taken twice. Six credits of film theory, five credits of electives, and an advanced production workshop of four credits round out the first two years.

At the end of the second year, during the fourth semester, every student must complete the comprehensive two-part exams. The first part is written. Students work with the production and cinema studies faculty to define a theory area. Each student develops six or seven questions to address in this area. All questions must be approved by the faculty and are then researched by the student. Come exam time, students are given three hours to answer three or four of their questions. If there are any problems with the written exam, students will be asked to follow up with a separate oral presentation about the topic in question. Students also submit a research paper written for any class. The second part of the exam is a one-hour oral review of the student's work in the program thus far. This is presented to the faculty. Students are expected to screen at least two films. Also expected are two short papers associated with these projects. Papers should contextualize the films. As with the written portion, if there are issues, a student is given a second chance to address the subject again, this time in written form. Although it is a possibility, as yet no one has ever completely failed his comprehensive exams. At exam time students also propose their thesis ideas. If approved, semesters five and six of the third year are mostly devoted to thesis projects. Only six additional elective credits are taken over these final two semesters. Once a thesis is completed, students also present a thesis defense to the faculty and the entire student body.

There is no student film festival, but community screenings are held at the end of every semester. A public screening is required of every MFA thesis. Students often join forces to screen together. Outside of the program, many grads are involved with the Iowa City Documentary Film Festival.

▶ **THE PRICE**

| | |
|---|---:|
| $6,959 resident tuition for three years | $20,877 |
| $9,600 per year rent and living expenses for three years | $28,800 |
| Average film costs | $15,000 |
| **Total** | **$64,677** |

The small number of students accepted into the University of Iowa makes it possible for the program to provide each with a strong financial package. Everyone is admitted as a resident and thus pays the lower tuition rate. Each is awarded a teaching or research assistantship. Stipends vary according to the level of assistantship awarded (one-third or one-quarter) and the hours worked, but both come with the lower tuition. A one-third TA position provides a stipend of almost $11,000 for thirty hours of work each week. In the second year one student is given the Iowa Arts Foundation Fellowship. This is a full-tuition award that requires no teaching and comes with an annual stipend of $14,000.

Iowa City is a small college town situated amid the cornfields of the Midwest. The entire town can be biked in less than twenty minutes. The university is so dominant that sometimes it's difficult to determine where the campus ends and the town begins. And like many a college town, the party scene is huge. Although there are several multiplexes and plenty of restaurants and bars, the college is the main source of most activities outside of eating and drinking. This also means that competition for nonuniversity jobs is fierce. The norm for grad students is to stick with the TA positions and take out loans rather than vie with 30,000 undergraduates for outside jobs. There is little film work beyond the local cable channels. Most students live in the city and pay around $500 for a one-bedroom apartment. Grad students tend to prefer living in the historical district on the eastern side of the city and get around via bike or public transportation. However, the weather extremes, stifling hot in the summer and frigid in the winter, can make biking tough at times. While living outside of town is less expensive ($500 for a house!), it makes a car necessary. Locals are not at all jaded, and no one seems to care where you film.

### ▶ THE LOWDOWN

Forty applications are received for Iowa's four openings each year. The admissions committee looks for some film and video experience but is most drawn to students who are interested in the scholarly as well as the artistic aspects of film. Production students will be in theory classes with PhD Cinema Studies students, and the committee wants to be certain that they will be able to hold their own in this environment. Applicants must submit a research paper or another form of scholarly writing along with their statement of purpose and creative portfolio. Although the program professes not to specifically support any one film genre, anyone who indicates an interest in narrative features would not be accepted. Rarely is a student admitted straight from an undergraduate program. Students in their late twenties are more common, and there have even been students in their fifties.

In the first two years, six production courses are required, but the number of films made in each course is up to the individual student. This was as few as six for some students but upward of twenty for others. All films tend to be on the short side (well under five minutes). The program does not specifically consider itself as solely experimental, but there is little support for narrative film. The faculty and most students focus on experimental nonfiction and animation. There is one documentary filmmaker on staff, but even her projects tend to be experimental. The head of the program, Leighton Pierce, is known in the experimental film world, and some students come to specifically study with him. But once here, students are permitted to do whatever they want, and some have pursued the narrative route. Students do work together periodically and will collaborate on ideas, but for the most part everyone works alone on their films. This is not just a result of the program's minimal size but also rather the personal nature of films created at Iowa. Students regularly process films by hand or push into other areas like podcasting or installations. Collage filmmaking and manipulating video or film techniques are standard fare. Any medium is acceptable if you can make a case for it. The program does encourage students to cap their theses at thirty minutes, but this, too, is flexible. One recent student completed a seventy-minute documentary. It is best to think of Iowa as a program of artists simply using film as their medium. Most students intend to move into teaching.

Iowa's intentionally loose structure is not for everyone. It lends itself to remaining at the university beyond three years, with four years being the standard. There are only three full-time professors, yet students report they are surprisingly difficult to connect with in person. This could be because they are working filmmakers or because they seem to adopt a very hands-off approach with students. The most persistent students can establish relationships with the professors, but it takes some effort. Those who do so report that it is well worth the time. Students take a real variety of classes but single out Sound Design and Digital Animation as excellent production choices. Most find the theory classes taken with the PhD students to be very demanding.

There is not an abundance of equipment, and all of it is shared with undergraduates, but no grads seem to find this inconvenient or limiting. With so few students, the demand is light, and because projects are very small in scope, less equipment is needed. Reservations are usually honored, and grad students have flexibility in checkout times. There are a couple of Arriflex SR cameras, some BLs and Ss, lots of Bolexes, and even a few Super 8 cameras. The equipment room staff tries to keep the equipment in good shape, but none of the 16 mm cameras are very well maintained. There is a high-end DV camera, but the Panasonic DVX100, of which there are several, is increasingly popular. Students often wind up purchasing their own video cameras. The sound and lighting packages are acceptable. There is one large soundstage and one smaller shooting studio. Flatbeds and Moviolas are still available for editing, but Final Cut Pro is the mainstay, and there are sixty computer stations equipped with it. There are also six Avid stations and three ProTools suites. All post is accessible 24-7.

The program wants to groom teachers and seems to be successful at it. Ninety percent of Iowa grads enter academia.

*Some of the worst things about the program:* If you are not into shooting in cornfields, you might go a little stir crazy. Iowa is really in the middle of nowhere. Because of its size you won't be exposed to much diversity in terms of classmates or instructors.

*Some of the best things about the program:* The right students will find the freedom liberating. If you are interested in teaching, your prospects are very good upon graduation.

# UNIVERSITY OF MIAMI

School of Communication
P.O. Box 248127
Coral Gables, FL 33124-8127
305-284-2265
http://com.miami.edu/graduate/
   mfamotionpicturesproduction.htm

| | |
|---|---|
| Tuition: | $26,880 |
| Enrollment: | 23 |
| Deadline: | March 1 |
| Focus: | Independent |

## ▶ THE PROGRAM

The University of Miami has offered undergraduate courses
in film for decades. The MFA has existed only since the
early nineties, and the two-year program is divided into
three areas of specialization: production, producing, and
screenwriting. Twenty-three students are admitted into the
program annually: ten students total in screenwriting and
producing, and thirteen enrolled in production.

Incoming students who do not already have experience with 16 mm film or Avid editing are required to pay
extra to attend the school's intensive Summer Motion
Picture Production Institute prior to the first year. This
session runs for five weeks and offers six undergraduate
courses. The institute is a crash course in 16 mm film
production and digital post. Students make several short
sync-sound films and cinematic exercises. Generally
about half of all incoming students have to go through
this summer session. Students may skip the summer institute if they can demonstrate a proficiency in 16 mm
production.

Film studies, screenwriting, producing, and production students all share the first-year curriculum, which con-

sists of standard foundation courses. The program is front-end loaded with four classes in the first two semesters and three in the last two. In the first year, students take Cinematography I and II, Film Culture I and II, Postproduction, Directing, Writing the Short Film, and an elective. The Directing course deals more with film composition than working with actors. Each student makes one 16 mm film in the cinematography course and completes it in the editing course.

Second year, in addition to a thesis, requires at least one more film studies class and Production Management. Nine elective credits can be taken in any area. Any student who intends to direct a narrative film must take Acting for the Camera as one of these electives. Students try to shoot their thesis films in the fall and edit in the spring. The last semester is thesis post and elective or independent study credits.

The program pays for some film and processing and tape stock. Students can add to this, but "less is more" is the motto around here. The school contributes $3,000 toward each thesis film.

▶ **THE PRICE**

| | |
|---|---|
| $26,880 tuition for two years | $53,760 |
| $1,000 per year rent and living expenses for two years | $2,000 |
| $1,500 car insurance and maintenance for two years | $3,000 |
| Average film costs | $15,000 |
| **Total** | **$73,760** |

Some graduate assistantships are available to second-year students. These provide 50 percent tuition remission and a stipend of $3,750 for half-grad assistantships. In return, GAs assist professors in the classroom for eight hours a week. Almost everyone who applies gets at least a quarter assistantship.

Every spring, the head of the program, Paul Lazarus, takes twenty students to Los Angeles for a six-credit course taught at, but not by, UCLA. The three-week course serves as an introduction to the film industry. Students tour studios and attend lectures by industry professionals, many of whom are also University of Miami alumni. There is also a large alumni reception for networking.

The Canes Festival is a three-day event that screens both grad and undergrad films. The best of this fest are also screened in Los Angeles at Paramount Studios. The city of Miami hosts its own International Film Festival, and there are also two shorts fests in Miami and Fort Lauderdale.

The university is just twelve miles from the beach. Coral Gables is to Miami as Beverly Hills is to Los Angeles: posh houses, perfect lawns, and a bit of a Stepford attitude. One student suspects that everyone uses the same lawn service. It is predominantly a residential area, so a car is necessary, even for those who choose to live on campus if they want to have any sort of social life. Public transportation is weak at best. It is more difficult to film in Coral Gables than Miami as the city is more restrictive. But outside of Coral Gables, Florida has amazing locations. From tropical islands in the Caribbean to vibrant urban locations in the Cuban part of town; from stunning underwater spots in the Keys to scenes of Old South urbanity up around Pensacola. All this and great weather for shooting all year round—except, of course, during hurricane season. There is a very active nightlife center in the clubs in Miami Beach.

Many students choose to live in South Miami, which is less expensive. A one-bedroom apartment here will run about $700 compared to $1,000 in Coral Gables. Of course, the farther one moves from Coral Gables, the more Latino the neighborhoods, and language becomes an issue. Spanish is spoken in 53 percent of the homes in South Florida. Yes, it's possible to get by not speaking any

Spanish at all, but life is significantly easier for the bilingual. South Florida is home to lots of commercial production.

Students can work part-time after the first semester. Jobs do exist within the university, but just as many work outside of it in retail or restaurants. There are some production jobs, mostly in post.

▶ **THE LOWDOWN**

About ninety students apply for the production program each year with another twenty applying for screenwriting or producing. The admissions board looks for GRE scores of 1,000 and a 3.0 GPA. As with most schools, there are letters of recommendation and an essay, but no portfolio requirement. They seek people who are good students from good schools, but they also want artists who have something to say. So, while they look at GPAs and GREs, they put more emphasis on the written materials. About half of the applicants are straight from undergraduate programs.

Paul Lazarus believes it is imperative to have a solid grasp of what has transpired in film for the last one hundred years, so film history, theory, and analysis are some of the most valued components of the curriculum. This is not an auteur program. Film is taught as a collaborative process, very much in line with the philosophy of the president of the university, who is pushing for greater interdisciplinary activity between programs. The positive end result for film students are fruitful collaborations with other students in various disciplines.

Most students, including directors, choose to master a secondary bread-and-butter skill like sound or editing. These jobs are the most plentiful in Miami's commercial sector should a student elect to stay after graduation.

Students find sharing equipment with undergrads to be a constant source of frustration. The reservation system is flawed, so reserving equipment does not necessarily mean it will be there when you show up to check out. The program has been slow to embrace video. There are Bolexes, a few Arriflex BLs, CP-16s and a lone, overly used Arriflex SR—aka the "good camera"—that all grad students share. This has led to more students shifting over to the newer Sony PD150s, Panasonic DVX100s and HDV cameras. About half of all thesis projects are now shot on video.

Postproduction fares better, thanks to the program's four new Avid Nitrous systems, Avid Express, and one ProTools station. Editing time is limited to the hours between 9:00 a.m. and 9:00 p.m. Many students resort to purchasing their own computers to edit. The program is in the process of updating their ProTools lab. There is a soundstage.

Faculty runs the gamut. Students complain that some just collect a paycheck, while admitting that others are truly committed and helpful. The cinematography instructor is a very active DP locally, and there's an award-winning documentary filmmaker. The directing instructor is theater-trained but has no film experience. Students are unhappy that they do not get to work with actors in his class. There is real enthusiasm for the new sound instructor and the postproduction design expertise he brings to the table.

Miami just welcomed a new dean into the school. This is always guaranteed to instigate changes, and Sam Grogg, who comes from AFI, is a Hollywood transplant with strong credentials. He himself is now teaching writing and producing. There is a sense among students that good things are on the horizon.

**Some of the worst things about the program:** For a program that feels strongly enough about film to provide 16 mm stock and processing, there should be more than one camera students trust.

*Some of the best things about the program:* There are some really committed instructors and a fair amount of flexibility in courses. Students are groomed to think independently and are not beholden to any Hollywood formula. They have ample opportunity to master secondary skills. The great locale for shooting shouldn't be discounted. No one will be looking at a Snow Shoveler credit in these parts.

# UNIVERSITY OF NEW ORLEANS

Department of Film, Theatre, and Communication Arts
2000 Lakeshore Drive, PAC 307
New Orleans, LA 70148-3520
504-280-6317
http://ftca.uno.edu

| | |
|---|---|
| Tuition: | Resident: $3,292 |
| | Nonresident: $10,336 |
| Enrollment: | 40 total |
| Deadline: | July 1; November 1 |
| Focus: | Independent |

## ▶ THE PROGRAM

For over thirty years the University of New Orleans has been graduating MFA students with film degrees. But business as usual was significantly altered in 2005 with the arrival of Hurricane Katrina. As with the rest of New Orleans, this university is very much still living in the aftermath. Although the school was mercifully spared from the hurricane's wrath (in terms of facilities and equipment damage), the program has been impacted in other ways. Many students withdrew after the hurricane and have not returned. There has also been a substantial decrease in the number of new applicants. Thus, the program's size has shrunk considerably. It is entirely possible that it will take several years before it completely rebounds and again achieves its desired numbers. Despite this fact, the faculty remains committed to students and returning to pre-Katrina normalcy. Students who are willing to live in some chaos outside of the campus will find that within its walls, the Department of Film, Theatre, and Communication Arts is functioning and back in the business of instructing filmmakers.

UNO is a three-year program of sixty credits. Two of those years are course work; the third year is mainly for thesis production. At this point there is no deadline that mandates acquiring a degree within a certain length of time, so students can hang on for years. Enrollment is carefully monitored to achieve a total program size of forty students. This means that the number of new students admitted is in direct correlation to the number of students who graduate each year.

During the first semester, students who are accepted without any production experience are asked to simultaneously audit an entry-level undergraduate film production course, Introduction to Cinema Techniques, along with their other classes. In this course they learn all basic production techniques that will bring them up to speed for Intermediate Film Production, the graduate-level 16 mm course they take at the same time. The program provides four hundred feet of film stock for Intermediate Film, but students pay for processing. The film allotment must be adhered to. In this course all projects are only taken to the dailies stage; that is, processed but not edited. UNO has a very strong connection with the drama program that it grew out of. This has resulted in a series of required courses shared between the film and theater students. The first of these, taken this semester, is Performance and Direction, which allows students from each major to understand more about the other's craft by learning from their perspective. The last fall semester course is one in basic Digital Theory.

During the spring the incomplete Intermediate Production projects are finished in Post Production, the course where everyone receives their hands-on editing and sound-mixing training. Films average three to four minutes in length. There's a basic survey course in Film Criticism. Theater and film majors reunite for the dramatic writing course, Concept, Conflict and Character. Students can take one elective course. At the end of the spring semester, students screen their 16 mm film for the faculty. This project determines whether or not students will be invited to continue in the program. Those who are invited are appointed a graduate committee comprised of three faculty members who will continue to advise and supervise them during the remainder of the program.

In the fall of the second year, students go through comprehensive examinations. The comps are a big deal—a five-hour written examination that tests everything students should have mastered thus far. One week later, students must also give a one-hour oral defense of the written exam in front of their committee. It is only after students have passed the comp exams that they are considered candidates for the MFA degree, and they are green-lighted to develop a thesis. The committee chair will assist in this process and report back to the other committee members.

The fall is also when students take Development of Cinema (a basic history course) and two electives. If required, they audit Beginning Screenwriting. Finally, students preproduce their second-year films in the media development and planning course in the fall and then produce them in the advanced media project class during the spring. The spring wraps ups with Advanced Screenwriting and Form and Ideas in Media, the third of the joint courses taken by all theater and film MFAs.

Theses are preproduced in the fall of the third year in Studio Thesis I and completed in the spring in Studio Thesis II. During this time, students will take a graduate seminar in film, for which topics rotate, and three elective courses.

All told, each student makes a minimum of three films, including the thesis. However, students can retake upper-level production classes for elective credits as often as they want and make even more films if they desire. Most do. In addition to making their own films, they also crew for each other. Finally, every spring offers the chance to work on "the spring film." A $10,000 budget is provided to shoot for ten days over spring break. Usually this is a twenty- to thirty-minute narrative piece that is faculty produced and directed, but there have been occasions when a feature has been tackled. And recently three short student-directed Katrina films were shot. Whatever the length or subject matter, a crew comprised of advanced undergrads and grad students work side by side with their instructors on these films.

Katrina did have some unexpectedly positive effects on the program. Software manufacturers Final Draft and Movie Magic provided dozens of free installations of their screenwriting and budgetry software. The Silver Docs Festival offered to fly a student filmmaker to the fest. And finally, while other universities opened their doors to accept UNO students, the VP of the American Film Institute, Jonathan Estrin, initiated a partnership to help those who remained. This eventually evolved into an AFI pilot program that sent AFI faculty and artists in residence to UNO for two days of workshops. The experience was apparently positive for both schools, and UNO hopes some sort of permanent partnership may continue in the future.

There is a media showcase for the entire department every spring, but no specific end-of-year film festival exists other than those organized by students. Students can enter the Louisiana category of the New Orleans Film Festival, which takes place each October.

## ▶ THE PRICE

| | |
|---|---:|
| $10,336 nonresident tuition for one year | $10,336 |
| $3,292 resident tuition for two years | $6,584 |
| $9,600 per year rent and living expenses for three years | $28,800 |
| Average film costs | $8,000 |
| **Total** | **$53,720** |

Residents can shave $7,000 off that price tag. It is very easy to become a resident of Louisiana. Registering to vote or obtaining a Louisiana driver's license in your first twelve months should do the trick. Ideally you will take on a part-time job and pay some taxes. Becoming a resident will save $14,000 in tuition.

Typically, UNO film department scholarships amount to only a few hundred dollars each. But let's face it: this program costs less for three years than one year at many other institutions. And film students have had some success in winning the larger university-wide scholarships in the past. If you need the free ride, apply for one of the nine graduate assistantships available starting in second year and lasting through third year. The faculty awards these in second year because the university requires that instructors have eighteen hours of study before they are allowed to teach, the primary service performed by GAs. Film department GA positions provide full tuition and a $4,000 annual stipend. Typically, this funding will last for two years so that it does not impede academic progress for those who linger beyond three years. But if you need the extra time after you have completed all of your courses, you need only to register for one credit to continue to have access to all the facilities and equipment. There are also assistantships available in the various administrative offices on campus.

Living is inexpensive in New Orleans . . . or at least it was before Katrina. Housing is more difficult to find these days, and the prices have increased. What cost $400 prior to the floods is closer to $700 these days. These prices may drop as more housing becomes available, but it's difficult to say. UNO is a commuter school, and some of the areas that were most attractive to college students, like Lake View, no longer exist. Many faculty and students still live in trailers. And sadly, many available trailers lie empty due to governmental redtape. Luckier students have moved uptown into more gentrified, albeit costly, areas. This is a city completely in flux. It rebounds with each passing day, and the die-hard students who have remained still love the town. If you can look past the reconstruction and lack of services, the amazing music and food and the unbelievable resiliency and spirit of the locals make New Orleans unique among American cities. There are millions of stories waiting to be told, and who better positioned to tell them than filmmakers at UNO?

## ▶ THE LOWDOWN

UNO used to get about fifty-five applications annually. In any given year about a quarter of those were accepted, again based upon the total number of students. It's difficult now to project how many will apply or how many of those who left will return. For the near future the class size is up in the air.

The admissions staff intends to continue to search for the strongest candidates, but they have slightly changed their priorities. Competency in film used to reign over all other criteria. The new school of thought is that technical skills can be taught in the audited courses. In fact, reviewers believe that undergrad film majors are often simply technicians with little to express. An undergrad degree certainly won't prevent your acceptance, but reviewers prefer good students who are eager to learn and demonstrate some sort of artistic proficiency. A high GRE and GPA might not make you the best filmmaker, but they are heavily weighted because committee members feel they are indicative of what kind of student you will be. Remember, it takes a good student to pass the second-year comps in order to even continue in the program. Along the same line, the statement of purpose is carefully reviewed. For UNO, a command of written language that gives insight into your creative side and demonstrates your ability to articulate your ideas seems to have a correlation to those who can be good filmmakers.

The affordable tuition at the University of New Orleans attracts applicants who are budget-conscious. Students tend to make smaller, economical films. Documentaries are welcome, but this is a film program that has always been associated with a drama program and narrative work. The small size fosters a fun, tight-knit group of people.

Considering that the program operates on a minuscule budget, the equipment, which is shared with undergrads, is good. Students will work with one of a few CP-16 cameras or the souped-up Arri SR loaded with accessories including video tap and excellent prime lenses. There are plenty of standard and 24p digital video cameras to go around. There is a noncredit summer workshop to train students to use the Steadicam. The lights and sound packages are up-to-date and plentiful, and there's a grip truck available to transport them. Students can film on one of two nice-sized soundstages—if they can sneak in between the features that regularly book them. New Orleans recently changed its tax code, and feature film production is up these days. Through the NIMS Center Studios in New Orleans, the university has a feature film intern placement service to assist with the process. NIMS is also putting the finishing touches on its high-definition postproduction facility to attract postproduction work to the area.

Thirty computer stations are available for editing, and all of the computers are connected to a central server, so students can work at any station and need never carry around media. There's also a post suite with seven Avid stations and a finishing room with Avid Adrenaline. There is an audio finishing suite, and a whisper room for voice-overs and ADR.

The few of full-time faculty care about students but are a bit stretched. This leads them to be fairly strategic when working with students. Instructors are not directly connected to the current film industry, so there is little help they can provide you upon graduation.

Students are very pleased with the technical classes and the structure of the program. Perhaps it's the Southern effect, but it's not nearly as demanding or fast-paced a program as some schools. The one group project, "the spring film," is optional, and everyone is excited to be a part of it. Screenwriting is the weakest area in that there's just not enough of it.

*Some of the worst things about the program:* The faculty is overtaxed, so they are not always available. They can be so hands-off that students really are on their own. Hurricane Katrina has complicated things.

*Some of the best things about the program:* The price. The equipment is available whenever you need it. If you want to make a lot of films but are on a tight budget, UNO is worth a look.

# UNIVERSITY OF SOUTHERN CALIFORNIA

USC School of Cinematic Arts
University Park, LUC-404
Los Angeles, CA 90089-2211
213-740-3317
www-cntv.usc.edu

| | |
|---|---|
| Tuition: | $33,836 |
| Enrollment: | 50 per semester; 100 per year |
| Deadline: | Fall: November 15 |
| | Spring: September 1 |
| Focus: | Industry |

## ▶ THE PROGRAM

Founded in 1929, USC's is the oldest film school in the country, and is probably the most famous film school in the world. With well-known alumni like George Lucas and Robert Zemeckis to its name, people who know nothing else about film or film education will often tell you that USC has the best film school. And on this assumption, many people who want to go to film school apply only to USC, including countless people who really don't belong there.

One striking thing, if you spend much time in Los Angeles, is how many people you meet who went to USC as undergraduates purely because they wanted to get into the film program. Almost all of them discovered that they could not get into the film program and had to graduate in something else. It sometimes seems like USC only has students in its other departments because all the undergrads are killing time, taking political science classes or history classes while waiting to get into the film program.

USC's film program is a large and bustling school, with numerous experienced professors and vast facilities and stocks of equipment. It is a good place to learn about the technology and the business of film. And the size of the program allows students the freedom to go in many different directions as they learn about the medium. But it is not for everyone. It is heavily geared toward Hollywood-style filmmaking and focuses far more on getting jobs—on technical training and on pitching ideas to agents and studio executives—than it does on actually writing and directing compelling films.

The program offers MFA degrees in Animation, Interactive Media, Screenwriting, Producing, and Film and Television Production. (Note that Producing and Production, though they sound alike, are very different programs. *Producing* refers to the tasks typically done by a producer, of funding and organizing the making of films, where *production* refers to the technical aspects of shooting films.) Animation and Interactive Media are outside our scope for this edition; we'll focus on the latter three programs.

### Film and Television Production

This is the program most people want to get into, where George Lucas learned to make movies. While fifty new students enter in both fall and spring semesters, we'll trace the program for someone entering in the fall semester.

At the beginning of first year, the fifty incoming MFA Production students go through a week of orientation. One part of this orientation is the official lowering of expectations; a professor gets up in front of the entering class and tells them that the film industry is a great industry to be in but that few if any of the students in front of him will ever get in. There follows a lecture asking students to be realistic about what to expect of USC and what will happen after graduation.

The main class first semester is Directing I, or 507. (Most students refer to their classes by course number instead of name.) For the first twelve weeks of the program, each student writes and directs four short films. These films are shot on digital video, on Sony DV cameras; they tend to be simple, little more than sketches, but they have to tell a story, and do so visually, with a minimum of dialogue. The first exercise cannot have any dialogue; the second can have one word; the third can have one sentence; the fourth can have an exchange. On these projects, students break apart into groups of three and shoot a film each week, with each member serving as writer/director on one, cinematographer on one, and editor on one. Toward the end of the semester, after everyone has made four exercises, students make what is called the "group project." All students submit short scripts, and three are chosen by the faculty to be made as group projects. Students then pitch themselves to be producer, director, cinematographer, editor, and so on, for one of the films. These films are also shot on video and are not terribly complex productions, but they give students their first taste of what it is like to work collaboratively on a larger crew.

Also included in 507 are classes on working with actors. And a recent addition to 507 is safety seminars. There have been issues in the past where students were pushing themselves and their crews so hard that exhaustion and sleep deprivation became a real problem. This was thought to have contributed to a few traffic accidents involving film students. So the school now provides specific instruction in managing the stress and balancing production deadlines against safety. (This is not just a USC problem; it's as much an issue in the industry as a whole; see Haskell Wexler's documentary, *Who Needs Sleep?* [2006], for more on this very subject.)

Apart from 507, students only take two other courses in first semester: a writing course where they work on screenplays for short films, and a course called Concepts of Cinematic Production, where professionals of various positions—producers, editors, assistant directors, and so on—talk about their jobs. At the end of the semester students screen their 507 films and, based on these films, decide who to pair up with for the 508s.

In the second semester there is a class in screenwriting, and students take classes in film history and criticism. But the semester is dominated by 508, where each student makes a film no more than five-and-a-half minutes long. Working in pairs, for the first half of the semester one student writes and directs a film while the other produces, shoots, and edits. The 508s are shot over the course of four weekends; students screen their rushes for the class each Wednesday, with professors and classmates critiquing the footage and offering advice. After four weeks, these films are shot and mostly edited; at that point the pairs swap positions for the second film, with the second student in each pair writing and directing and the first producing, shooting, and editing. Late in the semester the students are allowed one additional weekend to shoot any pickup shots they may need to complete their films in one additional weekend. These films are shot on 16 mm film, on Korean War–era Arriflex S cameras; sync sound is not allowed, but students are encouraged to work hard on the sound design of these films in postproduction. The school provides 1,100 feet (about thirty minutes) of film for each project. The school pays for the telecine to convert the film to video, and students edit in a big room where the school has set up eigtheen Avid editing stations. Once the picture is locked, it is the director's job to do the sound design. The school provides ProTools sound editing systems for this.

Students say 508 is where you first start to get a real sense of what USC is about. On the 507 exercises students can do whatever they want, but the 508s have strict rules and limitations on them—and the critiques offered by professors and classmates can be harsh and often cause filmmakers to change their films in ways they do not necessarily like. The 508s give students their first real taste of compromise.

In the summer after first year, some students work as crew on thesis films to get experience, some work jobs to try to pay the bills. Many take classes during the summer semester; there are a lot of credit requirements for graduation, and it is hard to fulfill them all in second and third years while also making films. So many students, in an attempt to complete all the requirements within three years, fulfill some of these requirements in summer school.

In the first semester of second year, students take 532, Intermediate Directing, which is a prerequisite for 546, which is in a way the holy grail that all students hope to reach at USC. In 546, seven films are made by students and paid for by the school. At the end of each semester, students submit twelve-page scripts to be considered for the next semester's 546 class. Out of fifty or sixty submissions, four narrative projects are chosen by faculty to be produced (plus three documentaries, discussed below). For the most part, the writers of these projects do not get to direct them; other students group together in director-producer teams and pitch to shoot the projects. A team is chosen by faculty to make each project, and the remaining students then pitch themselves as crew members to the chosen directors and producers. As with the earlier courses, production on the narratives takes place on weekends, and dailies are screened and critiqued the following week. These films are shot on film, with sync sound recorded separately, so editors on these projects have to sync up the sound with the dailies before the screenings. Crew members in other positions meet in separate classes; all the production designers meet in one class, all the editors in another, etc. The school provides equipment, film stock, processing, and a few thousand dollars in funds. Each of the crew members generally pitches in a few hundred dollars toward a slush fund to cover anything not covered by the school's funds.

Three proposed twenty-six-minute documentaries are also chosen each semester for 546. These are submitted by students who have taken the prerequisite documentary prep class, Planning the Production. Because these films are documentary, because they are shot on digital video, and because of the prerequisite to submitting, the competition is less fierce for these, with fewer proposed documentary projects and fewer people interested in working on them. USC is not really known as a documentary program; few students come here specifically to study it, and some only go into documentary out of frustration when they aren't chosen to direct a narrative 546. But once students begin studying documentary, USC seems to prepare them rather well. At the end of the semester, a screening of the 546s is held; one night for the narratives, and one night for the documentaries.

Occasionally a student chosen to direct a 546 will decide to make that her thesis film, but for most students the restrictions on it—limited funds, limited length, compulsory use of a largely inexperienced crew—are too great to make it a suitable résumé piece. USC students expect their thesis films to be technically impressive, to show everything they can do in one solid piece. So, regardless of the 546, most students look ahead to third year and the thesis production classes, 581 and 582. But first there are all these academic requirements to take care of.

While at many film schools classes end after second year, at USC students seem to take even more classes in third year. Students have a lot of requirements to fulfill, many of them not really seeming to merit requirement status; ten units of critical studies courses seems a little extreme for a production program. A course in multi-camera TV setups seems like a great idea for an elective but seems odd as a requirement. And nobody seems sure why the nebulous Visual Expressions is a requirement. Regardless, students spend most of third year and often some of a fourth year fulfilling all of these course requirements. After all this time and all these classes, some students decide not to make a thesis film, and instead just write a screenplay as a thesis. But some are determined to come out with a highly polished thesis film, and for them there are three semesters of thesis classes.

The thesis begins with 551, Planning the Advanced Production, a preproduction course where students write and rewrite their screenplays under faculty tutelage, prepare budgets and schedules, and put together their production teams. The next semester is 581, where students go into production, followed by 582, where they complete their postproduction. Perhaps because there are so many alternatives to making a thesis film, the people who decide to make thesis films go all out. But the school puts a number of restrictions even on these films. For instance, 581s can be no longer than sixteen minutes. And as with all student projects, the school claims the copyright on the finished films. So even a student who spends tens of thousands of dollars of his own money on his 581 does not own the film and has to get approval from the school for public screenings.

The one exception is films made in course 586. Unlike the 581s, 586 films are free from restrictions. A student who makes a film in 586 can make it any length, and on any subject, and can spend any amount of money on it. And when it's finished, the filmmaker will own the copyright on the film. The catch is, in 586 the student is not allowed to use any of the school's equipment or facilities. Without school equipment and assistance, you might expect these films to be kind of stripped down. But in fact, 586s tend to be the most extravagant, expensive films that come out of USC; 586 is where students go when they want to show off and don't want professors telling them to scale it down. It is not unheard of for students to spend $100,000 on a single film.

At the end of each year USC holds its annual First Look festival to highlight student works. The school makes a big show of inviting producers and agents from the industry to come see the best of the school's student films. A few interns and low-level employees might show up to take a look, but little comes of it. The festival is mostly for the benefit of students and their families.

The school has an Office of Student-Industry Relations dedicated to advising students and helping them find internships and jobs in the industry. The office also organizes the annual First Look festival. And because the school owns the copyright on all student-produced works, the office handles any outside screenings of films, such as at film festivals or on television.

## Screenwriting

USC's screenwriting MFA can be seen as a less-expensive alternative to the Production program. It provides an in-depth focus on screenwriting plus a lot of the benefits of the Production program, but with a commitment of only two years. As we noted above, many people in the Directing program, once they are in it, decide not to make a thesis film and instead write a feature-length screenplay to quickly fulfill their thesis requirement and graduate. But with all of the course requirements in the directing MFA, they still spend at least three years, often more, completing the program. So if screenwriting is your interest, or if you are already making films in the real world and don't need the intensive technical instruction, you might give this program a serious look.

The program admits thirty students per year. In the first semester these students learn the basics of screenwriting, work on an outline for a feature, and also write screenplays for short films. They also take a class in acting and directing actors, and they even make films; screenwriters take the 507 course just like the production students, where they make the same four exercise videos and group exercise. The screenwriting students do not take this class with the production students—there is little communication between the divisions—but they do take it with the students from the Peter Stark Producing program, which makes for a nice opportunity for screenwriters to network and establish relationships with tomorrow's producers.

In the second semester students work on feature-length screenplays, either using the outlines from first semester or starting new ones from scratch. They also take courses in film editing and script analysis, and they learn to write in other genres, such as one-hour dramas or situation comedies for TV.

There are no classes to take in the summer after first year; students are just asked to come up with ideas for thesis screenplays to write in second year. At the beginning of second year the students pitch their thesis ideas to the class, and the faculty and other students give feedback on which they think are the most worthy of writing. Each student then chooses a project to write as a thesis screenplay. The rest of the year is spent writing this screenplay.

In order to complete the MFA, students have to fulfill fifty-six units, which is a lot for two years, especially considering that there aren't that many screenwriting classes to take. In the second year, students find themselves looking around for classes to take to fill the requirements. While many would like to take classes in production or in more technical aspects of filmmaking, most of those classes are reserved for students in the Production program and are not open to screenwriters. So screenwriters find themselves loading up on critical studies courses that don't necessarily interest them much. This is a cause of some resentment among the screenwriting students; at $1,000 a credit for ten required credits of critical studies courses, they are paying $10,000 to watch movies they could rent from Blockbuster.

At the end of second year, students turn in their screenplays, and the faculty read them. Most students pass and graduate at that time; a few students are asked to do one more rewrite over the summer before they can graduate.

The school doesn't do much to promote the screen-writing students. Students have taken it upon themselves to publish an annual booklet called *First Pitch*, in which they include pitches for their screenplays, and send it out to industry professionals. They also hold mixers where students in the various departments can meet. While the Stark and Production departments often host lectures by visiting filmmakers, the screenwriting program rarely sees visits by A-list screenwriters; students have taken it upon themselves to fill this gap and organize occasional lectures by working screenwriters.

But for all that, students seem fairly positive about the program. One thing to be aware of, though, is that the Screenwriting program does not require past writing experience in its students. The teaching starts from scratch, which is great for new screenwriters, but students who come in having already written screenplays or made short films often find the entire first year frustratingly basic.

## The Peter Stark Producing Program

The Stark program is a two-year MFA program that is designed to not only teach students what they need to know to launch careers as producers in Hollywood but to seamlessly move them out of school and into those careers. Each year the program admits twenty-five new students. These people often have no experience in film; sometimes they have little knowledge of film. But they share the aggressive, hypersocial personality of a producer.

Appropriately, the first thing new students do upon arrival at the Stark program is go to a cocktail party; the new students join the previous year's students, now entering their second year, for an evening of liquor-lubricated meeting and schmoozing. The next day classes begin. In the first week of classes the students watch short films made by the previous year's producing students in their 507 class. And they begin an intensive load of courses that teach a wide range of film-related subjects. In the first semester, while the students take courses in legal and organizational aspects of producing, they also take a course in film history, and in 507 they make short films with the screenwriting students. In the second semester, the producing students make films. They form into four-person groups and take turns as writer, director, cinematographer, and editor. Shot on 16 mm film and edited on Avid, these films generally run around eight minutes. Meanwhile the classes in producing get pretty wonky; they delve into entertainment law and into the minutia of the complex business deals that determine how films are made and distributed, and how the various participants profit from them.

In the summer after first year, all of the Stark students are placed in summer internships at studios or production companies in Hollywood. These internships tend to be much better than the typical Hollywood internship—students are placed with high-ranking studio executives and producers and are often given tasks that have some importance—and students speak highly of the experience. The program actually encourages students to turn these internships into real jobs; all classes in the second and final year of the program are held in the evening, so many students are able to work day jobs while completing the program.

In the second year, students continue on with their course work and also work on their thesis projects. The thesis generally consists of a full production package: a shooting screenplay, plus contracts and legal agreements, production schedules, and business plans. The expectation is that students will see these projects through to completion once they are out of USC.

Students and graduates speak highly of the program. Unlike the vast majority of film programs, as much effort goes into getting students into careers after school as goes into teaching them how to produce. Starkies permeate Hollywood, so to come out of the Stark program puts you in a club that provides entry at all levels of the film industry. Virtually every studio and production company has a few Starkies on staff.

Certainly the Stark program is not for everyone. But for those who are by nature suited to producing and who are driven to make their way in that field, there are few better ways to start.

### ▶ THE PRICE

| | |
|---|---:|
| $33,836 tuition for three years | $101,508 |
| $20,000 per year rent and living expenses for four years | $80,000 |
| $2,000 per year maintenance and insurance on a car for four years | $8,000 |
| Average film costs for directors | $20,000 |
| **Total** | **$209,508** |

You can save money in the usual ways; get out promptly in three years, don't make a big, expensive thesis film, shoot your thesis on DV instead of film; make it a documentary instead of a narrative. But it's a private school in a big city, so it's going to be expensive, no matter what.

Note that the Stark and Screenwriting programs are two-year programs with no thesis films, so attending one of them instead of the Production program costs about $97,000 less. For many people this is a pretty good deal; you probably get about 80 percent of the benefit of attending Production—the contacts, the experience, the degree, and the USC name—but in half the time and at half the cost.

Few students live near the university, which is in an unpleasant part of town. Most live a few miles north of the school, in the happening Los Feliz and Silverlake neighborhoods, or west along the 10 freeway, in West L.A. or Santa Monica. One-bedroom apartments can generally be found for around $1,000 to $1,200 a month. Needless to say, when you live in Los Angeles, and especially when you live ten or fifteen miles from school, a car is necessary.

## ▶ THE LOWDOWN

The application process is pretty straightforward: a personal statement, two writing samples, a portfolio list where you describe your major creative works in chronological order. If the school is interested in you they may ask you to send copies of some of the works you list here. Sometimes students will be interviewed by faculty, but this won't happen to everyone.

Overall, the Film and Television Production program is a jumble of sometimes conflicting intentions. The elements of the program the school boasts about the most are not really its strongest points, and there are things it is very good at that people often don't learn about until they arrive.

Most people who do Production at USC have dreams of being the next George Lucas, of being a filmmaker both visionary and successful. But the faculty seem to see the program as more of a trade school, whose intention is to give students specific skills—editor, cinematographer, sound designer—that they can use to get jobs in the industry. Many students realize somewhere along the way that the thesis is not really necessary to this and leave the program without making a thesis film, many without even graduating. The narrative thesis films that are made at USC tend to reflect the school's priorities; they tend to be technically flawless, with beautiful cinematography, editing, and sound design, but at the same time they tend to be a bit soulless, the works of well-trained technicians who want to show off all they can do but don't necessarily have a lot to say. Often students find ways to cram three or four different stories, in three or four different genres, into a single short film—the clear point being to demonstrate the filmmakers' range as technicians to people who might give them jobs, not to show their ability to write and direct compelling original stories for the screen.

So while the school does not really advertise itself as a place to study specific technical fields like cinematography or editing or sound design alone, it is the people who choose to focus on technical skills who probably get the most out of the program and who are most likely to forge careers for themselves in the years after graduation. And while the school does not advertise itself as a documentary program, students tell us the young working professionals who teach documentary are often better teachers than some of the older career professors on the narrative faculty. And it is true that the documentary filmmakers coming out of USC these days are quite good: Jeffrey Blitz, the director of the Academy Award–nominated documentary *Spellbound* (2002) is a USC graduate, as is George Hickenlooper, director of *The Mayor of Sunset Strip* (2003) and *Hearts of Darkness* (1991). But on the narrative side, USC Film and Television Production students primarily learn to be highly adept with the equipment, how to get along in the industry, how to pitch, how to schmooze, how to take meetings, and how to negotiate deals. The one thing that most students don't seem to get out of the Production program is a strong ability to tell compelling stories in the visual medium.

*Some of the worst things about the program:* The school's focus is on technical training and preparation for working within the industry. As such, students in the writing, producing, and directing specializations spend far more time learning how to compromise their ideas in order to appeal to the

UNIVERSITY OF SOUTHERN CALIFORNIA

tastes of other people than they spend learning to have strong personal voices and clear visions to express in the medium of motion pictures. This is a program about the technology and business of film; any art that happens is usually incidental.

**Some of the best things about the program:** The USC name is probably the best thing. Whatever the reality, the popular conception is that USC is the best film school in the country, and if you tell people you studied film there, they will generally be impressed. Because it's such a large program and has been around for so long, there are countless USC graduates in all levels and all aspects of the industry. This makes networking and taking meetings easy, as virtually any company you go to will have a few people around with whom you can compare notes on USC. USC does a good job of preparing students to make their way in Hollywood. The technical training is top-notch; if you want to be a sound mixer, an editor, or a cinematographer, no school will give you better training or access to better facilities. And a strong case can be made for it as a top-notch documentary program.

# UNIVERSITY OF TEXAS AT AUSTIN

Department of Radio-Television-Film
1 University Station A0800
Austin, TX 78712-0108
512-471-4071
http://rtf.utexas.edu

| Tuition: | Resident: $4,826 |
| --- | --- |
| | Nonresident: $10,968 |
| Enrollment: | 12 directors |
| | 7 screenwriters |
| Deadline: | December 1 |
| Focus: | Independent/documentary |

## ► THE PROGRAM

The University of Texas at Austin offers MFA degrees in screenwriting and film production. The screenwriting program is a two-year program devoted to writing narratives for television and feature-length film. The film production program is a three-year program where students learn through constant hands-on experience with film and video equipment. The screenwriting program admits seven students per year; the directing program admits twelve. It is a small graduate program in a large university, which provides the best of both worlds: the intimacy of a small school and the enormous resources and social life of a large one. In the past few years UT has brought in a number of new faculty members, many of whom specialize in documentary, and a large amount of new digital video equipment has been added, bolstering its position as one of the leading documentary programs in the country. The school tries to ensure that graduate students get a well-rounded education by requiring them to take courses outside of the film department. Students are not only required to take a number of electives, they are actually required to declare a minor in another field of study.

The first year begins with documentary. Students learn documentary technique and, as exercises, make short documentary videos about one another. This serves the dual purposes of teaching students the technique of documentary and introducing the students to one another. In a screenwriting course students begin working on scripts for narrative films they will make later in the program. In the second semester students begin to work in narrative and to shoot on film. Students take courses in narrative production, cinematography, and sound, and shoot five-minute-long narrative films on 16 mm film.

From second year on, students choose whether they want to work in documentary or narrative. Though the faculty is fairly evenly divided between the two, two-thirds of each class will usually choose to work in narrative. The second year revolves around a single film, the prethesis. At the beginning of the year each student chooses a three-member faculty committee to oversee her prethesis project. A narrative prethesis should run between ten and fifteen minutes; a documentary up to half an hour. All documentaries and most narratives now shoot on video. Once a student has chosen a committee, the committee reviews the script; the script must be approved before the student can proceed into production. Students then work on their scripts through the first semester, shoot in the winter, and edit through the spring. Students continue to take a full schedule of classes while they make these films, including advanced courses in nonlinear editing and digital sound design. The main production course and other required courses are scheduled to support students as they make their pretheses; the first-semester courses center on writing and preproduction, while the second-semester courses center on production, editing, and sound design. The process of making documentaries is so different from that of making narratives that the school has lately been experimenting with breaking the students apart into separate sections, with all of the students making narratives meeting and discussing their work in one section and all of the documentarians in another.

The prethesis is supposed to be finished by the end of the year, when each student shows a fine cut to her committee and also turns in a report about the project. This report includes the shooting script, budget information, and a discussion of the making of the project. At the review students also discuss the thesis films they plan to make in third year. Many students have not finished their prethesis by this time. The school generally doesn't allow students to use the equipment during the summer, so students either set up their own Final Cut Pro systems and edit at home or take the summer off and resume editing and mixing when school starts again in the fall.

The school encourages students to use the summer to write their thesis projects and to arrive in the fall of third year with a script in hand. Thesis films tend to be ambitious projects but are not supposed to run more than thirty minutes (though the school does not strictly enforce this time limitation). As in second year, about a third of these films are likely to be documentaries, and many students choose to work in video rather than film. As in the previous year, students attend a production class that revolves around the making of the thesis film, but they are otherwise free to complete their elective requirements.

Few students finish their films before the end of third year. Most continue working on their films at least through the middle of the fourth year. While students usually finish all of their required course work in three years, there is one final course that students do not take until they are nearly finished with their thesis projects. This course guides them through writing their thesis reports and prepares them to present those reports, along with the films, to their faculty committees. The faculty encourages students to discuss in these reports not only their films but also how the program helped or hindered them. These reports are kept by the department and are made available to younger students so they might learn some of the older students' lessons.

## ▶ THE PRICE

| | |
|---|---|
| $10,968 nonresident tuition and fees of for three years | $32,904 |
| $14,000 per year rent and living expenses for three years | $42,000 |
| Average first-year film costs | $1,000 |
| Average prethesis film costs | $5,000 |
| Average thesis film costs | $15,000 |
| **Total** | **$95,904** |

Quite the bargain, really, especially for a full three-year program. It is not easy to become a resident of Texas if you are not one already—you have to live in the state for a year without taking any classes before you can gain resident status—so if you are not a resident already, you should not expect to be able to become one. If you are a Texas resident, however, you can shave about $15,000 off the above figure.

But even for an out-of-state student, UT is a great value. The tuition is incredibly low, and Austin itself is a fairly inexpensive town. Rents for one-bedroom apartments near school run around $600 or $700 a month. It is a good idea to have a car, but it is not necessary. Most of what Austin has to offer is accessible by foot or public transportation, so you will really only need a car during film shoots. It is possible to survive by borrowing or renting a car on the occasions when you need one. On the other hand, if you do own a car you will be inordinately popular with your classmates who do not, especially around production time.

The school is pretty good about finding funds to help students; many get free tuition for their entire stay. Because the school has a large undergraduate film department, it offers many teaching assistantships to graduate students. Twenty-hour assistantships provide full tuition remission plus a stipend; ten-hour assistantships provide half that. There are a few more assistantships available to graduate production students in other departments. The Business School, for instance, needs a few technicians around at all times to keep their video equipment running. Generally, the school has enough TA-ships that almost everyone who applies for one receives one. The university offers a number of general fellowships, which graduate production students have had luck winning in the past. But for the most part, students have to cover their own film costs.

▶ **THE LOWDOWN**

This is officially a three-year program, though many students have to stay around beyond third year to finish their thesis films. Long stays are discouraged but grudgingly tolerated by the school.

The school receives more than one hundred applications a year. Of these, twelve new students are admitted each fall.

For your application to be considered, you have to have an undergraduate degree, with a GPA of no less than 3.0, and very good GRE scores. You have to send in two applications, one to the graduate school and one to the RTF program. To Graduate Admissions you have to send an application, transcripts, and official GRE reports. To the RTF department you have to send copies of all of the above, plus three letters of recommendation, a statement of purpose, a résumé, and samples of work. Officially, the sample of work should be a writing sample, but the admissions board will look at paintings, photographs, and even films and videos. The admissions board looks for applicants with a creative bent, preferably in writing, and not necessarily with experience in film. A strong writing sample is as likely to help you get in as a reel of previous film or video work.

Students may work in either film or video; the school has ample equipment for both media. It is good-quality equipment, though the best film cameras are in short supply. The school has one Arri 35 BL camera, and two Arri SR 16 mm cameras, one that shoots Super 16 mm and one that shoots regular 16 mm. For video work there are two Sony PD-170 cameras and a Canon XL-1. Students have to schedule time with the better cameras well in advance, first getting the approval of the faculty, and then the agreement of the equipment room. The time students get with the equipment is not set as it is at many schools: the faculty decide how much time each student needs with the equipment based on the complexity of the project she is making. The school has three film soundstages, three television studios, and twenty-four Final Cut Pro editing stations. All audio work is done in ProTools. The school has two animation stands: an old one that the school has had for years and a fancy newer one. There are also a number of title stands, so students don't need to tie up a full animation stand just to shoot their titles.

With a large undergraduate department, and with three classes of graduate students, Austin has films in production almost all the time. Students say that the way to get the most out of the program is to work on as many of these films as possible; it is the best way to learn how to make films. The school makes an effort to hire working filmmakers as professors. All are good filmmakers, but not all are great teachers. Students tell us that the professors are best in one-on-one communication—sitting in cafés discussing scripts, or sitting at editing stations discussing cuts.

Austin is in direct competition with a number of other schools for students; it makes a very strong case as a great school for any kind of filmmaking. But it has one major handicap: its location. While there is some production happening in and around Austin these days—well-known filmmakers Robert Rodriguez and Richard Linklater live and work in the area, and a former military base outside of town has been converted into a film studio—it is not Los Angeles. The school is now making an aggressive effort to work around this problem. The school maintains an outpost on the Universal Studios lot in Los Angeles, and students can choose to take classes there for a semester, and get to know their way around Los Angeles, while still in school. Every spring the faculty chooses two hours' worth of student work and screens them for the industry in Los Angeles.

Probably the most innovative response to the problem of location is Burnt Orange Productions, a new Austin-based film production company created to help students get experience working on professional films. Students can submit projects developed at UT to Burnt Orange for consideration; some of these films are produced. Not all productions are written and directed by UT students at this point, but students benefit by working as crew on all productions.

Every spring, the South by Southwest, or SXSW, festival is held in Austin. In addition to being one of the top-tier American film festivals, it also is a major festival of music and new media. And every year it is timed to take place during UT's spring break, so students are free to either work in the festival or just attend, meet filmmakers, watch movies, and listen to bands from all over the world.

*Some of the worst things about the program:* While Austin is a great town, and people love living here, its location thousands of miles from where most films are made makes the transition from school to a career in filmmaking difficult.

*Some of the best things about the program:* UT Austin is an especially strong school for documentary. The professors have a wealth of knowledge and experience, and there is ample equipment for any production. And for all that, it is still one of the least expensive film schools in the country.

# UNIVERSITY OF UTAH

Division of Film Studies
375 S 1530 E RM 257b
Salt Lake City, UT 84112-0380
801-581-5127
www.film.utah.edu

| Tuition: | Resident: $4,664 |
| | Nonresident: $14,766 |
| Enrollment: | 5 |
| Deadline: | April 1 |
| Focus: | Independent/documentary |

## ▶ THE PROGRAM

The University of Utah's MFA film program is a two-year program that accepts only a handful of students each year. It is largely geared toward documentary filmmaking, though students are welcome to make narratives or experimental films. The faculty takes a hands-off approach, providing equipment and guidance but largely letting students pursue projects that interest them.

With so few graduate students, there aren't really any graduate-level courses; all classes are undergraduate classes that graduate students attend (and later serve as TA for). The school assumes that all graduate students have already made films and does not spend much time offering introductory courses. Students start out in their first semester with a course in documentary, each making a ten-minute documentary video over the course of the semester, and a course in film history. In the second semester, students move on to an intensive course in directing, where they write scenes, cast actors, and team up in crews to shoot the scenes on video, and they take a videography course in video production technique.

Students generally stay around over the summer after first year; the school offers a summer course in postproduction that meets once a week and allows students to continue using the school's equipment to finish up their first-year projects. Students also generally meet with professors during the summer to discuss the thesis projects they will be making in their second year. Sometimes students even begin shooting their thesis projects during the summer.

In second year, students take an intensive yearlong course in production that guides them through shooting, editing, and completing their thesis films. Some students finish their films and graduate at the end of second year; others take one or two additional semesters to complete their films and graduate.

## ▶ THE PRICE

| | |
|---|---:|
| $14,766 nonresident tuition for one year | $14,766 |
| $4,664 resident tuition for one year | $4,664 |
| $10,000 per year rent and living for three years | $30,000 |
| $1,000 per year maintenace and insurance on a car for three years | $3,000 |
| Average film costs | $10,000 |
| **Total** | **$62,430** |

You have to have lived in Utah for two years without being a student in order to be classified as a resident. However, with such a large undergraduate population and so few graduate students, every graduate student gets either a full or half TA-ship in second year. Full TA-ships pay full tuition plus a $7,000 stipend; half TA-ships allow recipients to pay resident tuition, and the school pays half of that, plus a $3,500 stipend. So even nonresidents only have to pay nonresident tuition for one year, and everyone gets some of their second-year tuition refunded. Utah residents who get to pay resident tuition first year can shave $10,000 off the above total.

In addition to the TA-ships, the school also gives out a handful of tuition scholarships each year, plus some small production grants and work-study assignments. Everyone in the program gets some sort of financial help from the school. And Kodak has taken to donating a few thousand dollars' worth of free film stock every year for students to use.

Salt Lake City is an inexpensive place to live. One-bedroom apartments can be found for $500 a month or less; shares for around $300. Most students live a ways away from campus and drive to school for classes, so a car is a necessity. And, anyway, you need a car to take advantage of all the great exterior locations Utah has to offer.

▶ **THE LOWDOWN**

The school receives about thirty-five applications each year, from which three to five new students are accepted. The faculty looks for applicants who are already working in film or video. Once in a while an applicant will come along without much experience, but who shows promise, and the school will suggest he come to the university, take an undergraduate film course, and see how it goes.

The equipment is not always the newest, but it is reliable, and there is enough of it that students have virtually unlimited access at all times. The school has Aaton and Arri 16 mm film cameras, and an Eclair that was recently converted to Super 16. But with the nearest film processing labs a thousand miles away, shooting film is a problem in Salt Lake City. These days more students shoot video, especially for documentary work, and the school recently added some new Sony DVCPRO-50 video cameras to support this and is looking toward getting some HD cameras. Students edit their thesis films on five Avids the school owns; other films are generally cut on Final Cut Pro.

A local equipment rental company, Redman Movies and Stories, is owned and operated by a Utah film school graduate and has an ongoing relationship with the school. Redman will often give students good deals on equipment rentals, so if the school doesn't have the specific equipment a student needs, Redman will usually be able to provide it at a good rate. Also, when Redman has extra equipment that they no longer need—old C-stands, grip equipment, lighting gels—they will often donate it to the school.

Late every January the Sundance Film Festival takes place in Salt Lake City and nearby Park City, and for two weeks the world of independent film comes to town. Students either volunteer at the festival or just attend screenings; it's an exciting time of year and an integral part of the education here. And the program offers a course, Film Festival Workshop, where students discuss and analyze films they see in the festival.

*Some of the worst things about the program:* People either love or hate Salt Lake City. A conservative town dominated by the Church of Jesus Christ of Latter-day Saints, bars and liquor stores close early, and nightlife, though improving in recent years, is still kind of scarce. On the other hand, few cities offer more to those who enjoy nature.

*Some of the best things about the program:* The program provides a great deal of freedom to student filmmakers. The faculty does not dictate the kinds of films students may make, and students get nearly unlimited access to equipment. It is probably best for documentary filmmaking; much of the equipment is especially good for documentary work, and several faculty members are experienced documentary filmmakers. This is also probably the film school with the best local skiing.

# UNIVERSITY OF WISCONSIN—MILWAUKEE

Peck School of the Arts

P. O. Box 413

Mitchell Hall Room B70

Milwaukee, WI 53201-0413

414-229-6569

www3.uwm.edu/arts/programs/film

| | |
|---|---|
| Tuition: | Resident: $9,116 |
| | Nonresident: $23,482 |
| Enrollment: | 12 |
| Deadline: | January 1 |
| Focus: | Experimental |

## ▶ THE PROGRAM

Founded in 1984, the University of Wisconsin–Milwaukee's MFA is not a program for novices. Experienced filmmakers who have projects they are dying to work on may find there is no better school for them. An undergrad film degree or expertise in the technical aspects of film production is required.

This is an unabashedly unstructured two-year program that seeks free-minded, freethinking citizens of the world. No commitment is made to any genre, but the overall vision is experimental. The idea behind the school seems to be to find a very few promising students, give them access to a lot of equipment, and see what happens. It is a film school without walls, where students are encouraged to follow whatever paths interest them and to make whatever projects they want, in whatever media they think best on whatever subjects they fancy. There is an assumption that students will constantly produce creative work during their time here, but there are no specific requirements regarding that work.

Students must choose some elective courses in film studies and film production and select twelve credits of Complementary Study. Complementary Study is almost like a minor; it is a separate field of study taken while studying film. Students also select an advisor for this course of study. (This is in addition to their film advisor.) Areas of study run the gamut from creative writing to photography or even languages or architecture. UWM wants well-rounded students able to discuss art in a broad context.

The only required courses are the graduate seminars, Professional Practice, and Advanced Research in Film/Video classes. The seminars form the center of the program. These are the common classes that students take during the first three semesters, with a different instructor each semester. Depending on the term, a seminar can be a combination of production, lectures about production and filmmaking skills, and discussions and critiques of student work. One recent class completed a large video installation.

Also required are six credits of Professional Practice. This is a project-oriented course that supports student work in internships, production of a media project for a nonprofit organization, or as media event curators. Most students find the curator aspect of this course most attractive. They can volunteer for the Milwaukee International Film Festival, the student-run Underground Film Festival, the weekly Experimental Tuesdays screenings, or the UWM-hosted Milwaukee International Lesbian Gay Bisexual Transgendered Film/Video Festival. Carl Bogner, the LGBT programmer and a UWM instructor, works with grad students to teach festival programming and administrative responsibilities. He also helps students curate two other monthly screening series, one on campus and one in town.

The final requirement, Advanced Research in Film/Video, is the thesis supervision course taken three times during thesis preproduction, production, and postproduction.

Students generally make several short films are usually made each semester. These might be part of a course or an independent project or just something the filmmaker feels inclined to do. These are usually very personal, small projects, and students incur all costs. All creative work is reviewed and discussed at the end of the first year by a graduate review committees of four professors. Students meet with their committee after their first year and then at the end of each semester thereafter. The goal is to keep every student on track for graduation. Students must propose their theses to the committee and gain approval before beginning work. Review committees are made up of a principal advisor plus two other film professors and the complementary study professor. Students tend to develop close working relationships with the members of their committees.

The second semester of second year is supposed to be when students finish their thesis projects. In fact, many students only begin their thesis project in this semester and return for another year to finish. There is some pressure on students to finish in two years, since the school has a cap on the total number of students it can support both financially and artistically. The number of new students is adjusted according to the number of current students; those in their third year may begin to feel like guests who have overstayed their welcome. On average, about half the students finish in two years.

There is no film festival. Projects are usually screened at the end of each term. Every thesis must have a public screening. They sometimes coordinate this with Carl Bogner. Or several students will join together to put on their own event. In the past these have been held at the Student Union Theater or even at a local Landmark Theater.

## ▶ THE PRICE

| | |
|---|---:|
| $23,482 nonresident tuition for one year | $23,482 |
| $9,116 resident tuition for one year | $9,116 |
| $10,800 per year rent and living expenses for two years | $21,600 |
| Average film costs | $2,000 |
| **Total** | **$56,198** |

That is, if in fact you had to pay full tuition, which you won't. Milwaukee accepts few students so that it can extend generous support packages to every incoming student. Most are awarded teaching assistantships. For residents this equals full tuition and a stipend of $7,000. If they are nonresidents, TAs are only charged resident tuition and then additional cash is given via the Chancellor's Awards to defray remaining tuition costs.

If there are not enough teaching assistantships, the school also offers a package that includes everything but the teaching assistantship. This amounts to about $14,000 of nonresident tuition. Again, scholarship money is added to that amount to help cover remaining tuition and provide a stipend. While they are not there yet, the goal is to have everyone at a similar level so that students graduate with a debt-free MFA.

Milwaukee has been described as a "twenty-minute city." You can travel to most places within its boundaries in that amount of time, and nearby Lake Michigan is worth the trip. It is a good idea to have a car, but it is not strictly necessary. A car is handy to move crew and equipment to locations, but in the winter, when batteries freeze and roads and parking lots are buried under yards of snow, cars can be more trouble than they are worth. The bus service is adequate. A nice one-bedroom house can cost as little as $600; two-bedroom apartments might run $700. Apartments farther away from the campus can be found for under $500. Many students choose to live in River West, an inexpensive artists' community about a mile away between downtown Milwaukee and the school. This area has a mixture of funky coffeehouses and shops, cool restaurants, and decent music venues.

## ▶ THE LOWDOWN

Milwaukee receives fifty applications per year. While an exceptional recently graduated undergrad might be accepted, most are older. One class included a successful Brazilian television personality who also happened to be Brazil's Woman of the Year, and a respected Turkish film critic among its ranks. UWM is extremely selective and generally only accepts people who have a working knowledge of and some experience in filmmaking. You must have a substantial portfolio of work to even be considered. If the faculty sees an applicant they think is particularly interesting who might be able to get up to speed with some undergraduate courses, they may make an exception, but that is fairly rare. This is because no real effort is made within the program to instruct in technical areas, save maybe After Effects software.

Because Milwaukee stresses independent and experimental filmmaking, they make a point of not admitting people who want to make Hollywood-type films. It is not that they hate Hollywood, only that they are not interested in teaching Hollywood filmmaking when there are so many other schools that do and that do it well. Early on, the program decided to go in a direction different from larger, more established programs. It carved out a niche for itself and developed its program according to what the school thought to be most successful at serving students. It is a very individualized program that takes pride in the amount of one-on-one attention it provides to students and the level of financial support given to incoming and continuing students.

No matter what students choose as their primary genre, UWM films do not follow a traditional approach. Most filmmakers work alone or use very small crews. Students don't compete for funding or equipment. They just work on projects that more often than not blur the lines of traditional narrative and experimental. A recent grad submitted his thesis to the Next Frame Student Film Festival as an experimental film, and the judges recategorized it as a documentary and awarded it first place.

Budgets vary, but students tend to be a frugal bunch working in short form. Films are split about evenly between 16 mm and video, with most posting digitally and distributing on DVD. Installations have recently become popular.

Considering its size, Milwaukee is reasonably well-stocked with equipment. There are Bolexes, Arriflex 16Ss and CP-16Rs, and a single Arriflex SR, which is reserved for grads. The school recently purchased a high-def camera. A wide variety of microphones and recorders are available. There is a ProTools workstation with an isolation booth. Through the Music Department, a sound-recording studio is accessible. There are five digital audio workstations with Logic and ProTools and twelve Final Cut Pro stations. Students still have the option of cutting film on a Steenbeck.

The school has its own black-and-white film-processing lab. Students pay a $20 lab fee each semester and then have access to unlimited black-and-white reversal processing free of charge. University of Wisconsin–Madison processes color reversal film for five cents a foot. Together these two schools (Milwaukee and Madison) make a pretty good film-processing lab; everyone we spoke to was happy with the quality of the labs' work. Students who want to shoot negative have to send their footage away to labs in New York, Los Angeles, or Seattle.

There are two optical printers. The printers are not set up for color correction, so they are only for use with black-and-white stock. The school has two Oxberry animation stands, which are more often used for titles than for animation. There are two lighting studios with lighting grids and Mole Richardson fixtures, and both one hundred-seat and three hundred-seat theaters.

Despite the small size of the graduate program, the entire department has always been pressed for space. The current facility is not even on campus. Renovation is about half complete on the Kenilworth School of the Arts Building, a major new facility that will include graduate studio space, a lighting studio, and individual student space and is slated to open in 2007.

There's also the Kenilworth project, a new residence for grad students. Students now have the option of living closer to campus in a building right next to the new studio facilities.

Students rarely work outside of their TA positions. Most manage to live on the stipend. If necessary, they can also take on summer TA assignments. It makes sense for the many students who want to teach when they depart.

Although it has grown over the years, the faculty is small. There are a few technical classes in animation and sound, but for the most part students are left to their own devices regarding the equipment.

This program is absolutely suited to self-motivated artists with clear visions of what they want to do. All the equipment is there for students to use, but there is little structure dictating when and how to use it. If you have found you work best under tight deadlines and strict guidelines, this is probably not the program for you. Likewise, if what you want in a film school is a pathway into the industry, Milwaukee is not the place for you. The school does not teach how to make Hollywood-style films, nor does it offer any hints on how to get into the Hollywood system.

If you talk to the faculty about their students, they almost sound like proud parents. Any professor can name any student or former student and can tell you exactly what he did while at UWM and exactly what he is doing now. That is not surprising, considering the size of the program. This small size gives students some big benefits. Students can check out production equipment almost anytime they want. There are almost as many teaching assistantships as there are graduate students, so almost everyone gets the opportunity to teach undergraduate courses. And because there are nine faculty members for twelve students, students get an unusual amount of attention.

What Milwaukee does best is stay out of your way. It gives you access to equipment and moral support but leaves the rest up to you. If you have the vision and force of will to make the films you see in your mind, if you want support and feedback from professors but don't need to be told when you are doing it all wrong, if you know what films you want to make and just need enough school to help you make them, then there is probably no better school for you.

*Some of the worst things about the program:* Winter in Wisconsin can be painful. If you are into any genre other than experimental, you will find structure and training lacking.

*Some of the best things about the program:* The small size and the close communication between faculty and students. The availability of equipment. Everybody gets to teach. It's cheap!

# After Film School

► **OK. I'VE GOT MY DIPLOMA—NOW WHAT?**

Graduation from film school can be an exhilarating joy ride or it can be depressingly anticlimactic. After you screen your film you may get interest from producers and agents. You may get meetings, perhaps representation, perhaps interest in your talents as writer or director.

Or you may not.

The single most important thing we want to impress on you here is that you must actively work to maintain your network of classmates. Of your classmates, one or two may get meetings or find agents. At that point they may kind of disappear from your life, as they move off into a new existence of taking meetings and giving pitches. And if they do, don't feel a need to pester them to keep them as your friend. They will resurface eventually, when they discover that they can't go it alone and still need their collaborators from film school.

The majority of graduates will have no such luck, and for them the community of classmates is an even more vital resource. Keep those friendships active. Meet with one another at least once a week and throw around ideas: hatch schemes, brainstorm plans. Make short films.

We know that's not what you want to hear right now. You want to hear how to make your first feature and launch your career in film. And we're about to go into that. But be aware that there are some rough spots ahead, and you are going to need the support of your friends from film school.

OK, now, about that movie . . .

## ▶ YOUR FIRST FEATURE

There are three general routes to making a first feature: the Hollywood route, the independent route, and the documentary route. Which route you take will be determined to some degree by the school you went to and the kind of films you want to make. But it will also depend a great deal on what you are comfortable doing, where you are located, and how much money you can put together on your own.

## ▶ THE HOLLYWOOD ROUTE

If you're like most graduates, your ideal is to find someone else to pay for your first feature. Naturally, you want to avoid taking on financial risk for your films whenever possible. But, as we've been saying, it is very rare for this to happen for first-timers these days, and whether it is at all feasible depends on whether or not the screenplay you have written has marketable elements that would make it attractive to investors. Below are a few examples of elements that could make your film attractive.

### Is It a Horror Movie?

Production companies love horror movies. Horror movies cost very little to make and almost always make money. Teenagers, who make up the largest segment of the moviegoing public, will pay to see any horror film. Even if it doesn't have well-known actors, even if it gets terrible reviews, boys—and an increasing number of girls—will flock to it. So production companies are always looking for the next no-cost horror movie that becomes an enormous hit: the next *Night of the Living Dead* (1968), the next *Halloween* (1978), the next *Blair Witch Project* (1999), the next *Saw* (2004). If you have an original concept and a screenplay with some genuinely scary elements, you may be able to find a production company to back it.

## Is It Another Genre with a Devoted Audience?

Horror movies are not the only ones with an enthusiastic and more or less critic-proof audience. There is a small but devoted audience for movies on gay and lesbian themes. There are large festivals devoted to these films, and these films will often play in art houses in major cities and then move on to a brisk trade on video. Movies with overt religious themes often become profitable without ever playing in traditional theaters, playing instead in church basements or selling directly to fans on DVD. And many films with overt political themes, whether to the political left or right, find financial success through DVD sales to their respective niche audiences. And sometimes a movie that focuses on characters of a specific ethnic group will build publicity in festivals and then open in cities that have communities of that ethnicity.

## Can You Get a Star?

Is there an actor you would like to perform in your movie, someone known, but not a top-level star, who could advance his career through a juicy role in your film? If you can contact the actor and say, "I wrote a part specifically for you," the actor (or more likely the actor's representatives) will probably be willing to at least read the screenplay. If the screenplay is well-written, and the role challenging, and the actor likes you, he may be interested in playing the role. If so, you can ask the actor to sign a letter of intent, saying that if you can get the money to make the film, then he will appear in it. You can then approach production companies with a package—a completed screenplay with a bankable star attached to it and you attached to direct—which will be far more attractive to producers than you alone. Actors who have been working in Hollywood for some time will usually have relationships with producers—many have their own production companies—so, depending on the actor's enthusiasm for the project, there is also the possibility that he will be able to help you find funding. Recent instances where young filmmakers got funding for their first narrative features by tailoring lead roles to specific actors include Kimberly Pierce's *Boys Don't Cry* (1999), Patty Jenkins's *Monster* (2003), and Bennett Miller's *Capote* (2005). Each of these films took actors who were recognizable but not big stars (Hilary Swank, Charlize Theron, and Philip Seymour Hoffman, respectively), and gave them roles they could turn into career-defining performances. Each of these three films was the first feature film for its director, and each won an Academy Award for its star.

### Is Your Project Appropriate for the Sundance Lab?

The Sundance Institute holds a semiannual directors/screenwriters lab, where a dozen or so filmmakers are invited to Utah to spend time developing their projects under the mentorship of a staff of professors and filmmakers. If your project is accepted into the Sundance Lab, producers will be much more interested in looking at it and in talking to you about funding it. But Sundance specifically looks for projects that are challenging, that push at the edges of entertainment. Projects developed through the Sundance Lab are often about groups that are traditionally underrepresented in film or about people on the fringes of society or on the fringes of human experience. If your project is edgy and provocative, maybe even a little hard to watch at times, then you should apply to Sundance. If your project is a romantic comedy or a monster movie, it's probably not worth applying.

But the best advantage you personally could bring to the table when going the Hollywood route is the experience of having already made a feature. And this catch-22 is why it is unlikely you'll be going the Hollywood route on your first feature, and why it's much more likely that you will be taking . . .

▶ **THE INDEPENDENT ROUTE**

Making a feature-length narrative film on your own is one of the hardest things you'll ever do. It is fraught with risk both financial and emotional and will push you to the very limits of your endurance. But it also offers the most freedom you're ever going to have in filmmaking. As soon as other people start giving you money to make films, they'll start telling you what you can and cannot say through your films. And the more money you take, the less you get to say. As long as you are paying for a film yourself, you will be completely free to say what is on your mind.

But how do you do it?

First, you need a screenplay. And it'll have to be a manageable screenplay. The action of the screenplay will have to take place in limited locations, locations to which you can easily gain access. It should involve only a few characters and take place over a brief period of time (so you have fewer costume changes and continuity issues to keep track of).

Next, start delegating. While young filmmakers usually want to be writer/directors, because your resources will be so limited, it's best to separate the two disciplines on this film. If you are going to direct this film, put someone else in charge of developing the screenplay. You can work on the screenplay together at the beginning, but once you move into preproduction you will have to focus on casting and rehearsals, on securing locations and equipment and crew and donations of food from friends and families and local restaurants. It's far better that, as you come up with new dramatic ideas in rehearsals with actors during the last weeks before production, you discuss them with the screenwriter and delegate the actual writing to her, rather than attempt to do the rewriting yourself. In the end, audiences don't care if you are the writer/director. They only care about whether or not the movie is good. So don't allow yourself to be distracted by petty concerns about credit. Just delegate whatever work you have to in order to get the movie made.

Then, put together a team. Having recently finished film school, you know a bunch of skilled, energetic young filmmakers who want to make movies and who have time on their hands. You probably have a computer configured as an editing system. And you probably either own or have access to a DV or HD camera. You may still officially be a student, and have access to the school's equipment, and be covered by the school's liability insurance. So what else do you need?

You need a producer. If you don't already have one, get one. You can't produce this film yourself. Find someone who knows about the logistics of film. If that's not a possibility, then ask everyone you know for referrals until you find one. If that doesn't work, then ask the most organized, together person you know to do this for you, and buy her a bunch of books to read about producing. However you do it, get a producer on board, and agree that you're going to make this film together and that you will do everything it takes to get it done.

Be specific in all your discussions of the film. Set a date for the first day of shooting and tell everyone about it, even if you can't imagine right now how it's going to happen. This may sound strange, but think of it this way: it is your job to have a clear vision of this film as a finished project, and to express that vision so transparently that the people around you start to see the finished product clearly as well. Speak about the film in absolutes, and with complete confidence. For instance, if you say to a classmate, "I'm thinking I'd like to make a feature, maybe sometime this summer," he's likely to respond, "Awesome. Good luck!" and that will be the end of it. But if you say, "I'm making a feature this summer. Caroline is producing, and Matthias is the DP, and it's a thriller Amy wrote called *American Wristwatch*, and we start shooting August 1 in Trenton, New Jersey," the response will be different: "I have an uncle who owns a lot of real estate in Trenton; maybe he can help you with locations." Or "My dad's a watch collector, and we have tons of old watches you could use as props." Or, "Hey, I'm free in August. Can I come to Trenton and help out?" Each specific response may or may not be helpful, but that's not really the point. The point is, people around you see this project as real and specific. They start to see it as inevitable, as something that is going to happen at a specific time and in a specific place—and as something they should be involved with as a way of escaping their drab, humdrum lives. If you do a good job of this you may find yourself on August 1 directing your first feature without quite remembering how it all came together.

Next, you need money. If you shoot on digital video you won't need an enormous amount of money, but you're going to need some. You should pay your most important crew and lead actors something, even if it's just a token amount. And providing food is vital; it's a small thing, but if you don't provide meals and snacks, your crew and cast will become cranky, and your film will suffer. So if you were going to shoot your film in twenty days, and were going to spend about $1,000 a day on meals, salaries, props, wardrobe, and transportation, you'd need about $20,000 to get through production. Daunting, but not undoable.

Don't get hung up on film. People sometimes think that it's only a real movie if it's shot on film, preferably 35 mm. While it's true that film looks better than video when projected in a movie theater, on a low-budget film like yours, the slight improvement in image quality when viewed on a large screen is not worth the enormous amount of money and time required. Digital video cameras require very little additional light and can be repositioned very easily. This will allow you to work very quickly and efficiently. You can take all the time you would have spent setting up lights and instead spend it working with the actors on their performances. On this kind of film, getting exceptional performances from your actors is by far the most important thing.

Try not to spend your own money, and don't take on any additional debt to make this film. Get friends and family to buy shares if you can. Dip into savings if you absolutely have to, but don't go into debt, especially not credit card debt. The press loves to print stories about filmmakers who bet it all, maxing out dozens of credit cards in order to make their debut features, and who became successful filmmakers as a result. The unspoken message is, this is fun, and it works. But for every filmmaker who succeeds this way, there are literally thousands of other filmmakers who did exactly the same thing, whose films did not make it past the festival circuit, and who may die before they emerge from the debt.

Debt is especially dangerous for recent film school graduates, who are often already burdened with student loans, and for whom the additional debt load seems like relatively small change. There's a point in most film students' lives where they say to themselves, "I already have $100,000 in student loans; what difference will it make if it goes up to $120,000?" This is in some ways the most dangerous point in a filmmaker's career. Try to remember, SallieMae is not your friend. Taking on debt for film school is already a big risk. Taking on debt to finance a low-budget indie film . . . Well, that's just crazy.

If you only have money to pay a few of your crew members, then pay your DP and your sound person first. The film has to look good, and it has to sound good, so pay what you must to get good picture and sound. Sound is almost always an afterthought at this level of filmmaking, and filmmakers often wind up spending huge amounts of money later trying to fix their bad production sound. Also, be willing to pay to have a still photographer on set much of the time. This may seem like a minor thing, but when your film is finished, when it comes time to publicize it at festivals or for a release, you will need high-quality photographs. If you don't have eye-catching, print-quality press photographs, then your film won't be featured in newspapers or magazines, and audiences won't know about your film and come to see it.

Also be sure to set some money aside for postproduction. This is much less of a problem than it used to be, since most festivals and many independent theaters will now screen video. (Until recently, if you shot on video, you'd have to pay around $50,000 to transfer your video to film before any festival would screen it.) These days you can do the picture and sound editing on a home computer and can directly output a digital videotape or DVD that a festival can screen. For more money you can get an online edit and professional color correction, but that's not necessary for most festivals. But you still should spend the money necessary for an experienced composer to write a good score for you, and a skilled sound mixer to give you a quality sound mix.

OK, so that's the independent route. But suppose even that isn't an option. Suppose you went to a very small film school and don't have many people who can help you make your film. Is there any hope? Sure! There is the third option . . .

## ▶ THE DOCUMENTARY ROUTE

Why would you want to make a documentary? Two reasons: they're less risky to make, and they often turn out to be better films. And, anyway, making a documentary is an experience every filmmaker should have, and this time after film school is an ideal time to get that experience.

Documentaries generally require fewer crew members and less money than narrative features. If you are making a documentary, you will probably need at most a cameraperson and a sound person for production. A producer to collaborate with is always helpful, especially if your documentary involves significant travel or a large number of subjects. And you will want an editor to work with you to construct a film from the footage you shoot; it is very difficult to edit a documentary you shoot. So that's at most four people to shoot and edit your entire film, and if after finishing film school you don't have four friends who can fill these positions, then you might as well just forget about this whole film thing right now.

Also, there is money available for documentaries. If your documentary deals with any kind of social issue, any kind of scientific, medical, or governmental subject, any specific group of people, or almost anything else in the world, there are specific grants you can apply for. This is a large source of money that is not available to most narrative films.

A few things to keep in mind, though. Be sure to get a signed release from every single person who appears in your film. Have them sign it at the time you shoot with them; don't expect to catch up with them later. Why is this so important? If your movie is good, and companies want to distribute it in theaters or on television, the first thing they will ask you is if you can prove you have the rights to the people and stories portrayed in your film. If you are missing even one person's release, it will endanger the deal. Also, be especially aware of music rights. If there is music in your film—even if it's something as innocuous as a cell phone ring tone in the background—you may have to pay thousands of dollars for the right to use that music.

Well, we said there were three ways to make a feature, and that number three is the way to go if you have little money and few collaborators. But what if you have no money and no collaborators?

▶ **OTHER**

One thing about movies: there is always another way. In recent years numerous filmmakers have found ways to make films using only what they had. Jonathan Caouette's *Tarnation* (2003) was pieced together entirely from home movies and videos, cut together in the editing program iMovie that comes free with every Macintosh computer. *Tarnation*'s total production budget is said to have been $300. Neill Dela Llana and Ian Gamazon, in their film *Cavite* (2005), devised a concept for a narrative film that they could make entirely by themselves; Gamazon plays the lead role of an American man in the Philippines whose mother has been kidnapped. For almost the entire length of the film, he walks through the slums of Cavite, told where to go and what to do by the unseen kidnapper on his cell phone. Most of the movie was made with Gamazon and Dela Llana as the entire crew, with Gamazon starring. If all else fails, you, too, could probably come up with a way of making a film using only the people, equipment, and locations available to you. All it takes is some creativity.

Animation is another kind of film you can make with little money and few collaborators. You're not going to make a feature this way, but it is a way to go on making short films even if you have no other options. Computers make animation much easier than ever before, whether 3-D animation with applications like Maya or Combustion, or 2-D animation with Flash.

The people who have enduring careers in Hollywood are the ones who find new ways to make movies when none of the old ways work. Be creative, and keep making movies any way you can.

## ▶ OK, I'VE MADE MY FIRST FEATURE— NOW WHAT?

If you succeeded in going the Hollywood route and got backing from a production company, then you don't need any further advice from us. Your production company will handle arranging distribution for it; you'll probably be asked to do some promotion of it when it comes out, but otherwise you're done and can get to work on your next film, which should be fairly easy now that you've made one feature. The one additional bit of advice we have is, get your next feature going before your first one is released. Even if you are sure it's great, it could get bad reviews, and bad reviews can end a budding film career. But bad reviews won't stop a production that's already under way, so always try to have your next project started.

If you made an independent narrative or a documentary, then it's time to go back to the festival circuit. Luckily, thanks to that thesis film you made that played on all those festivals, you know programmers and will be able to let them know you now have a feature to send to them. (One of the best things about being on good terms with programmers is that they will often waive your application fee. If you apply to fifty festivals, and every one has a $50 application fee, you're paying a couple thousand dollars just in fees. So fee waivers are important for the low-budget independent filmmaker, and they are only possible if you know the programmers personally.)

One thing to be aware of is the festival pecking order. When your film premieres in a festival, it is nailed into position in the pecking order. Festivals higher in the pecking order will no longer want your film; you can only go down from there. As a result, you want to premiere your film as close to the top as you can; you want to see if you can get into Cannes or Toronto or Sundance first. If your film is rejected by the top-tier festivals, then you can apply to the second-tier festivals, such as Tribeca, SXSW, or Los Angeles Film Festival. If all of the second-tier festivals reject your film, then you can move on to the regional festivals, such as the Hamptons or Santa Barbara or Hawaii. For every festival that accepts you, be aware of where it stands in the pecking order, and try to gauge whether or not the invitation is worth accepting. Attending festivals is often expensive; the first- and second-tier festivals are generally worth attending, as that is where you will meet people who can help you make your next movie. The lesser festivals can be great fun but are unlikely to help your career in any substantial way.

Also, don't forget that there are many specialized festivals for which your film may be suitable. Gay and lesbian festivals such as Los Angeles's Outfest are great places to take films that address gay and lesbian subjects. There are festivals that specialize in comedy (the Aspen Comedy Arts Festival), documentary (Columbia, Missouri's, excellent True/False Film Festival), films by and about Asian, Latino, Jewish, and black experiences, and many others. These festivals can be a blast, but be sure to try to get into the general festivals first before you apply to the specialized festivals. Otherwise you risk getting stuck in the niche festivals and being seen only by niche audiences.

As a feature filmmaker you will be treated as an honored guest at any festival you attend. You will be invited to most of the parties and will have the opportunity to meet other filmmakers, producers, critics, journalists, and programmers from other festivals. Audiences will see your feature for the first time, and you'll begin to build a reputation through reviews in the press, word of mouth, and—best-case scenario—awards. And you will meet independent producers and distributors, giving you the opportunity to befriend them and get them involved in your next project. If you are lucky, you will get a distributor to give your DV film a limited release. But that's not the most important thing; the most important thing is to impress the independent producers enough that they want to talk to you about funding your next film.

And that, dear reader, is how you begin a career in film in the early years of the twenty-first century.

## ▶ GETTING A JOB

So say you aren't ready to make a feature just yet. Say you've tried, but it's just not happening right now. How about just getting a job and making some money, paying off all those loans for a bit? Here, too, you have some difficult choices to make.

In many cases you won't want to include your MFA on your résumé. Ironically, an MFA in film will probably help you more outside of Hollywood than inside. To someone not in the film industry, your film degree is kind of interesting; it indicates that you are not aimless, that you have devoted yourself to something. It suggests that you are adaptable and are capable of working over long periods of time in adverse circumstances in order to complete difficult tasks. For a job in middle management, a film degree is certainly no worse than a degree in history or sociology, and is probably better.

But to someone in the film industry looking to hire an employee, your MFA degree makes you suspect. People in the industry have a preconception that MFA students think they are better than everyone else, are liable to not take their jobs seriously, and if put into positions where they can communicate with powerful people, might promote their own careers to the detriment of their employers. (It bears mentioning that this preconception is not always inaccurate.) Several people we know, who have MFAs in film and who work in film and television production, do not include their degrees on their résumés. They found that when that was included on their résumés, they were rarely hired. It was only when they removed the MFAs from their résumés that they started getting work.

## ▶ FILM WORK VERSUS NONFILM WORK

Generally, your choice after graduation will be to either take a job in film that works you long hours for virtually no pay, or to take a nine-to-five job outside of film that helps you pay off your loans and gives you some free time to write.

The best thing you can do once you are out of film school to keep your filmmaking career going is write screenplays. But if you are working sixteen-hour days as an intern, you won't get much writing done. The advantage of a nine-to-five job is you are free to write and to get together with your film school collaborators and hatch plans. It can be frustrating to be nowhere near the industry eight hours a day, but if you have the discipline to write in your free time (and perhaps even on the job during your lunch break) it can be a productive way of passing the time until you can get your first feature going. If you do choose the office work route, it is especially important to maintain your film school support group. Weekly writing groups can keep you focused and can help provide deadlines and a sense of purpose. Without this kind of support, it is easy to be sucked into the world of business and to lose track of your film aspirations.

# Benediction

Now comes the hard part.

The decision whether or not to go to film school is a tough one. We hope we have helped to make your decision easier by providing you with as much information as we could. It may not be much, but it is a lot more information than we had when we were faced with the decision.

Many people apply to all of the schools, and go to whichever accepts them. We both did this, and, as it happens, we both wound up at NYU. Knowing what we know now, we may have decided differently. But we hope that you will now be able to decide on a school that is right for you, to apply to it in a way that will get you accepted, and to use that school to advance yourself toward your ideal career.

One thought we'd like to leave you with: Film school is all about the student film. You may dedicate several years of your life and tens of thousands of dollars to bringing your thesis film into existence. No matter how much time, money, and sweat you put into this film, it is important to remember one thing: *it's only a student film*. It may be the greatest student film ever made, but it will not make you an internationally known filmmaker. It will not get you a three-picture deal. It is just one small step at the beginning of a very long journey. Don't go into it intending to re-create cinema; just tell the best story you know how to tell, and tell it as well as you can.

And when you finish, remember that there are many more graduates each year than there are jobs. You can't expect to direct, nor to get any other high-level job, for some time. You may find yourself assisting a low-level development executive at a low-level production company. You may find yourself doing humiliating work for sixteen hours a day. Or you may find yourself completely unemployed.

This is where your strength and determination will be tested. Keep your network of classmates active. Keep brainstorming ideas and hatching plans. Above all, keep writing. It may take a few years, but if you keep working at it, you will make it.

We hope that we've helped provide some insight into what lies ahead for you in film school and beyond. Maybe you've decided not to bother; maybe you're only more determined. Whatever your choice . . .

Good luck!

# Glossary
# of Common
# Film School Terms

**A AND B ROLLING.** Also called conforming or checker-boarding, this is a process for hiding the physical cuts in film by splitting successive shots onto two separate reels and then making a new print from those reels. In addition, A and B rolling also makes possible effects like dissolves, wipes, and fades.

**ACTOR.** A difficult person.

**ANSWER PRINT.** A first print of a finished film struck from the A and B rolled negative that includes both the picture and the mixed soundtrack. After the answer print has been checked for flaws, the next step is to make release prints. Mind you, this is film terminology and is not something a lot of film students deal with in the digital video age.

**ARRIFLEX.** Arri is short for Arnold and Richter, German manufacturer of high-quality 16 mm and 35 mm cameras. All Arri cameras have a registration pin, so even the bottom-end models provide a very steady image. Arri cameras include the 16S (nonsync); 16 BL (crystal sync); 16 SR, 16 SR-II, and 16 SR-III (internal crystal sync with microprocessor-controlled movement). Typically, when a school has Arri cameras for students to use, they will brag about it; if a school doesn't tell you the kind of cameras it has, it probably doesn't have Arris.

**ARRI KIT.** An Arri kit is a light kit very popular with film schools. It consists of four 1,000-watt tungsten lights, with stands and scrims, all in one box. Each kit is the size of a thirty-inch TV and weighs about twice as much. To show off their strange Teutonic sense of humor, the Arriflex company put a flimsy little handle on the box, like what you'll find on a Samsonite makeup kit, and dubbed the kit "portable." If you like your back, you will not try to lift an Arri kit by the handle.

**ASSISTANT DIRECTOR OR AD.** The AD has to keep communication flowing between everyone in the cast and crew, no matter how much bitterness may have developed. The AD has to butter up the people who are being difficult and has to make sure the shoot stays on schedule. In many ways it is the hardest job on a film crew.

**AVID.** Refers to any of the digital nonlinear editing systems made by Avid Technologies. For many years Avid was the dominant nonlinear editing system. Apple's Final Cut Pro, much less expensive and somewhat easier to use, has taken a large chunk of Avid's market share. But Avid still has the reputation of the system professional editors prefer.

**BEST BOY.** On a film crew, the first assistant electrician, who answers directly to the gaffer.

**BOOM.** On a shoot, the person who aims the microphone at where the sound in a shot is coming from. Gets to stand around chatting nonchalantly with actors and actresses during the long lighting setups. As a result, tends to be oversexed.

**CINEMATIC MASTURBATION.** See *Experimental film.*

**CINEMATOGRAPHER.** The person on a shoot who is in charge of how the film looks. The cinematographer dictates the kind of stock to be shot, the position and intensity of lights, the gels and filters used, and all the other details that determine the overall appearance of the film. In student and low-budget films, the cinematographer also operates the camera, but on professional shoots, the cinematographer generally has a camera operator doing his bidding and rarely actually touches the camera.

**COMEDY WITH NO LAUGHS.** Film students love to make comedies. But many don't have the ability to actually write anything funny. The comedy with no laughs is a genre of film marked by an amiable lightness of spirit; nothing bad happens to anyone, no character is ever in any peril, and in the end whatever small inconvenience the characters have encountered works out OK. A comedy, apparently, except that the audience never has reason to so much as chuckle. We estimate that nearly 50 percent of all student films fall into this genre.

**CP-16.** A 16 mm camera made by Cinema Products Corporation. Small, light, and quiet, this camera was designed to be used by television news crews in the days before video. When video made them obsolete, every television station in the country did the same thing: they donated their CP-16s to the local university and took hefty tax deductions. As a result, the CP-16 is still the most common camera in film schools. Cinema Products' newer models include the GSMO, a terrific small, microprocessor-controlled, crystal-sync 16 mm camera.

**CRYSTAL SYNC.** No two analog machines ever run at exactly the same speed. So to make sound and image run together as one, motion picture cameras and sound recorders have to be forced to run at exactly the same speed. One solution to this is crystal sync. Quartz crystals oscillate at an extremely precise rate when an electric current is sent across them. Manufacturers of motion picture cameras and sound recorders have put motors into their machines that use the oscillations of quartz crystals to dictate the speed at which they run.

This is only of use in analog equipment; all digital technologies run at the same speed and do not require additional crystal sync mechanisms to make them run at speed.

**DAILIES.** On a film shoot, the first positive print of a day's footage. On a typical film shoot, exposed negative film is rushed to a film processing lab at the end of a shooting day. Late that night the lab processes the negative, exposes a workprint off of it, and processes that workprint in time for the DP and director to see it first thing the next morning. Also called rushes.

**DAT.** Digital audiotape, a digital audio recording format. For most production work, DAT is now being replaced by hard drive–based recorders.

**DAYLIGHT SPOOL.** A metal spool with 100 feet of raw 16 mm film wound on it. The metal spool blocks all light from reaching the film, so it is not necessary to use a darkroom or a changing bag to load it into a motion picture camera.

**DIRECTOR.** The person ultimately in charge of all artistic aspects of a film's production.

**DP.** Director of photography. See *Cinematographer*.

**DOUBLE SYSTEM.** The use of separate equipment to record a scene's sound and picture, i.e., a Nagra records the sound while a camera records the picture. Some cameras, like the CP-16 and the Arriflex 16 BL, have the capability of recording sound inside the camera, directly onto the film. This is known as single-system sound. Today, digital video cameras can record high-quality sound along with the image, so many projects, especially documentaries, use single-system again. But on feature films, sound is still generally recorded on a separate device from the camera.

**ECLAIR.** Eclair International makes a variety of good-quality film cameras. The model most often found in film schools is the NPR, a rugged 16 mm crystal-sync camera. A more recent camera you might come across is the Eclair ACL.

**EDITOR.** A person who can be happy spending all day every day locked in a small, dark room. In documentary, editors often function like writers, creating stories out of apparently random footage.

**EXPERIMENTAL FILM.** If it doesn't tell a story, if it isn't a documentary, if it isn't animated, if it's so strange that you can't think of a single thing to say about it—well, it's an experimental film. Many students making their first film want to make a film that will redefine the medium of cinema, that will defy the audience by not telling a story, that will assault them with shocking images, and that will challenge them with dense, inscrutable symbolism. These are, er . . . experimental films. OK, we admit we're being a little disingenuous. In fact, experimental film is an offshoot of painting and photography, not of cinema. Taken in that context, these films can be quite interesting (we admit a particular fondness for the films of Maya Deren). But too many filmmakers, when they are just starting out, use experimental film as an excuse for laziness: Why go to all the trouble of inventing intriguing characters and putting them in a thoughtful story when you just can splash cool images across the screen?

**FLATBED.** An automobile-size machine on which reels of picture and sound film run in sync across a broad, flat tabletop; film can be cut and spliced on the tabletop. Digital editing systems are so much more efficient that flatbeds have become obsolete in a few short years.

**FOLEY.** Sound effects created in a recording studio.

**GAFFER.** The chief electrician on a film crew, who oversees the setting up of lights according to the director of photography's instructions.

**GRIP.** Grips are in charge of anything that moves on set. On student shoots, most everyone has to be a grip.

**INTERNSHIP.** A specialized employment program to help children of the very wealthy.

**MAG FILM.** Magnetic film. This is 16 mm or 35 mm film that is with magnetically coated like audiotape. It was traditionally used in the editing and mixing of film sound but has been replaced by ProTools.

**MISE-EN-SCÈNE.** A French term that means both "everything in your film," and "I know more obscure film terms than you do."

**MOVIOLA.** Moviola editing machines come in two types: upright and flatbed. Upright Moviolas are compact machines, about the size of a small refrigerator, that allow for the editing of one image track and one soundtrack simultaneously. Upright Moviolas were replaced as an industry standard by flatbed editing machines, which allow editing of more soundtracks at once and provide a larger viewing screen.

**NARRATIVE FILM.** A film that tells a straightforward story.

**NEGATIVE.** Film that exposes a negative image, from which positive prints can be made. A lab processes a negative, exposes a positive workprint from it, and processes that workprint. In film, the advantage of shooting negative stock, as opposed to reversal stock, is that the negative remains untouched while you cut your workprint. When you have finished editing your workprint, you then go back to the negative and, wearing cotton gloves, cut it and A-B roll it to match your edited workprint.

**NONLINEAR.** For most of their history, films have been edited in a linear fashion. That is, one shot is taped to another in a single, very long strand of film. Computer technology has made it possible to edit in a nonlinear fashion. A nonlinear editing system allows an editor to order and reorder shots and scenes the way one can rearrange words and sentences in a word processor.

**OFF-LINE EDITING.** Off-line editing equipment allows fast and simple editing of video materials by using low-quality copies of high-quality video. Time on online editing equipment that edits and outputs video at the highest quality can be expensive. So an editor will often edit a project off-line and, when finished, output an edit decision list. This EDL is then taken, along with the high-quality original tapes, to an online editing system which uses the EDL to quickly and automatically cut together a broadcast-quality version of the piece.

**ONLINE EDITING.** Editing of video materials at broadcast quality.

**PRODUCER.** The person on a film ultimately responsible for all business and organizational decisions related to its production. But—and we can't emphasize this enough—never, ever say to a producer that this is what she does.

**PROTOOLS.** A powerful digital audio recording and editing system made by Digidesign, now owned and distributed by Avid Technologies.

**REGISTRATION.** A term that refers to how steady the image is that a motion picture camera exposes. Good registration is achieved by cameras that hold the film firmly in place in the exposure gate for the fraction of a second while an image is being exposed. Some cameras use a registration pin, a small pin in the exposure gate that thrusts into one of the film's sprocket holes and holds the film absolutely still during exposure. All Arriflex cameras have registration pins. Other cameras, like the CP GSMO and the Eclair NPR use a spring-loaded plate that presses the film firmly into the gate. Cameras that have no registration mechanism can give you a shaky image. This can be unnoticeable on small screens or video, but it can be nauseating when projected on large screens.

**REVERSAL STOCK.** The opposite of negative stock. Reversal stock exposes a positive image inside the camera. Processing is quick and cheap, because no workprint is necessary, but any cut you make on the film cannot be undone. Reversal film saw its heyday in television news before the advent of portable video equipment; it could be processed and edited in time for the 6 o'clock news. Now that all news is shot on video, reversal stock is used almost exclusively by film students, who like shooting film but don't want to have to pay the high cost of shooting negative.

**STEENBECK.** A common brand of flatbed editing machine.

**SUPER 16.** Ordinary 16 mm film has sprockets on both left and right sides of the film. In Super 16, there are no sprockets on the right side, and those extra millimeters of film can be used for image. This allows 16 mm film to hold both a wider and slightly higher-resolution image; the wider image and higher quality of Super 16 makes it an excellent production medium, which looks good whether converted to standard-definition video, high-definition video, or blown up to a 35 mm print.

**TELECINE.** The process of transferring film to video. The many different formats and frame rates of film and video make this a technically daunting subject.

**WALKING FILM.** A film in which an unnamed character walks around a city looking at stuff with a philosophical expression on his face. A perennial favorite with film students, who are traditionally good at bringing together actors, crew, and camera equipment at a location, but who sometimes neglect to write actual stories.

**"YOU JUST DON'T GET IT, DO YOU?"** The archetypal bad line of dialogue: It means nothing, nobody ever says it in real life, and you can't turn on the TV without hearing it at least once. Runners-up for the archetypal bad line: "Are you nuts?" "What is it with you?" "Wait a minute, let me get this straight!"

# Need More?

Things change quickly in the film industry, and film schools have to evolve in order to keep up. In an effort to assure that *Film School Confidential* provides the most up-to-date information on these ever-changing programs, we have set up a website. The Film School Confidential site contains information that came in too late to be included in this book, and links to the websites of all of the MFA film programs in the country. You can even send us comments and criticism. Stop by any time!

www.filmschoolconfidential.net